Praise for *The Way of the Prisoner*

"If you would like to be on the most extraordinary of all journeys, *The Way of the Prisoner* may help you, as it helped me. Sane, balanced, seasoned by hard-earned wisdom and faith, it will surely become a classic on contemplative prayer."

—**Reverend N. Gordon Cosby**,
The Church of the Saviour, Washington, D.C.

"Lord Buddha would delight in this book. Jens, whom I've known during my prison visits, brings needed clarity and precision to these explanations of how to deconstruct the self, a job we all need to do in order to awaken our blissful inner being, or, as he puts it, 'to break through the self to reach God.' "

—**Venerable Robina Courtin**, Director,
Liberation Prison Project

"Soering's book stands as astounding gift. His words plead with many different voices, and his hint of autobiography distills a fearful essence for others. As a guide to Centering Practice it reflects hours, months and years of waiting, then pondering. As a loving call to prayer for all imprisoned by superficial, myopic concerns with self—while sensing a need for closeness with the Transcendent—this bold record of a spiritual journey demonstrates what can happen when contemplative prayer is systematically cultivated.

"Not surprisingly, the book also stands as a plea for action. Soering teaches us about contemplative practice. His words witness through Centering Prayer that we can learn to act for others."

—**Victor A. Kramer**, Ph.D., Executive Director,
Aquinas Center for Theology–Center for Catholic Studies,
Emory University; Founding Editor, *Merton Annual*

"Soering has a keen theological mind; his mastery of scripture and classical Christian theology and spirituality is indicative of a depth of study and personal engagement that is quite phenomenal, yet he makes the key concepts and theology so understandable, so readable, and so inviting for a hungering pilgrim. As one who has struggled with Centering Prayer, I found Soering's writing to be so encouraging and heartening that I have started the practice anew. Surely other beginners, as well as those who have invested themselves in the discipline over the years, will find *The Way of the Prisoner* equally rewarding....It is rare indeed to find an author with so penetrating a mind, combined with so generous a spirit."

—**Reverend Richard A. Busch**, Ph.D.,
Professor Emeritus, Virginia Theological Seminary;
Co-director, Servant Leadership School,
Church of the Saviour, Washington, D.C.

THE WAY OF THE PRISONER

BREAKING THE CHAINS OF SELF THROUGH
CENTERING PRAYER AND CENTERING PRACTICE

Jens Soering

LANTERN BOOKS • NEW YORK
A DIVISION OF BOOKLIGHT INC.

Lantern Books, 2003
1 Union Square West, Ste. 201
New York, NY 10003

Printed in the United States of America

Library of Congress Cataloging-in-Publication Data

Soering, Jens.
The way of the prisoner : breaking the chains of self through centering prayer and centering practice / by Jens Soering.
p. cm.
ISBN 1-59056-055-8 (alk. paper)
1. Contemplation. 2. Soering, Jens. I. Title.
BV5091.C7S63 2003
248.3'4—dc22
2003014869

To my fathers, Klaus and Bev

ACKNOWLEDGMENTS

Special thanks to: Samuel Patton Hand Brasfield and Harvey Crews, for editorial guidance and support from the very beginning; Robert Papa and Katie's dad, for vital encouragement in the early stages; Gary Gutman, Mark Markivich and William Robinson, for essential technical support throughout; Richard Busch, Tilden Edwards and David Hilfiker, for public endorsements and personal recommendations that lifted me out of the editorial slush piles— every unpublished writer should be so lucky as to have backing like yours; Ann Rainey, for absolutely indispensable "midwife"-services; Father Thomas Keating, for graciously making a crucial connection; and Sarah Gallogly, my editor, for smoothing the road surface of *The Way* so others can travel on it more easily. I will always be grateful to all of you.

CONTENTS

FOREWORD

Over a year ago a friend of mine asked me to read and comment on the manuscript of this unusual book. In reading it I found myself entering the hidden world of the prison, through the story of a highly intelligent German citizen convicted of murder in a controversial and well-publicized trial, a murder of which he continues to declare his innocence. I also found myself entering the world of someone converted to a deep Christian spiritual life with the daily help of contemplative Centering Prayer. Beyond that, I saw that his daily life with others in the prison has been transformed through what he calls "Centering Practice." This is a way of life focused on self-emptying, as St. Paul speaks of it in Philippians 2, in the context of Jesus' self-emptying on the cross, with its God-given purification and compassion for others.

Reading *The Way of the Prisoner*, corresponding with Jens and visiting him in prison has taught me much about his struggles, insights, spiritual practice, and prison experience. I have felt his passionate concern to help others face the truths of their own prisons (and he believes that we all live in our own form of prison), and to help us see how turning to God and self-emptying through

Centering Prayer and Centering Practice can lead us to authentic spiritual living.

I have also felt his passionate concern for the plight of the millions of people in prison. The United States has a higher proportion of its population in prison than any other country in the world. The punitive rather than rehabilitative focus of prison life so prevalent today easily breeds hardened criminals and lost souls. The term "penitentiary," a place to learn repentance, has become a euphemistic name for a place where violence, fear, brutality and despair are bred instead. The system is in desperate need of reform, for the sake of the prisoners and of our society. Jens has strong feelings about the need for people to follow Jesus' advocacy of visiting the prisoner, not only literally through developing personal relationships with prisoners, but also in terms of working for a more just and rehabilitative justice system.

The book weaves together all three of these major themes: Jens's own gripping story of his controversial conviction and his experiences with other people in the many prisons in which he has been held over the years, his practice of Centering Prayer and Centering Practice, and his advocacy for restorative justice and communication with prisoners. For people who have little awareness of what goes on behind prison doors, Jens's personal experiences are revealing and give evidence of the great need for a major change in the way the criminal justice system works. His experiences especially reveal some amazing ways that God's Spirit can break through the fear, violence and despair of prison life. His writing can stimulate the reader to better appreciate and become involved in the prisoner's world and to understand some of the practical ways one can do that.

Jens's detailed description of Centering Prayer and Centering Practice shows how he has taken a popular form of contemplative prayer today and, from his own experience, come to a particular understanding of it and of its implications for daily living. I think that when we practice a particular form of prayer for a long time, it often has a way of evolving into an understanding and practice that is different for us than it was when we began the practice, and different perhaps from the understanding of those from whom we learned the practice. The subtle interactions of God's Spirit in our spirit over time create a personal uniqueness that can redefine the original boundaries of the prayer.

In this sense, every prayer in time becomes unique and beyond the naming, and so it is with Jens, in his adaptation of Centering Prayer. At the same time, the particular guidelines for a form of practicing prayer can be more tangible, as they are in this book. Jens connects his own personal appropriation of Centering Prayer's form and understanding with what he has gleaned from his reading of some of the historical classical writings on various forms of contemplative prayer. He feels strongly that his own experience and understanding can be valuable to others who undertake such prayer. Contemplative prayer, he feels, is vital to deepening spiritual life and communal well-being in our world today, and I heartily concur with that from my own perspective.

Reading this book will likely stretch your understanding of prison life, your own form of prison, and the way through and beyond prison in the light of contemplative prayer and practice. Jens steadily invites this stretching to happen in the light of the Gracious One who inspires these movements in us and who invites our full communion. Along with these benefits, you will be exposed to the electrifying story of a very articulate, impassioned person writing from his prison cell, as other Christian spiritual writers beginning with St. Paul have done through the centuries.

Reverend Tilden Edwards, Ph.D.
Author, *Living in the Presence, Living Simply through the Day,*
Spiritual Friend and *Spiritual Director, Spiritual Companion*
Founder and Senior Fellow, Shalem Institute for Spiritual
Formation, Bethesda, Maryland

PREFACE

ONE DAY AS WE were lunching together in November 2001, my friend the Reverend Beverly R. Cosby asked if I would read a manuscript on Centering Prayer. The author, he explained, was a young man serving a life sentence in prison and hungry for feedback on his work. At that time I did not know anything about Centering Prayer. I had heard some sermons on the topic but had never felt drawn to that spiritual discipline. Bev persisted, believing that my having served as Professor of Continuing Education and Director of the Doctor of Ministry program at Virginia Theological Seminary, and now (in retirement) acting as co-director of the Servant Leadership School in Washington, D.C., meant I could offer this young writer a unique perspective. I agreed to read Jens's work, and as I read I formed these two convictions: first, that *The Way of the Prisoner* was worthy of publication, and second, that I would begin practicing Centering Prayer.

Jens's book spoke to me with its integrity and passion. I was struck by his grasp of the biblical, theological and spiritual foundations of the contemplative tradition, and moved by his authentic tone, emerging out of his own despair and brokenness. Jens's embrace of Centering Prayer literally saved his life and even enabled him to benefit from seventeen years of hard time. This prayer practice shapes his discipleship, offering him a new way of understanding, a new way of living: self-emptying service. The book reflects this pastoral sensitivity and generous spirit. By using his life as an example of the principles of Centering Practice, Jens shows how readers can transform their crosses, their prisons, whatever they may be, into the means of their salvation. These issues are of immense importance, yet they are presented in a highly readable style, with a light touch and a wry sense of humor.

In response to my feedback on *The Way of the Prisoner*, Jens and I began a correspondence. Usually his letters include practical encouragement and theological reflection on aspects of Centering Prayer. In the early days of our correspondence, I drove frequently from northern Virginia to Charlotte, North Carolina, to do some teaching. Since Brunswick Correctional Center was not far from my route along Interstate 85, Jens suggested a visit.

I remember very well the occasion of our first meeting—the tall fences, the coils of razor wire, the clanging doors, the patdown, the waiting, the dreary atmosphere of the visitors' area. We sat at a small table. Jens appeared younger than I had imagined. He wore steel-rimmed glasses, his hair was cropped short, and he seemed to be in good shape. He was bright, articulate. As a way of initiating our conversation and getting past the initial awkwardness of the moment, I asked how he had become acquainted with Bev Cosby, our mutual friend who had recently died. Jens described a Christian who came to the Lynchburg, Virginia, jail, befriended him, believed in him and faithfully communicated with him for thirteen years. At one point, I recall, Jens paused as if to gain his breath and said simply, "I loved him so much!" In that key moment, the spontaneity and sincerity of his remark showed me that Jens was a person to be trusted. We would be friends. To this day our letters and visits continue.

Reading the book, corresponding on a weekly basis and visiting Jens bi-monthly have provided for me a relationship with a very special human being. Jens has a rare gift: the ability to deal with deep issues of the human spirit. He always concludes that prayer does not lead to withdrawal, but rather moves us to go out into the world with renewed compassion and strength. Since being incarcerated, he has become a Christian and is a practicing Roman Catholic. He continues to be an invaluable spiritual guide to me in the practice of Centering Prayer.

Reading *The Way of the Prisoner* and knowing Jens has changed my life. It has opened me up to a new way of thinking about God and a new way of engaging in prayer. It has also given me an introduction to a "hidden world"—the prison culture in which 2.5 million Americans live. Acting on the scriptural admonition to visit the prisoner has provided a direct personal experience of seeing life in a new light—a light that would have seemed strange prior to my contact with Jens. This has awakened in me a growing involvement in prison issues and reform. In addition, I believe my teaching of Paul's prison epistles in the Servant Leadership School has been enriched through an awareness of the brutalizing and dehumanizing character of life behind bars.

The Way of the Prisoner continues to be a resource for me, and I anticipate using it as a text in the Servant Leadership School. My prayer is that this amazing book will serve as an introduction to Centering Prayer and Centering Practice for you as it has for me.

Reverend Richard A. Busch, Ph.D.
Professor Emeritus, Virginia Theological Seminary
Co-director, Servant Leadership School, Church of the Saviour,
Washington, D.C.

INTRODUCTION

I AM A PRISONER—and, since you felt moved to pick up and examine this book, you probably are one, too. Maybe you have had to give up your career to care for an aging relative. Perhaps an accident or crime scarred you emotionally and physically. Or your spouse may have died, leaving you alone and in debt. Chains of some sort have been laid upon you and taken your freedom away.

My prison is literal, not metaphorical—Brunswick Correctional Center in Lawrenceville, Virginia—and in January, 2001, the United States Supreme Court denied my final appeal, my one last hope for justice and liberty. Your prison may be less obvious than mine, but to you it is just as real. And even if you, unlike me, have some hope of release in the future, we have something in common for now: these walls that enclose us, these bars that surround us.

The purpose of this book is to remind you of one way to lose your chains. You already know this way, for it is Christ's: he chose to become a prisoner, went willingly to his execution, and thereby overcame the world. If we obey his call, "Follow me," we too may find that the very fetters that now bind us are leading us to a greater freedom.

The key word in the last sentence is "may." During seventeen years in eleven different penitentiaries, I have seen pain produce despair far more frequently than hope. What saved me from bitterness is a specific Christian method of praying and living, practiced by Jesus himself as well as by monks, nuns and lay people for two thousand years. Since liberation is this method's goal, it seems apt to call it the Way of the Prisoner.

Christ gave us a road map to this path when he said, "If anyone would come after me, he must deny himself and take up his cross and follow me" (Matthew 16:24, NIV).[1] Emptying the self and opening the soul to God is the aim of Centering Prayer, and taking up our crosses, our chains and our prisons as contemplative prayer-in-action is what I mean by Centering Practice. These complementary techniques liberate us, not by breaking our bonds, but by melting away the self that feels bound. Once the wrists vanish, the manacles fall to the ground and we are free.

While that image may seem like merely poetical or wishful thinking, Centering Prayer and Practice are eminently practical and realistic. Some of the greatest minds in history have trained themselves in contemplative disciplines *because they work,* and over the millennia these men and women have left us increasingly detailed directions into the interior. So specific are these maps that they can be followed even from a prison cell!

The only condition we must meet before setting out on this journey is a truly deep-seated, existential recognition that there is no other path out of our prisons. Your child will always have Downs Syndrome. Your best friend cannot return from that short drive that ended in the morgue. And my two life sentences will never be finished. No amount of exertion, no anger or tears, no planning and scheming can free us. Only when we recognize this are we ready to "be still before the Lord and wait patiently for him" (Psalm 37:7).

Centering Prayer

Centering Prayer is a modern adaptation of the ancient practice of contemplative prayer. During the first sixteen centuries of Christianity, the contemplative path was considered by many to be the truest and purest way of following Christ's footsteps, but this heritage was first suppressed and later simply forgotten in the doctrinal disputes that followed the Reformation. Only in the 1970s, in response to the growing popularity of Far Eastern meditation techniques, did a small group of Trappist monks at St. Joseph's Abbey in Spencer, Massachusetts, turn back to medieval classics such as *The Cloud of Unknowing*. Having distilled their recovered knowledge into a deceptively simple practice they called Centering Prayer, Fathers Thomas Keating, William Meninger and Basil Pennington then led retreats, gave lectures, wrote a number of fine books themselves and eventually organized a national movement through Contemplative Outreach, Ltd. Their absolutely indispensable "Method of Centering Prayer," by Father Thomas Keating, is reproduced in its entirety in this volume's Appendix.

For those unfamiliar with Centering Prayer, the actual technique can be summed up in four words: silently repeat one word. Everything else is commentary—useful, nourishing, but nonetheless commentary. In some ways, all you really need to practice this disciple successfully is Father Keating's "Method" in the Appendix! However, the path of inner silence can often be arduous and lonely, so you may benefit from my personal experiences with the technique and the scriptural and historical reflections I provide. If you are wondering whether you can trust a prison inmate to provide an accurate presentation of contemplative spirituality, perhaps you will feel reassured by the words of Father Keating himself, who wrote me:

> [*The Way of the Prisoner*] is not quite what we teach in Centering Prayer, but that is okay with me since what you teach could be a better starting point for people who do

not have a certain level of preparation when they are first
introduced to Centering Prayer. I personally am happy
when persons like yourself, with considerable experience,
provide certain nuances to the Centering Prayer practice
as we present it.

I confess that I myself did not have "a certain level of preparation when [I was] first introduced to Centering Prayer," so I spend
considerable time in this book teaching the methods I used to ease
my way into the deep pool of contemplation. If you doubt whether
you could ever master such an esoteric discipline, then my gradual
approach may be right for you, too.

What differentiates this book from others on Centering Prayer
is the approach and context. From Anthony of Egypt to Thomas
Keating, most Christian contemplatives have practiced silent
inner prayer within sequestered religious communities in order to
avoid the distractions of worldly difficulties and tragedies. I, on the
other hand, began my Centering Prayer journey at the harsher of
Virginia's two supermax prisons, where murderers schemed to rape
me and the guards fired their shotguns almost every other day.
Thus, I can personally attest to something the monks and nuns in
their monasteries and convents may have missed: contemplative
prayer brings Christ's "peace . . . which transcends all understanding" (Philippians 4:7) even, in my case, within a couple of hours
of being shot with a rubber bullet. My unusual background has
led me to emphasize a somewhat overlooked aspect of the
method—seeing and using mental distractions during contemplation *positively*, as new opportunities to deny the self—and this, I
hope, will benefit all practitioners, not only those in difficult
external circumstances.

Centering Practice

Many books on Centering Prayer discuss how to bring the spirit of contemplation to daily life through practices such as:

- performing simple physical tasks purely in the present moment, without the normal background chatter of the mind—*just* walking or *just* doing the dishes;
- consciously renouncing our emotional attachments (perhaps to our appearance or clothing) and aversions (such as that carefully nursed grudge against our coworker) and with them our desire to control the world (to get what we want and keep at bay what we hate);
- surrendering our time and ourselves in a spirit of humility when our plans or opinions are challenged by someone sent by God to shake us awake.

These techniques are all beneficial, but they are not what I mean by Centering Practice.

Instead of extending a contemplative attitude to commonplace activities, Centering Practice seeks to use the energy required for enormous existential problems to stimulate spiritual progress. As with Centering Prayer, the key here is focused awareness and concentration—not on a prayer word, but on the cross, the prison God has given us for our purification.[2] Why are some people transformed through their chains, while others are broken by a sibling's suicide, the loss of an uninsured home to fire, or yet another decade of bars and locked doors? Because the former confront their pain squarely and experience it fully, instead of avoiding, denying or distracting themselves from it. That is what differentiated the two thieves who were crucified with Christ: one sought to escape the significance and meaning of his own imminent death by joining in the taunts directed at Jesus, while the other faced his guilt, his end and God's judgment—and was saved (Luke 23:39–43).

A contemplative attitude, whether in prayer or on the cross, always requires seeing the truth clearly. Excavating the layers of self and selfishness during Centering Prayer is often very painful, and Centering Practice does not promise the experience of a dopey, hazy bliss while we monitor our T-cell count, empty our paraplegic parent's bedpan or undergo a strip search and cavity search by a guard who hates us. Instead, we must follow Christ in fully admitting our pain ("My soul is overwhelmed with sorrow..."), our reluctance ("...may this cup be taken from me...") and our despair ("My God, my God, why have you forsaken me?") even as we too try to do our Father's will for us (Matthew 26:38, 39; 27:46).

If we experience it honestly, pain can batter and grind down the structures of the self as effectively as do contemplative practices, and this is where Centering Prayer and Centering Practice reinforce each other. In my life, the various ordeals of my imprisonment actually followed a pattern paralleling the three stages of contemplation and thus prepared me well for intensive Centering Prayer. And just as genuine contemplation means seeing mental distractions positively as opportunities to deny the self, so does truly bearing our cross mean using pain as a chisel to break through the self to reach God.

Of course this process hurts; every additional day behind bars is a new agony for me, and whatever chains you bear will continue to tear at you, too. But alcohol or drugs, fantasies of revenge, or wishful thinking merely turns pain into meaningless, pointless suffering that leads nowhere. The only sane alternative, Centering Practice, has helped me survive and even benefit from nearly fifteen years of incarceration. If I managed to convert the instruments of my torture into steppingstones on the spiritual path, surely you can as well.

———

Overview

Book I uses Christ's temptation in the desert and his transfiguration on the mount to introduce the reader to the key concepts and theology underlying contemplation and self-emptying service. This theoretical survey is followed by a description of the actual method of Centering Prayer as well as a case study of two individuals' respective failure and success in applying the principles of Centering Practice to their lives' tragedies.

The first Intermezzo lays out the bare facts of my criminal case to allow you to make an informed judgment on my trustworthiness and to provide the raw material for a Centering Practice analysis of my mistakes at the end of Book II. This material is not an integral part of *The Way*, so you may skip it entirely if you wish.

Book II examines the process of progressive self-emptying that lies at the heart of both prayer and practice, as exemplified in the great *kenotic* hymn in the second chapter of Paul's Letter to the Philippians. Next, we study methods for navigating the subtle transition from concentrative Centering to contemplative expansion or opening. We then turn to my own case to uncover an early, failed attempt at self-emptying—or self-destruction.

A second Intermezzo describes one particular contemplation session of mine that meant and still means a great deal to me. My hope is that this chronicle of a special "experience" will encourage you to try this discipline yourself.

Book III presents four spiritual principles derived from Christ's crucifixion that allow all of us to transform our crosses, our prisons, into the means of our salvation. My own prison journey serves as a case study for this discussion of Centering Practice because at least some of my experiences behind bars correspond to the kind of tragedies you may find enchaining you at present: if you have been diagnosed with a terminal illness like AIDS, for instance, then learning how I coped with three years on *de facto* death row will hopefully be of practical benefit to you. At the conclusion of our shared Way of the Prisoner, I present a scripturally based spiritual exercise that will help you integrate Centering Practice into your own life's journey.

About the Author

Occasionally, TV news programs show interviews with orange-clad convicts proclaiming fervently, "I *know* Jesus has forgiven me." Because so very few inmates attend prison church services—perhaps 25 out of 730 at this facility, for instance—I tend to believe these rare statements of faith. But this book is not an emotional account of *my* conversion behind bars. Instead, it is about *your* conversion—to the twin disciplines of Centering Prayer and Centering Practice, and to the healing and forgiveness the Spirit offers all of us prisoners through them.

As far as forgiveness for my own, specific sins is concerned, I do recognize that God's mercy extends even to me, though I simply cannot understand the joy some believers clearly feel in this context. Sin terrifies me because there is nothing we can do to undo the damage already done. While Christ's sacrifice atones for my guilt, that does not change the harm my sin did to others and to myself. To me, that is cause for regret, not joy, and so I struggle with the concept of forgiveness. If you share with me this more reflective, less exuberant approach to spirituality, then this book will, I hope, appeal to you.

As you will read later in this volume, the sin I speak of is not the crime for which I am imprisoned. Several years have passed since I have claimed to be innocent, for I do not feel that I am. However, I am not guilty of the crime of which I was convicted.

While my subject here is Centering Prayer and Practice, not courtrooms and evidence, it would be unnatural if you did not want to know more about the source of this book's spiritual message—if you did not, in fact, wonder whether a convict such as myself can be relied upon to tell you the truth. While I passionately want to communicate my religious experience to you, I fear you may judge my message by the charges against me. Therefore, in the following pages, I will use my life as an example of the principles I wish to discuss regarding Centering Prayer and Practice. This will allow you to draw your own conclusions about the subject and the author simultaneously.

For now, I simply ask you to keep in mind that mistakes do happen in the criminal justice system: hardly a month goes by without DNA tests freeing yet another inmate after years of incarceration. There is no DNA evidence in my case, unfortunately, but even without it my attorney, Ms. Gail Starling Marshall, developed "the moral certainty" that I am in fact innocent.[3] And Ms. Marshall is no soft-hearted fool, but a former Deputy Attorney General of Virginia.

The subject of this book is not, however, the possible miscarriage of justice in my case, but how the Way of the Prisoner, Centering Prayer and Centering Practice, can free those of us who must carry chains. I have come to believe that in this context questions of guilt and innocence are almost irrelevant: we must all bear our crosses, whether we deserve them or not. The real question is whether we have the courage to move on from regret and, through contemplative spiritual practices, come to know the Truth that can indeed set all of us prisoners free.

———

Note

This is a serious book on the most important and serious of subjects. While *The Way of the Prisoner* will certainly inspire you, it is by no means light bedtime reading. My aim is to give you all the spiritual tools you need to revolutionize your life, to introduce you in depth to these tools' history and theory and to give you beginning, intermediate and advanced training in their use. By the time you finish this volume, you should be so well versed in all aspects of Centering Prayer and Practice that you will advance far more rapidly and unproblematically than I did. But learning and then using the skills of this discipline requires a willingness on your part to grapple with weighty, challenging material.

I hope this "warning" arouses a mixture of relief and excitement on your part: at last, someone is taking you and your life seriously instead of fobbing you off with spiritual palliatives. No doubt even as you read these words, someone is writing *Contemplative Prayer for Dummies*—but you are not a dummy, and your soul requires heartier fare than chicken soup.

Sparking off or setting in motion your contemplative practice is all I can really hope to do, of course. Just as reading diet books will not help you lose one pound if you refuse to change your eating habits, so will this volume bear no fruit without your active engagement in these spiritual disciplines. Right now you are holding in your hands the key that will open your prison's locks—but you are the one who has to use this key.

Notes
1. *Holy Bible, New International Version* (East Brunswick, NJ: International Bible Society, 1973, 1978). All Biblical quotations in *The Way of the Prisoner* refer to this edition except where another source is given.
2. Please see the Postscript on Centering Prayer terminology.
3. In a letter to my parole board, Ms. Marshall wrote, "There have been only two occasions in my thirty-five years of practice when, after a thorough investigation and review of the trial transcript of an individual convicted of a heinous crime, I have concluded, to a moral certainty, that the person was innocent of the crime for which he was convicted and serving time. Jens Soering . . . has spent his last eighteen birthdays behind bars for a crime he did not commit."

BOOK I

WHETHER OUR PRISONS take the form of a chemotherapy regimen, a job loss without hope of reemployment or an actual penitentiary, those of us who wear chains do not want inspiration and comfort as much as information and answers. Can Centering Prayer and Centering Practice really bring us freedom? Who else has tried this method, and did they succeed? What are the precise steps we must take to follow the Way of the Prisoner? This volume will give detailed, practical answers to all of these questions, but before we can embark on this journey, we will have to pay the price of admission.

That price is the full and complete admission to ourselves that the old quick-fix solutions have not worked and never will. As long as we attempt to cure only the symptoms without addressing the fundamental cause of our imprisonment, we cannot find true and lasting freedom. We have to make up our minds to get serious about losing our chains.

Realistically, most people refuse to make that kind of commitment and instead prefer to accommodate themselves to their prisons. With a little reflection we can all think of many such men and women: rather than surrender their old ways of living and thinking, they stay in abusive relationships, addictions or prestigious jobs they secretly hate. Even in my penitentiary most convicts have accepted the bars and locks, because real change takes real courage.

Fortunately, as Christians we are heirs to a spiritual discipline that has a proven, two-thousand-year track record of bringing true change, lasting freedom and the deepest possible intimacy with God. Centering Prayer and Centering Practice are merely modern names for this ancient method of praying and living, perfected by holy men and women who began their journeys no wiser or better than we are. It is a serious practice for serious people, not some New Age fad or hazy mysticism.

What our spiritual forefathers and -mothers discovered was that the root of all prisons, whatever external form they take, is the self; that this self can be dissolved or overcome through nonconceptual contemplative prayer as well as radically self-sacrificial service; and that sincere, dedicated application of these twin tools of the soul will break our chains and unite us with God. In a similar vein Paul wrote, "You were taught . . . to put off your old self . . . corrupted by its deceitful desires . . . and to put on the new self, created to be like God" (Ephesians 4:22).

That may sound vague and speculative, but even our age of false fame and cheap glitter has produced two widely known figures whose very lives validate these lofty metaphysical assertions: the Dalai Lama and Mother Teresa.

I have chosen the XIV Dalai Lama, Tenzin Gyatso, as an example only because everyone has heard of him; no doubt he would be the first to say that thousands of men and women across the world, many of them Christians, have made as much spiritual progress without gaining any fame. Liberation from all prisons of the body, heart and mind is the explicit goal of Buddhist meditation, and in this volume we will touch on the instructive parallels between those Eastern techniques and Christian contemplation. While Buddhism does not aim at *theosis* or divinization/divine union, anyone acquainted with the Dalai Lama's writings and speeches can easily recognize the profound inner freedom animating his life and words. It is precisely this spiritual quality that has allowed him to turn his very difficult external circumstances—persecution, escape, exile and homelessness—into a shining source of inspiration for others.

Mother Teresa began her amazing journey as a kind of exile, too, joining a religious order in Ireland only to be sent to India. In the not-too-distant past England punished its criminals by transporting them to foreign lands, so Mother Teresa's mission to Calcutta could easily have seemed like a kind of punishment to her. Certainly the prospect of tending the sores of lepers every day for the rest of one's life sounds as distressing as any prison you or I must face! Yet Mother Teresa's cross purified and transformed her to the point that she glowed with the presence of God within and drew thousands of others to follow her.

Both the Dalai Lama and Mother Teresa have often said that they are far from special, that anyone can do what they did in the areas of meditation/contemplation and service. This is not false modesty but a simple truth confirmed by the lives of countless men and women, past and present. We can use *their* spiritual disciplines—the practical, step-by step methods of Centering Prayer and Centering Practice—to travel in their footsteps. One of the reasons why I will be telling you a little about my inner and outer life in each Book of this volume is to illustrate that even a convict can successfully follow the Way of the Prisoner.

But, as I said earlier, there is a price of admission for this journey: we must abandon our old ways of thinking and living completely if we want the kind of freedom and peace the Dalai Lama and Mother Teresa found. Losing our chains requires losing ourselves.

The time has come to take our first few steps on this road. In this Book we will study a few of the pathfinders of the past who mapped out our journey and refined our method. One of the most effective tools they developed was the fourfold practice of *lectio divina*:

- *lectio*: listening to the Word of God as revealed in the words of scripture;

- *meditatio*: reflecting on what this Word is telling us personally, today;
- *oratio*: responding to God through active or discursive prayer;
- *contemplatio*: resting in the peace Christ left us, opening our-selves to him in silence, and letting the Spirit pray through us and for us with sighs that words cannot express (John 14:27, Psalm 62:1, Romans 8:26).

All three Books of this volume are structured on these four movements from self to God, as a reminder of our rich Western contemplative tradition. The inward journey is a solitary one, but it need not be lonely if we draw on the wisdom of our predecessors. Before we study them, however, we must as always begin with Christ and the instructions he left us for prayer.

While the sixth chapter of Matthew records Jesus' instructions for what is clearly a formal verbal petition addressed to God, I personally do not believe it is mere coincidence that these same vers-es also serve as an elegant outline or summary of the contemplative process. Most contemplatives and mystics communicated their insights through highly condensed language like poetry or epi-grams, so Christ too may well have combined his teachings on both petitionary and silent prayer into one—a feat of literary and didac-tic compression worthy of the son of God. Since he generally pre-ferred parables and "speaking figuratively," it seems plausible that the Lord's Prayer also uses words with more than one level of meaning (John 16:25).

However, you do not need to follow me on this small leap of faith. None of the topics covered in the following chapters depend substantively on a derivation from the Lord's Prayer. You will lose nothing if you view my choice of introductory verses from that prayer as merely a quaint affectation or a convenient organizing principle.

———

Lectio

Our Father in heaven,
> hallowed be your name . . .

(Matthew 6:9)

Jesus, full of the Holy Spirit, returned from the Jordan and was led by the Spirit in the desert, where for forty days he was tempted by the devil. He ate nothing during those days, and at the end of them he was hungry.

The devil said to him, "If you are the son of God, tell this stone to become bread."

Jesus answered, "It is written, "Man does not live on bread alone."

The devil led him up to a high place and showed him in an instant all the kingdoms of the world. And he said to him, "I will give you all their authority and splendor, for it has been given to me, and I can give it to anyone I want to. So if you worship me, it will be yours."

Jesus answered, "It is written, 'Worship the Lord your God and serve him only.' "

The devil led him to Jerusalem and had him stand on the highest point of the temple. "If you are the son of God," he said, "throw yourself down from here. For it is written: 'He will command his angels concerning you to guard you carefully; they will lift you up in their hands, so that you will not strike your foot against a stone.' "

Jesus answered, "It says: "Do not put the Lord your God to the test."

When the devil had finished all this tempting, he left him until an opportune time. Jesus returned to Galilee in the power of the Spirit. . . .

(Luke 4:1–14)

About eight days after Jesus said this, he took Peter, John and James with him and went onto a mountain to pray. As he was praying, the appearance of his face changed, and his clothes became as bright as a flash of lightning. Two men, Moses and Elijah, appeared in glorious splendor, talking with Jesus. They spoke about his departure, which he was about to bring to fulfillment in Jerusalem. Peter and his companions were very sleepy, but when they became fully awake, they saw his glory and the two men standing with him. As the men were leaving Jesus, Peter said to him, "Master, it is good for us to be here. Let us put up three shelters—one for you, one for Moses and one for Elijah." (He did not know what he was saying.) While he was speaking, a cloud appeared and enveloped them, and they were afraid as they entered the cloud. A voice came from the cloud, saying, "This is my Son, whom I have chosen; listen to him."

(Luke 9:28–35)

Meditatio

1—Centering Prayer—Christ's Desert Temptations as Model
"Our Father in heaven…"—the longer I practice contemplative prayer, the more I have come to see the first four words of his son's prayer as all the truth that is worth knowing, all the truth there really is. Certainly the ultimate purpose of the inward journey can only be to learn as wholly and deeply as possible that the source of all being, each grain of sand and every galaxy, lies in the Infinite and Eternal. "Transforming union," the ultimate fruit of contemplation, means making each moment of our lives a prayer dedicated to this truth.

To know fully that God is *our* Father means recognizing the common origin and shared divine dignity of all created things, no matter how great or humble. Just like a worldly parent, our *Father* resembles each of us on a fundamental level and imparts his nature to us. Yet he is also completely unlike us, *heavenly*, mysterious and otherworldly: the *logos*, the I AM THAT I AM that Moses encountered in the burning bush, the universal principle "in [which] we live and move and have our being" (Exodus 3:14, Acts 17:28). Truly he is both "a God nearby . . . *and* . . . a God far away" (Jeremiah 23:23, emphasis added).

That seeming paradox is, I believe, one of his most powerful means of drawing humankind to himself. The I AM began as the Universal which, through the act of creation, gave birth to the particular in all its multitude; whereas we humans begin with our individual, seemingly separate existence and seek to rejoin the Whole. Our intellects must capitulate before the puzzle of the unity underlying all diversity and the diversity flowing into unity, because language, while capable of stating logical contradictions, cannot resolve them. Our souls, however, can be taught to absorb this divine mystery through the use of silent nonconceptual prayer, prayer that goes beyond words to reach the Word.

I like to think of contemplation, or Centering Prayer, as hallowing God's name in the spirit of the second line of the Lord's Prayer. To hallow means "to sanctify, consecrate, honor [or] revere,"[1] and that is precisely what we are doing with our Father's name, his essence or nature, when we make it the focal point of silent prayer. By returning again and again to his Word in order to quiet the inner whirlwind of our lusts, hates and thoughts, we recognize God to be our greatest good and call on him to lead us into the stillness.

Following God into the stillness is undoubtedly what Jesus thought he was doing when he "was led by the Spirit into the desert" in the second excerpt of our *lectio* section above. But instead of communing with his Father in silence, Christ found himself "tempted by the devil . . . for forty days" and engaged in a battle of scriptural quotations with the evil one. That was how I understood this scriptural passage, anyway, and for many years I paid little attention to it. Only when I was well into my thirties did I finally understand—and promptly burst into laughter. How could I have missed this for so long?

What brought on my moment of insight was, I think, the actual *practice*, as opposed to the *study*, of Centering Prayer. At that point I had just moved up from two to three daily sessions of twenty minutes each, and I was beginning to make the transition to contemplation. So it was real, first-hand experience of some length and depth that now led to a flash of recognition: Christ's temptations appeared to resemble my own struggles during Centering Prayer! Once I made the connection, the parallels were so obvious that I simply had to laugh.

And then sobriety returned, with doubt trailing in its wake. Could Jesus *really* have been practicing contemplation during his time in the desert? I knew that medieval monks and nuns had frequently described the hazards encountered during silent prayer in terms of temptations by the devil, but that did not necessarily mean those contemplatives and I were engaged in the same spiritual practice as Christ.

Yet the possibility was too exciting not to investigate further. If Jesus himself practiced contemplative prayer, then those of us on the inward path can look back even beyond the Desert Fathers of the fourth and later centuries to the son of God himself for guidance on our journey. What an opportunity this would be for us to walk in his footsteps—and what a challenge!

Of course we cannot know with absolute certainty what Christ's spiritual disciplines were, but even at first glance there are tantalizing hints:

- Luke tells us that "Jesus often withdrew to lonely places and prayed," so it seems reasonable to conclude that his plans for this solitary retreat in the wilderness centered on prayer as well (Luke 5:16; see also 3:21, 6:12 and Mark 1:35).

- Christ's instructions for verbal petitionary prayer *also* serve as a wonderfully succinct outline of the silent contemplative process. As noted above, each Book of this volume is structured on the Lord's Prayer as it reflects the purpose, arguably even the technique and certainly the three stages of contemplation.

- A comparative analysis of other contemplatives' experiences suggests that all were engaged in a spiritual practice similar to that of Jesus. In fact, I have been unable to find a record of an inward journey that does *not* contain some usually very clear form of the same three temptations Christ encountered during his prayer in the desert.

That last statement is not as sweeping as it may seem, since I do not claim to be a scholar but merely an interested layman. What I can offer is personal, front-line reportage from the *terra incognita* of the soul, as well as tales I have picked up along the way from other travelers into the dark interior. To test the theory that all of us, including Jesus, visited the same spiritual territory, it is helpful to examine the road maps brought back by five other contemplatives. The last four of these are Christians, but the first one is not.

Like Jesus, our initial case study was a young man who sought the Truth in wild, lonely places, and many Westerners today find his teachings more palatable than the New Testament's. For a dozen years before my own conversion to Christianity, I too considered myself a disciple of his. Eventually I came to see that, as close as he came to the Truth, he did not quite reach all of it. He was not God's first and only begotten son.

We will spend very little time on him here, just enough to glean those very valuable insights of his which contribute to our subject. But by beginning with him, I hope to interest those many, many seekers of truth who, like me, found a spiritual approach with him that mainstream Christianity seemed not to offer. One of the purposes of this volume is to demonstrate that we Westerners need not journey all the way to India to find this meditative or contemplative spirit. Meanwhile, let us make a little detour to the East . . .

2—Centering Prayer—The Buddha

Five hundred years before Christ's birth, a young Indian prince left his palace to seek wisdom. First Siddhartha Gautama visited the acknowledged holy men of his age and culture, Indian John the Baptists, and soon surpassed them all. Next he practiced ascetic techniques like fasting in the desert heat, but this too failed to bring true enlightenment. So at last he sat down under a *bodhi* tree and resolved to meditate until he found the truth. (In his tradition, "meditation" refers to a nonconceptual, wordless spiritual practice that differs from Christian "contemplation" mainly through the latter's intent to open the soul to a God whom Buddhists do not acknowledge. In *lectio divina, meditatio* means discursive reflection on scripture.)

During the first watch of the night, Siddhartha directed his awareness to the vast spans of eternity, which he envisaged as never-ending cycles of birth and rebirth. In that context, he realized, it is clearly futile to become attached to this one brief, impermanent life and its mundane concerns. Christ expressed this insight more concretely during his desert encounter with the devil: "Man does not live by bread alone," adding later that one should "not work for food that spoils, but for food that endures to eternal life" (Luke 4:4, John 6:27).

During the second watch of the night, Siddhartha explored the relationship between actions and their consequences, or the law of *karma*. He came to understand that our restless and ruthless attempts to satisfy our afflictive emotions—the wants and fears, greeds and hates—not only fail to bring us lasting happiness, but also propel us helplessly from one sin to the next and on to a kind of judgment after death: rebirth into a lower realm. Jesus too taught this great truth in, for instance, the parable of the rich man who built larger barns for his wealth and was called to account by God himself: " 'You fool! This very night your life will be demanded of you!' . . . This is how it will be with anyone who stores up things for himself but is not rich toward God" (Luke 12:20–21). Christ knew well the ultimate consequences of failing to "worship the Lord your God . . . only," so the devil's offer of the "authority and splendor [of] all the kingdoms of the world" was no great temptation (Luke 4:9, 6).

During the third watch of the night, Siddhartha saw that suffering can be ended by overcoming its root cause, a specific kind of ignorance: the false belief that there is a true, separate self that is independent from the rest of existence and can control its destiny autonomously. We believe in this spurious self because its lusts or hungers, its desires or aversions, and—most importantly and insidiously—its precious conceptual constructs or thoughts seem so real to us. But if we relinquish our attachments to these physical, emotional and intellectual manifestations of the self, then nothing remains but a clear, empty vessel that, at least for Christians, is ready to receive God's spirit through grace.

Jesus promised that his crucifixion and resurrection would teach believers to see through this illusion of a separate self and to recognize our essential union with the divine: "On that day you will realize that I am in my Father, and you are in me, and I am in you" (John 14:20). Like Siddhartha he showed no patience for the chief source of pride of our precious selves: the products of our intellects, whether clever arguments about the resurrection, sly techniques to evade oaths or any of the many other ways of "setting aside the commands of God in order to observe your own traditions" (Matthew 22:23–33, 23:16–21; Mark 7:9). Pride is in fact the cardinal sin of placing that illusory self in opposition to God to test him, and this is what Jesus refused to do when the devil tempted him to show off his powers to the crowd by leaping off the temple's steeple.

When morning came, the final obscurations were lifted from Siddhartha Gautama's mind, and he awoke to full Buddahood, *nirvana*, the unconditioned. Later he codified his experiences during that night in terms of three mental poisons, or *klesas*, he had vanquished: *greed* for physical pleasures, *hatred* and other afflictive emotions that ultimately lead to negative consequences, and *ignorance* of the transitory, insubstantial nature of all created things, including the prideful self. God's son communicated the same insights in terms of temptations by the devil, because that was what his time and culture could understand—but of course the point here is not to compare Buddha and Christ. What strikes me as significant is that Siddhartha definitely practiced something very similar to what Christians call contemplation. Given the remarkable parallels between his night under the *bodhi* tree and Jesus' desert prayer, it seems probable that both of them were engaged in silent, nonconceptual spiritual disciplines that differed very little.

A quick review of four Christian contemplatives' experiences will not only help to confirm the remarkable consistency of the pattern of three levels of temptations but also provide a useful preparation for more in-depth discussion later.

3—Centering Prayer—Four Christian Contemplatives

In the third century A.D. St. Anthony of Egypt left behind his sister and his fertile farm to live a life of solitary prayer in a hut on the seedier outskirts of town. There the devil tempted him with:

- memories of his property and the sensual and sexual pleasures he had forsaken. These visions, in all their lushness, were still just a dressed-up version of the simple *bread* the devil had offered Christ.
- recollections of emotional intimacy with friends and relatives, greed for money and the power it gave to satisfy his desires, and fantasies of the control and authority Anthony could have achieved by becoming a community leader. All of these are

merely less grand versions of the *authority and splendor* also offered to Jesus, appealing to the afflictive emotions' attachment to this world and the resulting desire to control it.

- fantasies of fame as a revered holy man. Christ would have recognized this as another form of pride in the self, tempting us to *stand on the highest point of the temple* to bask in the crowd's applause.

Next the devil tempted Anthony with culinary delights and other luxuries, the supposed greater good of helping his sister and, most insidiously, doubts about his capacity to survive the rigors of the spiritual life, a kind of inverted pride that tells the self it is unworthy of God's love.

After Anthony had passed all of these tests, he went to live in the town's tombs to confront directly his own physical mortality, an additional spiritual practice found in many Western and Eastern traditions. The devil indeed nearly killed Anthony in those tombs, but the saint emerged with God's blessing—only to lock himself into a desert fort for another twenty years of solitary contemplation! When he reached the age of fifty-five his friends tore down the fort's walls and found Anthony safe, sane and unaged. His life inspired thousands of monks and nuns to follow him into the desert.

Evagrius—whose pupil St. John Cassian brought this Desert Father's teachings to the West in the fourth century through his *Conferences*—called the three basic contemplative vices Christ and Anthony encountered "gluttony," "avarice" and "vainglory," a list Pope Gregory the Great later expanded into his famous "seven deadly sins." In his sixteenth-century *Dark Night of the Soul*, St. John of the Cross discussed these physical, emotional and intellectual/conceptual hindrances on the inner path in order of their moral importance, not their developmental sequence, since "all do not experience [them] after one manner, neither do all encounter the same temptations." But those destined to "pass to the Divine union of love of God" will, according to John, be subjected to a familiar triple set of trials during an extended "night of sense":

- a "spirit of fornication," or hunger for bodily delights like the bread the devil offered Jesus;
- an emotional "spirit of blasphemy," or anger at God for denying the splendor of spiritual pleasures such as visions; and
- a self-doubting "spirit of dizziness," in which the intellect refuses to surrender itself to the divine will, thus putting God to the test.

Once the "night of sense" passes there is a period of consolidation, followed by a "night of the spirit" whose effect is comparable to Anthony's confrontation with the devil in the tombs. After this nearly fatal battle, God explained that he did not intervene to succor Anthony because Anthony needed to lose the final vestiges of a possessive self that clings to divine consolations. John's final "night" similarly focuses on "purging the soul, annihilating it, emptying it or consuming in it . . . all the affections and imperfect habits" that separate us from God.

St. Teresa of Avila's *The Interior Castle* made an important contribution to Christian contemplative literature in the sixteenth century by analyzing the subtler, higher-level manifestations of Jesus' desert temptations. Buddhist insight, or *vipassana*, practitioners speak of *piti*, *sukha* and *ekagatta*: an almost sensual, giddy rapture during contemplation, which is followed by a deep, peaceful pleasure or joy, and finally a laser-like concentration without apparent distractions. Teresa referred to comparable contemplative states as (psychological) delights or (divine) consolations, and her great gift to us is that she, like the insight meditators, saw them as mere stepping-stones on the way to the "prayer of full union":

- At first the practitioner may be granted sensory or physical gifts of the spirit, such as hearing God speak, going into a bodily trance state resembling death or feeling herself corporeally transported to another place during a "flight of the spirit."

- Later the contemplative may experience two types of visions, which Teresa termed "intellectual" and "imaginative," since only the latter involves seeing God and the saints; however, even the so-called "intellectual" visions are in fact emotional phenomena whose primary characteristic is a comforting sense of the divine presence at one's side.

- Finally, to the most advanced travelers on the interior path "the Lord will reveal deep secrets," a divine knowledge directly imparted to the intellectual/conceptual faculties.

Although these spiritual gifts are God-given, the practitioner may easily be led astray by wishful imagining, by a restless chasing after yet more such inner pleasures, and by a devastating sense of abandonment when they are withdrawn. The only safe course in view of these dangers, according to Teresa, is the continual practice of profound humility and a complete abandonment to the divine will.

In any case, the true and ultimate goal of the inner journey is to overcome the self completely in the "prayer of *full* union." Here there is no awareness of a separate self whose will may be focused or not, but only a nonconceptual, imageless sense of the divine Presence within. While Buddhists recognize no God in their enlightenment or *nirvana*, they nevertheless capture some idea of this state when they speak of knowing without a knower, breathing without a breather. Even when not praying, the contemplative now sees "all things in God and God in all things," as the thirteenth-century German mystic and poet Mechthild of Magdeburg wrote.

Father Thomas Keating will presumably be extremely embarrassed upon finding himself placed in the company of Saints Anthony, John and Teresa. Nevertheless, I cannot overlook the same threefold structure of temptations or distractions during contemplation that he lays out in *Open Mind, Open Heart* and in this volume's Appendix. This reflects the pattern we already found with Jesus, Buddha and the three saints[2]:

- "Ordinary wanderings of the imagination and memory," at least in my own experience, almost invariably begin with the same physical hungers and lusts as Anthony's reveries or John's "spirit of fornication," whence they may wander anywhere. In fact, so many modern meditators and contemplatives write of being disturbed by thoughts of pizza that I have come to see that particular dish as the devil's ultimate refinement of the *bread* that tempted Jesus.

- "Thoughts that give rise to attractions or aversions" are based on the afflictive emotions, our greed for *authority and splendor*. However, I have found that emotional attachments are also the primary force behind Keating's "thoughts that arise from unloading of the unconscious," a sometimes very painful process (certainly in my case!). We can cling to our inner hurts and coping mechanisms with the same ferocity with which we can become attached to, say, our appearance.

- "Insights and psychological breakthroughs" and "self-reflections such as, 'How am I doing?' or, 'This peace is just great,' " are two varieties of intellectual or conceptual constructs of which we are so proud that we use them to *put God to the test*.

Centering Prayer and contemplation gradually reduce the self's attachments to these three devilish temptations, thereby creating an open space in the soul into which God can enter. Some of the Desert Fathers called this process *kenosis*, an ancient Greek word meaning self-emptying. In standard theology, *kenosis* refers to Christ emptying himself of his divine qualities to descend to the human level, but in the contemplative context it denotes the practitioner's relinquishment of selfish concerns—and even the concept of a "self" itself—in order to purify his soul and rise up to what

Keating calls "transforming union" with God. Yet the self is not an enemy whom we seek to destroy in prayer, according to the modern German contemplative Father Williges Jäger, a Benedictine monk who is also a licensed instructor of the Sanbo-Kyodan school of Zen Buddhism:

> [The practitioner of silent inner prayer] simply wishes to restrain the self within its proper bounds and to give it the weight it really deserves. For this reason [the contemplative process] aims to recognize the self for what it really is: an organizational center for the personality structures of each individual person, . . . a conglomeration of conditioning factors, . . . a collection of behavior patterns. . . . The experience of mysticism leads the person to the point where he no longer identifies with this superficial self and thereby becomes free for a reality in which the self no longer dominates. . . . The wave of self ebbs away, and in its place the ocean experiences itself as a wave. . . . Everything is both wave and ocean.[3]

To experience ourselves as "both wave and ocean" is something Jesus wanted us to share with him: "I pray for those who will believe in me through [the disciples'] message, that all of them may be one, Father, just as you are in me and I am in you. May they be in us . . . that they may be one as we are one: I in them and you in me" (John 17:20–23).

Again, we cannot conclude with absolute certainty that Christ himself practiced contemplative prayer, based only on the account of his temptations in the desert and the striking similarities between Jesus' experiences and those of other contemplatives. Yet the practice of Centering Prayer has taught me to trust my intuition in matters of faith. My glimpses of the I AM within have only been fleeting at this relatively early point in my interior journey, but I have tasted living water and will return to this well every day of my life. So why would the son of God deny himself the intimacy of sitting quietly with his Abba?

4—Centering Prayer—The Guises of God

Of course Christ's Abba is our Abba too by adoption, and when we sit quietly in contemplation with him, our hope is to know and be known by him as deeply as this is possible while we are still in the flesh. Just as no literal jailbreak would be complete without the motivating dream of Rita Hayworth on a Caribbean beach, so is ever-closer union with God the goal of the Way of the Prisoner. Before delving more deeply into the methods of Centering Prayer and Practice in this Book's *contemplatio* section, therefore, I think it would be helpful to examine more closely the object of our spiritual hard labor: not mere freedom to chase the same old worldly desires, but transformation into the Oneness with the Father which Christ already had and wanted for us too (John 17:22).

The God of the contemplatives is exactly the same as every other Christian's God, of course. Yet it is an obvious scriptural, historical and experiential truth that he reveals himself to individuals and indeed to cultures in different ways, depending on the person's or the society's level of development. To Jacob God appeared as a wrestling "man," to Abraham he came as an "angel," while to Moses and the Israelites he showed himself as a "pillar" of smoke or fire. None of these manifestations of the divine is necessarily truer than the others, nor do they contradict each other. Our Father comes to his sons and daughters in whatever way suits them best at their particular stage on the spiritual path.

Not every appearance of the I AM is equally complete, however. Depending on each person's or society's inner needs and outer problems, God may for example be seen primarily as a mystical, all-embracing Earth-Mother, with relatively less emphasis on divine Love's role as an exacting standard by which all our actions will ultimately be judged—and, where appropriate, punished. The I AM is always the same, but we—in other words, our selves—only perceive those sides of God that we feel we need at our current level of spiritual development or in our present life crisis. By means of this selective blindness, we in a sense create our own gods, not in our own image, but in the image of our wants and fears.

As we learn to relinquish those wants and fears in contemplative prayer along with all the other manifestations of the self, we are inevitably forced to let go of our old, self-based ways of relating to God as well. This deconstruction of our former ideas of the divine is especially difficult because it is precisely during times of stress—for instance, the psychological stress of *kenosis*—that we tend to revert to relatively more primitive but more comforting images of God. The scarier our inner or outer world becomes, the more we yearn for a divine Parent to smite the Philistine enemy hip and thigh or comfort us in his sheltering arms.

Distinguishing the true, formless I AM from the various disguises we create for it to suit our needs requires a systematic analysis of the relationship between our own and our culture's spiritual development, and the different modes in which God manifests himself to humankind. In *Invitation to Love*[4] Father Thomas Keating lays out a very useful scheme for doing precisely this, a system he in turn derived from anthropologist and author Ken Wilber and the theories of child psychologist Jean Piaget. Below I have adopted a version of Keating's ideas with additions and revisions so major that he may no longer recognize his thoughts in mine, but I cannot neglect to credit him with inspiring me. Again, my purpose here is not to construct yet another conceptual toy for our intellectual amusement, but to present you with a tool I myself have used to unlearn my former ideas of God.

I think it is helpful to think of humankind's and each person's spiritual maturation process as a series of covenants that follows our paradigm of the levels of *kenosis*. Every stage is marked by an act of relinquishment of self that opens the soul more and more to its Creator. Thus society's and each person's view of God becomes ever clearer, without the divine nature itself changing.

These ascending levels are not neatly separated in practice, of course, and at any particular point of a culture's development there may be many individuals who have either regressed much lower or progressed much farther than their fellows. What I am trying to elicit here is not some ironclad rule of the soul, but a general sense of how humanity and each human is drawn closer and closer to God through a process of self-emptying.

(This interpretation of Israel's covenants with its Creator is, of course, purely Christian in character and takes no account of the great progress of Judaic theology and religious scholarship in the intervening millennia. Our Jewish brothers and sisters share a common spiritual history with us Christians at least until the birth of Jesus, but I am in no way suggesting that the following analysis of God's relationship with his people *before* the coming of his Son is the only one—or, outside the context of this volume's overall argument, even the preferred one.)

5—Centering Prayer—The Covenant of the Rainbow— Genesis 9:1–17

Yahweh's first covenant with his people reflected a physical relationship with and understanding of the divine. Historically, humankind was at its most primitive level of social development, based on small family groups each headed by a patriarchal leader like Noah. Since human existence was completely dominated by immediate physical needs such as food and shelter, people recognized God in those natural forces, like rain or sun, which either provided or denied the essentials of life.

To worship this Provider humans sacrificed to him the first-fruits of their small flocks or of their early attempts at subsistence agriculture, as did Cain and Abel. Since each morsel of food was so desperately precious in those prehistoric times, such simple offerings were in fact the first attempt by humans to give away something of their selves—that is, their only means of physical survival—to their Creator. In Noah's case his righteousness was rewarded with the promise that humankind's physical existence would never again by destroyed completely. The symbol of this covenant was the rainbow, which combined in one the two natural forces determining humanity's fate: sun and rain.

On each individual human's level, the equivalent developmental stage is that of the two- to four-year-old, whose life is dominated by physical dependence on its parents much as Noah's culture required the divinely regulated cycle of seasons to provide reliable harvests. It is during these early years that psychologists locate the child's formation of a body-self as well as its power/control and affection/esteem centers. For the first time the child experiences itself as a being physically separate from its mother, with whom it had hitherto lived in an almost paradisiacal state of near union.

The same early experiences that can cause an individual's psychological development to "fix" at or become focused on this stage may also affect his or her spiritual maturation and view of the divine. No doubt all of us can imagine how an overly strict upbringing might lead a child to see God as an omniscient Policeman, and we may be able to recognize the same authoritarian relationship between Creator and creation in some of today's popular theologies. However, our task here is not to take the speck out of our brother's or even our culture's eye, but to recognize *our own* regression to this level of development especially at moments of physical or emotional crisis.

When the insurance claim adjuster denies coverage or the doctor delivers her sad-eyed prognosis, when the lawyer presents his bill along with the usual apologies or the drunk driver stutters out his sorry excuses—have we *really* stopped wishing, even for an instant, that God would drown these miscreants in a deluge of sewer water that would make Noah's flood look like a mere trickle? If not, then we have not yet absorbed the deeper meaning of the covenant of the rainbow. Only if we, like Noah, leave behind the old world of the self's possessions and attachments can we weather our lives' storms and finally encounter the Source and

Wellspring of all creation on a rain-washed mountain peak atop a brand new world.

6—Centering Prayer—The Covenant of Circumcision— Genesis 17:1–27

Yahweh's second covenant operated on the emotional level of the self-emptying paradigm. At the time God made his new pact with Abraham, humankind was about to progress to its next highest stage of cultural development: small patriarchal family clans were coalescing into larger social groups such as "nations," requiring at least rudimentary government in the form of "kings" (Genesis 17:6). What mattered most to early men and women now was identifying themselves as members of these new, more anonymous groups and differentiating themselves from their enemies through tribal markings or scars like circumcision, the symbol of this covenant.

Here we can clearly recognize the second level of the process of *kenosis*, reflecting the central role of the afflictive emotions: grasping and rejecting, wanting and hating, classifying the world into "mine" and "not mine." In its most megalomaniac form, this way of relating to one's environments seeks the "splendor and authority of . . . all the kingdoms of the world," to use the devil's turn of phrase (Luke 4:6, 5). If world conquest seems too large a task, we attempt to satisfy these afflictive emotional urges on a cultural level by identifying with our social groups' leaders—our sports team captains and presidents—and believing our club or country to be better and more virtuous than our opponents'.

While allegiance to a tribe and its king may be necessary for survival, such loyalty has no metaphysical significance—unless the tribe is a spiritual one and its chieftain is God. Thus, as with Noah and primitive humanity's food sacrifices, Abraham's covenant also reflected an element of rudimentary self-emptying, since members of this group did not swear fealty to the warrior with the strongest sword-arm, but to an invisible God who merely promised worldly rewards to distant descendants. Although the afflictive emotional mechanisms still operated by classifying others as friends or enemies of the tribe, at least that division was now based on spiritual criteria.

This stage of cultural development, translated to the realm of individual psychology, corresponds to the four- to eight-year-old, who must separate himself from his parents and establish a sense of his own emotional identity—often through automatic, unreflected opposition to authority. During these years children also learn which tribal rituals, markings or uniforms make them members of "their" family, school or social class, and how to identify others as "not their" sort of people. Even play activity at this stage often reveals over-identification with group affiliation. Another important feature of this developmental level is a strong interest in possessions—"But that's *my* toy, give it back!"—which reflects the establishment of the afflictive emotional mechanisms.

Interacting with or encountering God primarily through feelings may perhaps be seen in the currently popular emphasis on a "personal" relationship with Jesus, or in the medieval mystics' passionate pursuit of their divine Lover. Especially in times of trouble, it is undoubtedly comforting to think of the I AM as a warm, mothering, sweetly compassionate Shepherd who shelters his flock from all dangers. Yet such a view of God, though true so far as it goes, is just as incomplete as the earlier, partially accurate image of the divine Judge whom we must make offerings to receive protection. Writing in a related context, the apostle John pointed out that "God is greater than our hearts," which so often seek to possess what they love (1 John 3:10). Our purpose must be to detect and then discard these convenient but limited roles which we seek to assign to the Unlimited.

The more we lose ourselves, the closer we come to God and, in this case, the essence of the covenant of circumcision: "the Spirit . . . by [whom] we cry 'Abba, Father' " (Romans 8:15). An even better translation of the Aramaic "Abba" might be "dear

Father" or even "Daddy," and it is no coincidence that this suggests the personal warmth and intimacy that I think lies at the heart of the mystical approach to God. Some, like me, must learn to abandon ourselves to the nurturing embrace of divine Love, to accept the consolations our Father offers the members of his spiritual family. Such an act of surrender can be tremendously difficult for those with granite-hard, mountainous selves like mine.

Others may need to recognize that so long as we are in the flesh, we are separated from God to some degree and thus must cry Abba. The Greek word Paul used for "cry," *krazo*, means to "croak (as a raven) or scream, . . . to call aloud (shriek, exclaim, intreat)," all of which suggest a yearning that can never be fully satisfied in this world.[5] Indeed, it could be said that only the separation or distance between God and humans makes mutual love even possible, since any emotional tie requires *two* who are then bound to each other by their attraction. If we persuade ourselves that complete, permanent union with the I AM is possible on this side of death, we may therefore be seeking to circumvent God's wisdom of keeping our focus on the divine by never completely satisfying our desire for him. That may be a hard and painful truth, but even in spiritual matters, we Christians must "live by faith, not by sight" (2 Corinthians 5:7).

7—Centering Prayer—The Covenant of the Law— Deuteronomy 5:1, 2

Yahweh made a third covenant with his elect as Israel prepared to take its next step up the ladder of cultural evolution, corresponding to the intellectual/conceptual level in *kenosis*. No longer would God's people be a nomadic, homeless tribe led by a chieftain combining religious and secular functions, like Moses, but a nation of "decrees and laws" settled in their own land (Deuteronomy 5:2). From the simple decalogue delivered on Mount Horeb, this new kind of relationship with the I AM would eventually flower into the profusion of minute rules and traditions practiced by the

Pharisees, as well as celebrations of divine Wisdom as found in Job, many psalms, Proverbs and Ecclesiastes.

Whereas true worship had once consisted of food offerings and then of religious-tribal loyalty, Yahweh now demanded obedience to his commandments. This primarily intellectual task of understanding and conforming to divine law once again contained traces of self-emptying: instead of "everyone [doing] as [he] saw fit," humans were now required to do as God saw fit—or at least as his priests interpreted his laws (Judges 21:25). While scripture does not name a specific symbol or sign for this covenant, I think the temple in Jerusalem fittingly represents this attempt to approach Yahweh by "understand[ing] the way of thy precepts" (Psalm 119:27).

It is worth noting at this point that the third covenant did not completely supersede the two earlier ones but subsumed them and gave them new meaning. Both sacrifices and circumcision now became part of the temple ritual, with their own complex set of rules and codes regulating their correct performance. As we shall see, this process of integration and reinterpretation was in some ways repeated in the fourth and final covenant, that of the blood.

Including and successfully building upon earlier stages of development is, of course, a central concept in developmental psychology as well. That field's equivalent of the intellectual/conceptual covenant of the law is found in children over the age of eight, who experience the emergence of reason and personal responsibility as they enter full reflective self-consciousness. While they still have much physical, emotional and intellectual growing left to do, they now have all three basic components of a complete, adult personality.

In the spiritual realm, relating to God on a primarily mental or conceptual level can lead to rules-based religiosity, or to the counting of angels on pinheads and other fascinating theological endeavors. I assume that readers of this book at the very least will have flirted with the temptations of theology and either intuited the futility of this approach or, like me, struggled bitterly and been defeated. God "has . . . set eternity in the hearts of men; yet they cannot fathom what [he] has done from beginning to end" (Ecclesiastes 3:11).

Of course this does not mean that the academic study of things divine serves no purpose at all. At the very least, this intellectual approach to God avoids the error of forcing him into limited roles that fill our human needs, as in the earlier covenants of the rainbow and the circumcision. Whether there is any deeper meaning to be rescued from the covenant of the law—apart from the law of love, which is really the basis of the fourth covenant—I cannot say with certainty. Yet I also cannot deny the divine beauty that shines through truly great minds reaching for God, even if, like Sophocles, they are neither Christian nor Jewish:

> I only ask to live, with pure faith keeping
> In word and deed that Law which leaps the sky,
> Made of no mortal mould, undimmed, unsleeping,
> Whose living godhead does not age or die.[6]

8—Centering Prayer—The Covenant of the Blood— Luke 22:20 et al.

Yahweh's fourth and final covenant is, of course, that of faith in the redeeming power of his Son's blood. What may have moved God to initiate a new relationship with his people at that particular point in history was the great effusion of pharisaical rules and regulations that formed the ultimate, yet ultimately dead attempt to worship the I AM under the covenant of the law. Jesus certainly spent much of his preaching career on excoriating the pious Israelites of his day both for their uncompassionate legalism, which forbade healing on Sabbaths.

A new way for humanity to relate to God had never seemed more necessary, yet who can deny that even two thousand years later our society still does not live by the covenant of the blood? In most regards humankind hardly seems to have progressed beyond the atavistic tribalism of Abraham's age, as a quick glance at any day's newspapers will reconfirm. Perhaps only the eyes of faith, which recognize the evidence of things not seen and the substance of things hoped for, can detect the considerable progress that civilization has nevertheless made toward the standards Jesus set for us.

While faith replaced offerings, tribal allegiance and compliance with divine decrees as the new basis of humans' relationship with God, the fourth covenant still incorporated some elements of the three earlier ones by clothing them with new meaning. The early Israelite sin-offering or scapegoat was now transformed into the "Lamb of God, who takes away the sins of the world," national leaders like Moses were superseded by the son of God as "head of the body, the church," and the minutiae of the deuteronomic code were "fulfill[ed]" by Christ's law of self-sacrificial love, which "sums up the Laws and the Prophets" (John 1:29, Colossians 1:18, Matthew 5:7, 7:12). As followers of Jesus we too must "offer [our] . . . bodies as living sacrifices" to become, not mere members of Yahweh's tribe, but "children of God . . . born of God," obeying Christ's "new command . . . [to] lay down our lives for our brothers" (Romans 12:1; John 1:12, 13; 1 John 2:8, 3:16). Thus the self-emptying aspect, which was only implicit in the earlier covenants, now became the defining center and basis of worship for those of us whose "old self was crucified with [Jesus] so that . . . we will also live with him" (Romans 6:6, 8).

Thanks to C. G. Jung and his successors, psychology is the only scientific discipline to address such issues of meaning or belief and to recognize that there are some truths beyond the grasp of reason. It could even be said that we do not reach full maturity until we encounter the limits of our mental powers and find the courage to make the leap of faith. While some developmental psychologists may disagree that their field of knowledge intersects with theology or spirituality at this point, our purpose here is merely to elucidate very briefly an age- and growth-dependent hierarchy of ways of experiencing reality that reaches its apex, not in the processes of the mind, but of the soul. Certainly no reader of this book will have any difficulty admitting that "God made foolish the wisdom of the world, . . . [f]or the foolishness of God is wiser than man's wisdom" (1 Corinthians 1:20, 25).

Of course "[e]xpressing spiritual truths in spiritual words" is easy enough in the mellow light of one's reading lamp, but as noted earlier, we all tend to revert to more primitive relationships with God and the world whenever lightning threatens to strike our comfy armchair (1 Corinthians 2:13). Then we are quick to ask for the divine protection our regular church attendance has surely earned us, for the sweet consoling love that God presumably reserves for members in good standing of his spiritual tribe, and for the logical reason or grand design he is bound to have for visiting disaster on fine folks like us. Faith in Christ's blood, on the other hand, requires us to accept our crosses without protection, consolation or explanation as Jesus did and to "suffer with [Christ] . . . so that we may also be glorified with him" (Romans 8:17).

Whereas under the earlier covenants humans experienced the I AM through guises like the avenging Judge, the comforting Shepherd or "the Law which leaps the sky," Jesus taught that "God is Spirit" and, through his self-sacrificial death, then demonstrated this Spirit's essence: "God is love" (John 4:24, 1 John 3:16). But terms like "spirit" and "love" are so abstract and difficult to grasp that we humans needed Christ, "the exact representation of [God's] being," to reveal the divine nature to us concretely, as the Word made flesh (Hebrews 1:3). Blood is not only the sign or symbol of the fourth covenant but its living center, since it stands for the life Jesus gave out of love for us. Through the gift of faith, that higher form of knowledge beyond the senses, feelings and mind, we Christians thus can glimpse the creative and organizing principle of the universe "from whom all things are and for whom we exist" (1 Corinthians 8:6).

To resolve the paradox of "know[ing] . . . love that surpasses knowledge," Anthony of Egypt, Teresa of Avila and their colleagues decided to accept the invitation to "approach God with freedom and confidence . . . through faith" in Christ and encounter the I AM directly, without food offerings, tribal markings, religious laws or even the "exact representation" of the God who is Spirit (Ephesians 3:19, 12). Granting humankind complete, intimate access to God was, after all, the whole purpose of Jesus' mission: through him "the veil is taken away," and now "God lives in us and his love is made complete in us" (2 Corinthians 3:16, 1 John 4:12). As "God's children, . . . heirs of God and co-heirs with Christ," we do not even need Jesus to intercede for us, as he himself stressed in his upper room discourse: "I am not saying that *I* will ask the Father on your behalf. No, the Father himself loves you because you have loved me and have believed that I came from God. . . . Ask and you will receive" (John 14:26, 27, 24, emphasis added).

What prospective contemplatives are likely to ask is how we can know something as unearthly and infinite as God directly, and what the eternal, divine Spirit looks like when it does not take the form of the first and only begotten Son. In the next two chapters we will examine the answers to these questions given by scripture and by the contemplative masters themselves.

9—Centering Prayer—The Transfiguration

The synoptic gospels' account of the transfiguration of Jesus records a real historical event, a spiritual retreat "onto a mountain to pray," whose most plausible interpretation is as a mystical and contemplative experience induced in the three disciples by their divine leader (Luke 9:28). Significantly, it was "*as [Christ] . . . was praying*"—no doubt accompanied by Peter, John and James, who prayed with him on other occasions too—that "the appearance of [Jesus'] face changed, and his clothes became as bright as a flash of lightning" (Luke 9:29, emphasis added; cf. Mark 14:33). Following this initial clue, we can discern a trail of further evidence indicating that the disciples experienced an altered or special state of consciousness comparable to the progressively deepening levels of contemplation, which we will study in more detail in this Book's *contemplatio* section: relaxation, concentration and expansion.

Relaxation. According to Luke's account, Peter, John and James were "very sleepy" as the transfiguration began. His Greek word for "sleep," *hupnos*, would later provide our language with the root for hypnosis, but even in Luke's age this term carried the alternate meaning of spiritual torpor or deep relaxation.[7] In Matthew's gospel Joseph was also in *hupnos*-sleep when the angel appeared in a dream to explain Mary's unconventional pregnancy, while all three synoptic evangelists used *katheudo*, meaning to lie down to rest, for the disciples' ordinary, unspiritual sleepiness in the Garden of Gethsemane (Matthew 1:24, AV). Practitioners of Centering Prayer will of course recognize *hupnos* as a non-practitioner's awkward term for the deliberately generated state of relaxation with which each session of contemplation begins.

Concentration. After this trance-like period, Peter, John and James "became fully awake . . . [and] saw [Jesus'] . . . glory and the two men standing with him" (Luke 9:32). Their emotions and thoughts were still active, so they were assailed with mystical visions of "glorious splendor" and even recognizable figures like "Moses and Elijah" (Luke 9:31, 30). It is at this stage or level of prayer that mystics and contemplatives part company: the former become attached to these beautiful images of the divine, whereas the latter use concentrative techniques to follow Christ's three disciples into deeper spiritual states that do not depend on visual representations of God, but instead allow direct encounters with the I AM.

As Peter, John and James quieted their hearts and minds, the visions ended with the "men . . . leaving Jesus," and "a cloud appeared and enveloped them, and they were afraid as they entered the cloud" (Luke 9:33, 34). Matthew adds the interesting detail that the cloud was "bright," and all three evangelists use the word *episkiazo* for "envelop," meaning "to cast a shadow upon; i.e., to envelop in a haze of brilliance" (Matthew 17:5).[8] Clearly this cloud should no more be thought of as a natural puff of cumulus than the cloud in which Yahweh came to Moses just before issuing the Ten Commandments and again during the dedication of the meeting tent (Exodus 19:9, 34:35; cf. 1. Kings 8:10). Contemplatives as diverse as Pseudo-Dionysius and the unknown author of the four-teenth-century Carthusian text *The Cloud of Unknowing* tried to capture their experience of God during prayer with very similar word-pictures, since the term "cloud" conveys perfectly the form-lessness of the I AM as well as its paradoxical melding of shadow-darkness with diffused luminescence. Certainly such descriptions match my own glimpses of God in the final expansion phase of contemplation, as does the disciples' common reaction of fear upon first meeting the divine on such intimate terms.

Expansion. Finally, we read that a "voice came from the cloud, saying, 'This is my Son, whom I have chosen; listen to him'" (Luke 9:35). The fact that the I AM is not a cold, impersonal metaphys-ical force, but instead wants to communicate with us during silent inner prayer and reveal to us the nature of divine Love through Jesus, is something on which all Christian contemplatives agree. This is also what separates us from Buddhists and others who have not been granted the gift of faith: when they enter deep states of meditation, they apparently encounter emptiness or a void, not our Father's loving care and concern.

What makes Luke 9:35 somewhat problematic from the point of view of this discussion of Centering Prayer is that the gospel seems to claim God spoke in words, whereas most contemplatives report that their experience of the divine was non-verbal. While I do not doubt the accuracy of scripture, I believe there are some rea-sons to suppose that this communication from the I AM did not take the form of words *per se*, though the evangelists obviously had to use everyday language to communicate effectively with the widest possible readership. Instead of using the conventional

Greek term for "speak," *epo*, Luke employed *lego*, meaning "to lay forth; i.e., relate"—usually in words, but not necessarily so.[9] Moreover, his word for "voice," *phone*, means "a tone (articulate, bestial or artificial); . . . probably akin to [to lighten (or) show] through the idea of disclosure"; this again leaves considerable room for concluding that the I AM showed or disclosed its message non-verbally to the disciples.[10]

What God wanted Peter, John and James to know was, in any case, not a complex set of theological instructions or divine laws, but simply the world-saving truth that their seemingly human leader Jesus was in fact the son of God. That would have required no words, only sudden insight like that experienced by other disciples much later on the road to Emmaus (Luke 24:31). But even if, in the singular and special case of his son's transfiguration, God did use words during the three disciples' prayer, there can be no doubt that he has communicated a very similar message to all Christians wordlessly for two thousand years since then.

This message is, of course, that "the kingdom of God is among you" and even "within you," since the Greek preposition *entos* carries both meanings with equal weight (Luke 17:21). Peter, John and James needed to learn that they were in the presence of the firstborn son of God, and so do we—for now, through faith, we are all younger sons and daughters of God. Recognizing the holiness and divine origin of all creation, including Mother Teresa's lepers and you and me, is the ultimate fulfillment of the contemplative vision and of course the very heart of Christ's truth. That message requires no words, but only eyes to see and ears to hear (cf. Matthew 13:16).

10—Centering Prayer—The Masters' Views on Knowing and Finding God

So, let us examine what a few of our spiritual predecessors have written about both *how* contemplatives "know" God, and *where* they encounter him. One of the best descriptions of the former comes down to us through *The Mystical Theology* of Pseudo-Dionysius (also known as Dionysius the Areopagite), a Syrian monk of the sixth century who greatly influenced Meister Eckhart, Mechthild of Magdeburg, John of the Cross and Teresa of Avila:

> [L]eave behind you everything perceived and understood, everything perceptible and understandable, all that is not and all that is, and, with your understanding laid aside, . . . strive upward as much as you can toward union with him who is beyond all being and knowledge. By an undivided and absolute abandonment of yourself and everything, shedding all and freed from all, you will be uplifted to the ray of the divine shadow which is above everything that is.[11]

Eight hundred years later, Meister Eckhart expanded on the above in his wonderful Sermon 71 on Paul's conversion on the road to Damascus:

> A master says: "Whoever speaks of God through a simile speaks of him in an impure fashion; but whoever speaks of God by (using the term) nothing speaks of him properly." . . . Even if I take the light that is God as it touches my soul, this is wrong. I have to take it from where it bursts forth. . . . And yet, if I take it as it bursts forth, I still have to be freed from this bursting forth. . . . If we are to know God, it must happen without a medium. Nothing alien can enter into it.[12]

What strikes me as particularly significant about such descriptions of knowing God in "nothing" is that they mirror the process of *kenosis* in silent prayer. There we come to know that the so-called self is also "nothing"—nothing but a ragbag of hungers, lusts and noisy ideas which all together keep shouting, "me, me, me!" As we take note of our minds becoming distracted from our focal point during prayer, we learn by direct experience, over and over and over again, that there is a *real* me, a soul that calmly observes, and is entirely separate from, the physical, emotional and intellectual/conceptual manifestations of the self. And when we encounter the I AM during contemplation, we discover—again by direct experience—that God has a real existence quite apart from the roles our selves create for him, as we discussed earlier in this *meditatio* section. His true nature, however, is as far beyond words as our souls are beyond the pathetic self we so often think of as "the real me."

Rediscovering our being in its Source is why we sit in contemplation; it is an act of remembering as well as of unknowing or unlearning. And as we shed all those accretions that hid the true I AM and the true, inner self or soul, we find that the silence of awe is not only the most appropriate response to the mutual in-dwelling of God and human, but its very essence.

Mystery on top of inexpressible mystery! Nowadays theologians use the term "apophatic" to refer to such discourse based on the unknowability and transcendence of both God and of the human spirit, but the underlying principle goes back to the Mosaic command not to make images of the inscrutable I AM nor to misuse the divine name. "No one has seen the Father," Christ himself taught his disciples, and St. Augustine went further: "God should not [even] be said to be ineffable, for when this is said, *something* is said. . . . That is not ineffable which can be called ineffable" (John 6:46). "Detach yourselves from the image," Meister Eckhart wrote, "and unite yourselves to the formless being."

But the contemplative masters have at least left us some idea where to find the God who "lives in unapproachable light" (1 Timothy 6:16). In sixteenth-century France, for instance, Jean-Pierre de Caussade discovered him in much the same place I did, though obviously with far, far greater profundity:

This treasure is everywhere. It is offered to us all the time
and wherever we are. All creatures, friends or foes, pour it
out in abundance, and it flows through every fiber of our
body and soul until it reaches the very core of our being. If
we open our mouths they will be filled. God's activity runs
through the universe. It wells up and around and penetrates every created being.[13]

This revelation of divine omnipresence carries a logical corol-
lary that someone like me can only accept with difficulty: if "all
things [are] in God, and God in all things," as Mechthild of
Magdeburg wrote, then God is also in *me*. Personally, I find it easier to see Christ in another convict's face than in my own because
I practice the trickiest form of idolatry: self-hatred, the worship of
unrealistically high expectations for myself, which then justify the
secret pleasure of hating myself when I fail to meet them. Yet even
Jesus said, "If anyone loves me, . . . [m]y Father will love him, and
we will come to him and make our home with [*or*: our dwelling in]
him"—a teaching found over and over again in the New
Testament epistles quoted throughout this volume (John 14:23).
Meister Eckhart phrased this insight particularly beautifully in his
Sermons 59 and 12:

This is why God gives birth to himself into me fully, so that
I may never lose him. Everything I have by birth I cannot
lose. God takes all his pleasure in this birth, and he gives
birth to his Son in us so that we have all our pleasure in
it..., so that he might reveal to us the utter abyss of his
divinity and the fullness of his being and nature. . . . Such
a person stands in God's knowing and in God's love and
becomes nothing other than what God is himself.[14]

Elsewhere Meister Eckhart wrote, "The eye with which I see
God is the same eye with which God sees me." I believe this turn

of phrase was inspired by 2 Corinthians 3:18, which could easily serve as a sort of Contemplative Manifesto since it perfectly describes both the goal and process of silent prayer. The best translation I have found of this verse is Martin Luther's German one, but for our purposes here the New American Bible Revised New Testament serves almost as well:

> All of us, gazing with unveiled faces on [or: contemplating as in a mirror] the glory of the Lord, are being transformed into the same image from glory to glory, as from the Lord who is Spirit.[15]

"Gazing . . . on the glory of the Lord" is the essence of the deeper levels of contemplation, and our ultimate goal is "being transformed into the same image" of God that Christ bore. What I find truly striking is the New American Bible's alternative translation, which is Luther's primary one: "contemplating as in a mirror." Apparently the kingdom of God really is *within* us, visible in the nearest mirror if we look with the eyes of faith.

1 Corinthians 13:12 suggests that Luther's translation using "mirror" more accurately conveys Paul's own thoughts on this matter than the New American Bible's preferred one. In this well-known passage, the great apostle also reminds us that our intimacy with the I AM can never be total as long as we are in the flesh: "Now we see but a poor reflection *as in a mirror*; then we shall see face to face. Now I know in part; then I shall know fully, even as I am fully known" (emphasis added). John, the great visionary among the evangelists and epistle writers, also noted this dichotomy between the present reality of God in us and the future completion of this as-yet partial indwelling of the divine: "Dear friends, now we are children of God, and what we will be has not yet been made known. But we know when he appears [or: when it is made known] we shall be like him, for we shall see him as he is" (1 John 3:2, emphasis added). Of course John had experienced Jesus' trans-

figuration on the mount many years before he wrote those lines, so he had clearer insight into such matters than do we. But if the two-thousand-year tradition of Christian contemplative prayer holds true, then we do not need to climb a real mountain to find God. We only have to empty our selves so the I AM's cloud can descend into our souls too.

11—Centering Practice—Christ's Cross as Model

We cannot leave behind Christ's transfiguration without studying what happened afterwards: Jesus "came down from the mountain" and immediately resumed healing members of the "large crowd [which] met him" in the valley below (Luke 9:37). That same, seemingly counterintuitive movement from a mystical peak directly to an active and practical social ministry can also be seen at the very beginning of Christ's public career. As soon as he vanquished the devil in the desert, "Jesus returned to Galilee in the power of the Spirit, . . . taught in their synagogues" and began to drive out "evil spirits" (Luke 4:14, 15, 36). Presumably, he could have stayed in the wilderness to enjoy silent union with his Father in prayer, just as he could have remained on the mountaintop in one of the "three shelters" that Peter wanted to "put up" (Luke 9:33). But instead, the son of God went back to the messy, unspiritual world of sin and sickness to *intentionally* lay down his life in an act of divine, self-sacrificial love. And that was no accident.

Since Jesus repeatedly told believers that "anyone who does not take up his cross and follow me is not worthy of me," pain and death must also be at the core of our own spiritual identity as Christians (Matthew 10:38). Centering Practice is in some ways an attempt to come to terms with Christ's really quite terrifying call, *not* to perform convenient good deeds and be nice to one another, but to be flogged bloody, nailed to a stake and speared through the ribs. *That* certainly is what my life in the penitentiary feels like to me on most days, and no doubt your prison, whatever it may be, seems no better to you. Surely all of us have wondered, why would a loving God demand this of us? Can it really be true that "in *all* things"—even in our chains—"God works for the good of those who love him" (Romans 8:28)?

To answer those questions among others, I suggested in this volume's introduction that we can use our crosses, our prisons, our pain to grind down the self in much the same way as we do with Centering Prayer—hence the name Centering Practice. As with contemplative prayer, this idea is neither mine nor new but has its own lengthy tradition. One of my favorite contemplatives, the fourteenth-century German abbot Thomas à Kempis, wrote in *The Imitation of Christ* that

> God desires that you learn to bear trials without comfort,
> that you may yield yourself wholly to Him, and grow more
> humble through tribulation.... Be assured of this, that you
> must live a dying life. And the more completely a man dies
> to self, the more he begins to live to God.[16]

Here Thomas was writing of our old friend *kenosis*, self-emptying, not in the context of contemplative prayer only, but also of the prayer our daily lives and tragedies can become if we use our suffering to empty the soul of self.

What I call Centering Practice does not, however, allude to Biblical teachings that "a broken and contrite heart" leads to repentance, or that "[i]t was good for me to be afflicted so that I might learn [God's] decrees" (Psalms 51:17, 119:71). Such ideas are beautifully expressed in many well-known Old Testament passages, and they undoubtedly convey psychological, moral and even spiritual truths. But by now we are sufficiently familiar with the three levels of the contemplative process to recognize that these two concepts operate on the emotional and intellectual/conceptual levels, respectively: "heart" and "learn[ing]." Centering Practice, on the other hand, is modeled on the New Testament's central symbol and message: Christ's cross. On this cross his death was transformed into eternal life, and Jesus clearly wanted those who believe in him to participate in this painful yet glorious destiny too: "[W]hoever serves me must follow me [to the cross]; and where I am, my servant also will be" (John 12:26). What interests us here is precisely how we too can change our chains into blessings.

12—Centering Practice—*Kenosis* Leading to Self-Sacrifice

Might it be possible to use the contemplative approach in this context? Certainly Paul emphasized the self-emptying aspects of the crucifixion to the Philippians: Christ, "being in very nature God, . . . [nevertheless] made himself nothing . . . humbled himself, and became obedient to death" (Philippians 2:6–8). As with Thomas à Kempis, we can again recognize strong echoes of *kenosis* here. Applying this same principle to himself, Paul wrote:

> That is why, for Christ's sake, I delight in weakness, in insults, in hardships, in persecutions, in difficulties. For when I am weak [that is, when the self's spurious power is diminished] then I am strong [because in a self-emptied soul] Christ's power may rest in me.
>
> (2 Corinthians 2:10, 9)

The fact that our souls respond to two such widely differing experiences as contemplative prayer and worldly suffering with a similar self-emptying process is no coincidence and has important implications for our own spiritual development. What Jesus saw so clearly was not only that Centering Prayer and Centering Practice share a common basis of self-emptying, but that they are actually two parts of the same path, the former inevitably leading to the latter. He expressed this thought much more eloquently than I could do: "If anyone would come after me, he must deny himself *and* take up his cross," pray in inner silence *as well as* suffer and die (Matthew 10:24, emphasis added).

But why must contemplation in the desert *necessarily* entail crucifixion on a lonely hillside, not only for Christ but for all of us who would follow him? Why can we not simply stay in the wilderness and bask in the divine Presence? Because the essence of the God we worship is love, and the more intimate we become with him through silent prayer, the more he compels us to live out this love in the world.

As far as I can tell from my study of comparative religion, Jesus was the first of God's children to take this truth to its ultimate, fatal conclusion: embodying divine love in *every* breath means we do so even with our *last* breath. Learning how to follow his footsteps on this most difficult of journeys is the purpose of Centering Practice.

The key here is to understand the nature of Jesus' Abba and ours and what it implies. While Christ knew directly that "God is love," the rest of us need the gift of faith to intuit this truth (1 John 4:8, 16). If, from that base, we are also granted the grace of contemplative prayer, we can experience firsthand that the I AM THAT I AM within is benevolent and giving, not only sustaining but actually embracing or cradling us, and drawing us toward it. Some medieval mystical poets even went so far as to describe this divine attraction with metaphors of romance or passion.

Eventually our Lover makes his conquest, and the contemplative passes from experiences of God in prayer to the "transforming union" with the divine that continues both during and outside of contemplation. It is at this point that we reach the nexus between Centering Prayer and Centering Practice: now that we no longer just know God's nature but have subsumed our selves into Love free of self, we must somehow *live* the love with which we have become united. But how can mere human flesh embody the selflessly loving nature of God?

Christ was the first to understand that merely holding sermons on love, like so many other holy men and women before him, cannot be the best and truest embodiment of divine unselfish Love, because there is still a self that is preaching. "Faith without deeds is dead," his brother would later become fond of saying (James 2:26). Jesus was the first to take the logical, necessary next step by intentionally giving up the self's most precious possession: the life, the breath, the body it has temporarily borrowed from God. And Christ was the first to realize that, to be truly selfless, his death must serve others, since no soul but his own would profit from a quiet departure from this suffering world.

Jesus was indeed the first to understand all this, but his followers soon learned from him. "I desire to depart and be with Christ, which is far better," Paul wrote the Philippians (1:23). To him postponing his death actually seemed like the greater sacrifice and service. Yet even as he wrote those lines, Paul was already in prison and on the long road to Rome, where he too would die to serve his Lord and save his fellow man by his testimony (Philippians 1:12–14). He could not escape the fatal logic of the cross.

The greatest love, the love most like God's, is to abandon the self on that cross, to accept all the pain and to "lay down his life for his friends" (John 15:13). If we take the first step on the inward journey and practice contemplative prayer to overcome the self, we *must* end here, alongside Christ: giving ourselves away completely in self-sacrificial, suffering service to others, up to and including death. "To this you were called, because Christ suffered for you, leaving you with an example that you should follow in his steps" (1 Peter 2:21). Only on the cross can we achieve *true* "transforming union" with God, for only here can we embody divine love in our own human form.

The cross God sends you may not require you to literally give your life. But do not be surprised if it does: before the Nazis killed him, Dietrich Bonhoeffer wrote,

> The cross is laid on every Christian. The first Christ-suffering which every man must experience is the call to abandon the attachments to the world. It is that dying of the old man which is the result of his encounter with

Christ. As we embark upon discipleship, we surrender ourselves to Christ in union with his death—we give over our lives to death. . . . When Christ calls a man, he bids him come and die.[17]

Answering that call in the spirit of Jesus is the goal of the methods presented in this volume as Centering Practice.

Oratio

(Elijah) went a day's journey into the desert [and] traveled forty days and forty nights until he reached Horeb, the mountain of God. . . . There he went into a cave and spent the night. And the word of the Lord came to him: "What are you doing here, Elijah?" He replied, "I have been very zealous for the Lord God Almighty. The Israelites have rejected your covenant, broken down your altars, and put your prophets to death with the sword. I am the only one left, and now they are trying to kill me too." The Lord said, "Go out and stand on the mountain in the presence of the Lord, for the Lord is about to pass by."

Then a great and powerful wind tore the mountains apart and shattered the rocks before the Lord, but the Lord was not in the wind. After the wind there was an earthquake, but the Lord was not in the earthquake. After the earthquake came a fire, but the Lord was not in the fire. And after the fire came a gentle whisper. When Elijah heard it, he pulled his cloak over his face and went out and stood at the mouth of the cave. . . . The Lord said to him, "Go back the way you came, and go to the Desert of Damascus. When you get there, anoint Hazael king over Aram."

(1 Kings 19:4, 8–13, 15)

O Lord, give me the courage to follow you
    not only into the deserts of this world
        to feed and clothe the hungry and homeless,
        to comfort and heal the sick,
        and to visit those in prison;
but also into the wild and lonely places of my parched soul,
    which yearns for your living water
        more than the dunes of the Sinai long for rain.
O Lord, forgive me as I lose my way amid
    the ever-changing, whirlwind cravings of my body,
    the quaking of a heart torn between love and terror,
    and that false self whose flame distracts me from your light;
        you are in none of these, I know.
Thank you, O Lord, for calling me back to yourself when I fail,
    with the same still small voice
that guided Elijah out of the cave of his fears and despair
    to return to your service,
        both on the mountain of visions
        and on the plains of kings and battles.

Contemplatio

1—Centering Prayer—Seeing Obstacles as Opportunities

Luke's account of Christ's temptation in the desert passes over one crucial aspect of the experience that Matthew gets exactly right: "Jesus was led by the Spirit into the desert *to be* tempted by the devil" (Matthew 4:1). In other words, the son of God set out for the wilderness with the *intention* of facing his adversary in spiritual battle, since he had to know beforehand whom he would meet out there. For us too the whole point and purpose of contemplation is to deal with physical, emotional and intellectual/conceptual temp-

tations over and over again, until we have freed ourselves completely of these manifestations of the self.

That may sound grim and joyless, but it is not. We are pursu-
ing the most important goal imaginable—union with God—and
our road there is interesting, varied and challenging. Yet we risk
losing our way and becoming discouraged if we forget what exactly our purpose in prayer is—overcoming that old devil, the self—
and what it is not—"feeling" something or "understanding" something. The latter two are paths of the mystic who seeks God with
his heart and the theologian who pursues the I AM with his mind.
Contemplatives, on the other hand, have already intuited the
divine Presence within and now work to dismantle the wall of self
that separates our souls from that Spirit. To us, glorious visions or
subtle intellectual insights are only picturesque roadside scenery—
not our destination, or even milestones along the way.

So much Christian contemplative literature tells of the frustration, disappointment and self-doubt many practitioners felt
because their silent inner prayer brought no doves descending on
their heads, only an endless series of temptations and distractions.
I sometimes find myself wishing I could go back in time to tell
them that they need not have worried, they were performing their
contemplation absolutely correctly. They were *supposed* to be com-
bating the devil! Anthony of Egypt could have explained all this
to them: even after his terrifying yet liberating experience in the
tombs, he voluntarily had himself walled into a desert fort for
another twenty years of fighting evil spirits.

Anthony also would have appreciated two extremely useful
ideas taught by Buddhist *vipassana* meditators:

- "making friends with your [inner] noise" in the sense of
  familiarizing yourself with the temptations that affect you
  the most and developing a sense of compassion for your
  poor little self as it fights for survival by creating those distractions; and

- experiencing a "moment of delight" each time you encounter a temptation during prayer and overcome it, and enjoying each one of the million little victories over the self we must win before we achieve "transforming union."

Approaching the difficulties encountered during contemplation with this kind of constructive attitude—seeing so-called obstacles as new opportunities to deny the self and advance spiritually—not only makes prayer itself much more joyful and enjoyable, but also brings benefits such as increased dedication and consequently accelerated progress. Our task is difficult enough in itself even without creating a mind-set of dread and anxiety simply because we are encountering those devilish temptations which are in fact the very reason why we practice inner prayer.

To me contemplation is very much like jogging. Outsiders may regard these two disciplines as pointless exercises in masochism, but we who practice them know well the subtle satisfaction of conquering the self with sneakers or with prayers. Disciples of the track and disciples of the Way both understand that in some ways the journey itself is the goal, and that the race is never really finished as long as we are in the flesh. There is always one more second to shave off one's personal best, one more temptation to overcome. So we stay on the road and become lovers of solitude, of early mornings, of sweat physical and spiritual.

Those days when the wind is constantly at our backs and our sneakers grow wings, those sessions when our souls melt into their Source and we know *almost* as we are known—well, of course all joggers and contemplatives enjoy them! But secretly we love even more that feeling of braving cold drizzle and dodging mud puddles, of staying on Center despite the self's slyest new tricks. These are the times we make the most progress and hone our skills for the future. And, truth be told, doing battle against outer or inner storms is a grim sort of fun!

The key to progress in silent inner prayer is, in any case, not technique but intent. Our goal is to free our souls of their encumbrances, to open them up to God and unite them with their Wellspring. All of us must find our own individual methods for accomplishing this purpose, and all of us can learn from the experiences of others. That is why in this volume's introduction I suggested that the practice of contemplation must be nourished by a steady diet of spiritual reading.

If you have never tried wordless prayer before but now feel drawn to seeking the I AM in silence, try making a commitment to eight weeks of two daily twenty-minute sessions. Then, no matter how difficult or discouraging one individual prayer or even two or three days in a row may be, stay with the practice until the two months of your "enlistment" are over; your self is a ruthless enemy who will fight fiercely to maintain its hold over your soul, so the only fair test of this discipline is an overall evaluation after a considerable period of time. I suggest you keep a daily log for jotting down your impressions and monitoring your progress, something I now wish I had done when I began praying silently.

2—Centering Prayer—Relaxation, Concentration, Expansion

Acquiring the skills of Centering Prayer is one of the most difficult learning experiences we will ever encounter, because our mental faculties have never done anything remotely like this before. As a result, beginning contemplatives can expect the first six to twelve months of their practice to be even more torturous and unpleasant than, for instance, the initiation period for joggers, who have at least used their legs for walking in the past. I can offer almost no consolation in this regard, apart from the firm assurance that thousands of others have mastered this skill and found it more than worth the initial effort and pain.

But before we can even practice contemplation proper, we must become skilled in concentration, or maintaining a mental focus on one point for a sustained period of time. This is Centering

Prayer, as I use that term: a form or method of training the soul for the eventual transition to contemplative prayer, which is as formless as the I AM.[18] For me, this change occurred only nine months or so after beginning my journey, but I was able to devote a great deal of time and energy to prayer because prison freed me from external obligations.

Perhaps it was the very intensity of my still-unskilled effort that led to my nearly failing a crucial early test. For a while I became attached to the subtle mental states that concentration makes possible, in my case the ability to shift warmth and energy to different parts of my body during a visualization prayer on Christ's wounds. Other contemplatives report experiencing similar phenomena and insist that they must all be treated as distractions or diversions. Pleasant though they may be, they neither last long nor advance us at all toward our real goal of breaking down the structures of the self. We do not actually need deep levels of concentration, only enough to catch each link of the chain that is our self. The ability to sustain focus is our most important tool for dissolving that chain, but it must be used for its proper purpose: contemplation.

Each individual prayer session proceeds through the stages of relaxation, concentration and expansion. Relaxing the body and mind before praying is as important as stretching before jogging, while concentration clears the soul of background noise so it can focus on God. At the beginning of our journey, as we learn how to concentrate with the method of Centering Prayer, this is in fact all we do.

Only after acquiring this skill can we proceed in our prayer sessions to the expansion or contemplation phase, in which we actually do battle with the devil by:

- observing mental phenomena—the physical, emotional and intellectual/conceptual manifestations of the self—as they arise against the backdrop of the divine Presence within, like ripples across the pool of Silence;

- noting each mental phenomenon's basic insubstantiality: all of them are impermanent, unsatisfactory and lacking any independent existence;
- watching each one vanish or "self-liberate" as we see through it; and
- returning to our point of focus: a prayer word in Centering Prayer, or the Spirit itself in the contemplation I practice.

Although these four steps are listed separately here, they are actually performed all at once, in a split second. Most importantly, we do not use the will to attempt to banish mental phenomena by force, but instead allow them to arise into empty space created by our use of a focal point. Once we then note each phenomenon's lack of substance, it disappears immediately on its own.

This fourfold contemplative process is in fact what Christ practiced in the desert. Instead of entering into considerations of his caloric deficit due to fasting, for instance, Jesus saw through the devil's temptation to its basic insubstantiality ("Man does not live on bread alone . . .") and immediately returned to his contemplative focal point, his Abba (". . . but on every word that comes from the mouth of God," Matthew 4:4, giving the rest of the quotation abridged by Luke). The two gospels' narrative accounts only hint at the details of the technique that we will study in great detail later, but the essence of it is right there before us in scripture.

The mental phenomena referred to just now are, of course, the devil's temptations, the three ways in which the self manifests itself during contemplation:

- physically: "My foot itches so badly that I keep forgetting to Center on God";
- emotionally: "If only my coworker had not made me mad this morning, my prayer would be so much more peaceful"; and

- intellectually/conceptually: "Finally *I'm* getting it right, *I'm* thinking only of the prayer word and nothing else— wait, no . . . !"

It has taken us our whole lives, up until the point when we begin Centering Prayer, to build this strange and amazing thing we call our self, so we might expect to spend just as many years dismantling it step by step during contemplation. Fortunately, liberating our souls will not take quite that long, because the self lacks any real, independent existence. As we shall see later—and, more importantly, as we shall experience directly and sometimes painfully in contemplation—there really is nothing more to the self than our hungers, hates and clever ideas. It is "nothing but a bundle or collection of different perceptions, which succeed one another with an inconceivable rapidity, and are in perceptual flux and movement," as David Hume wrote. Yet this illusion is what separates our soul from God.

That is what we are teaching ourselves to see by focusing on one manifestation of the self at a time, noting the aspects of its insubstantiality mentioned above and then observing as it disappears. True, we will have to confront the self with its own nonexistence a million times during contemplation before we achieve "transforming union." But the process is progressive, so we soon begin to notice ever-larger changes in our prayers, our emotional relationships and our whole approach to life as pieces of the self crumble away.

3—Centering Prayer—Relaxation—General Considerations

The relaxation phase of Centering Prayer can be thought of as quieting primarily the physical manifestations of the self, whereas the concentration phase calms the emotional and intellectual projections of that little devil. While both phases serve to prepare the soul for contemplation in the expansion phase, they are enjoyable in and of themselves and bring their own medical and psychological benefits. A widening body of research indicates, for instance, that even simple relaxation techniques like transcendental meditation (TM) can lower blood pressure, reduce stress and lead to better mental health.[19] Certainly thorough relaxation is essential to fruitful contemplative prayer, as I personally have had to learn several times over: some of my own spiritual dry stretches passed only when I returned to the basics and took plenty of time in each and every session to relax and concentrate properly.

In its widest sense, relaxation includes lifestyle factors like physical fitness and mood-altering substances. For instance, I have stopped drinking caffeinated drinks, since I believe I can detect a noticeable difference in my prayers even hours after consuming a cup of coffee. As your own contemplative practice matures and you experience more and more moments of absolute Presence both during and outside of prayer, your soul, too, will naturally respond by jettisoning worldly barriers to God and his creation. This is not at all masochistic or ascetic, but is simply a healthy preference for divine living Truth, which feels so much better than the lies that drugs and TV feed us.

Having thus at least reduced some of the more obvious external obstacles to internal stillness, we can now turn to what may be the most important aid to successful, consistent relaxation before and during contemplation: the discipline of a regular prayer schedule. Conditioning the body, heart and mind to quiet themselves automatically at certain times each day is easy, since all of us carry accurate biological clocks, but training our selves in this way does require dedication, effort and the sacrifice of dubious pleasures like morning TV. Fortunately, Centering Prayer is so rewarding that after a few weeks you will wonder how doing the crossword over breakfast could ever have seemed preferable to sitting in silence with God.

The two daily twenty-minute sessions recommended for beginners should ideally be spaced eight to ten hours apart, at the beginning of the day and then again about halfway through the waking hours. This keeps the soul in contact with its quiet center at regular intervals during the day without conflicting too badly with the demands of daily life. Since contemplation requires alertness, attempting to pray late at night, when body, heart and mind are exhausted, is generally not recommended; I personally reserve this time for intercessory prayer.

Whether to engage in Centering Prayer when one "does not feel like it" on any particular day is a question that would not even have occurred to our spiritual forefathers and -mothers, but in an age and culture marked by hedonistic *self*-fulfillment, a few words on this subject are necessary. Let us recall, then, that the desires or aversions of the self are exactly what we hope to conquer through our practice, and that God waits for us even when we would rather find heaven in a pint of gourmet chocolate ice cream. Of course your self would much prefer for you to give in to culinary temptations, or remember last-minute chores, or feel strangely tired at prayer time—if you stay with your discipline, your self will eventually shrivel into near-nothingness!

4—Centering Prayer—Relaxation—Techniques and Suggestions

As far as relaxation during each prayer session is concerned, I follow all the usual preparatory practices—a darkened (but not completely dark), quiet room, secured from interruptions by a "Do Not Disturb" sign—with the one addition of earplugs, which I recommend highly. By blocking outer noise, you can focus exclusively on the inner manifestations of the self that separate you from God. Of course God may speak to you through the sparrow trying to build a nest outside your window, but quiet contemplation is *not* the appropriate time for experiencing the divine in nature.

Our next subject, posture during seated meditation, does actually matter, even if I do sound like Mary Poppins in this paragraph. Keeping the spine straight and all the vertebrae aligned is the best defense against the sleepiness all contemplatives occasionally encounter, but sitting up straight like our mother told us also aids the breathing process on which Centering Prayer is based. The standard head position during Centering Prayer is chin tucked, jaws (but not lips) slightly parted, and tongue relaxed fully against the incisors. Whether you rest your hands on the arms of the chair, place them together loosely in your lap or use one of the traditional Indian *mudras* does not matter, so long as your chosen position allows you to relax completely.

Proper relaxation also includes training the soul to enter the glide path down to deeper, stiller levels of consciousness when presented with certain external cues or signals. I have read that lighting a candle or incense works well for some, but I silently say an old Byzantine prayer at the beginning of every contemplation session:

> Serene Light,
> shining in the ground of my being,
> draw me to yourself.
> Draw me past the snares of the senses,
> out of the mazes of the mind.
> Free me from symbols, from words,
> that I may discover
> the Signified, the Word unspoken,
> in the darkness
> that veils the ground of my being.

Note that this prayer faithfully reflects the contemplative or *kenotic* paradigm: physical ("snares of the senses"), afflictive emotional ("mazes of the mind") and intellectual/conceptual ("symbols and words").

This or any other prayer of your choice can be used to "regularize" the breath, a useful practice taught in many traditions. On each odd-numbered line of the prayer, breathe in as deeply as you can, hold your breath for a few seconds, and then exhale as deeply as possible on each even-numbered line, for a total of five complete

breaths over the ten lines of the prayer above. (The usual recom-
mendation is for ten, not five, of such full breaths.) This exercise
clears the lungs, energizes the soul and once again warns the self to
quiet down.

Classical *lectio divina* does not work for me as a preparatory
practice, but you may wish to try it. This is the traditional method
of prayer that has supplied me with the structure of each Book of
this volume: *lectio* (scriptural reading), *meditatio* (discursive reflection), *oratio* (verbal prayer) and *contemplatio* (silent prayer).
Personally, I tend to slip back into *meditatio* during the time that
should be devoted to *contemplatio*, but your experience may differ.

Once actual prayer begins, there may be a period of several
minutes during which aching knees, itchy feet or twitching eyelids
may bother you. This will be especially common in the early
months of your spiritual practice, but even long after you thought
you had conquered such crude hindrances, the devil will occasionally revert to these oldest of tricks. If you experience genuine pain,
you must of course move, but if discomfort is all you feel, you
should try to sit with this sensation at least for a while before you
shift your position. More than likely, this is merely one more
attempt by your self to distract you from prayer, and if you simply
let this physical phenomenon go like all the other manifestations
of the self, it will pass as quickly as it arose.

Although the above procedures for relaxing in preparation for
prayer require considerable space to describe in writing, they are
performed quickly and easily in practice. Centering Prayer in itself,
even without the deeper satisfaction of contemplation during the
expansion phase, is so rewarding that, like me, you will find yourself looking forward to your quiet time with God on almost all days.
The dirty laundry can wait half an hour; right now, it is time to "go
into your room, close the door and pray to your Father, who is
unseen" (Matthew 5:6). So turn down the lights, breathe deeply a
few times, and prepare to meet your Maker! He wants to meet you,
too, and asks neither for great ceremony nor for "many words . . .

babbling like pagans" (Matthew 6:7). Just one word, repeated
silently, will do.

5—Centering Prayer—Concentration . . . But Not Too Much Concentration

Silently repeat one word—how easy that sounds if you have never
tried Centering Prayer! Just one brief attempt, however, will
demonstrate that this spiritual discipline may be the most challenging skill you will ever attempt to master. And then one day,
after endless hours of frustration, the knowledge will dawn deep
inside you that you were never meant to *master* this spiritual practice at all, but that you must let your self go and let the Word master you.

It is this intent of surrendering to divine Love, this insight into
the ultimate purpose of the Centering process, that differentiates
Christian contemplatives from the practitioners of other concentrative methods. As far as the mechanics of the technique are concerned, not much separates us from the Hindu *yogi* focusing ever
more deeply to reach states of absorption far more profound than
in any Christian prayer form; or the Zen *roshi* mindfully seeking the
void, *nirvana*, the unconditioned; or the medieval mystic longing
for ecstatic union and divine visions; or the modern transcendental meditation (TM) student in search of inner tranquility; or the
Olympic athlete hoping to beat a record through visualization
exercises; or the mid-level executive trying to reduce his high
blood pressure with autogenic stress management techniques. All
of them begin their journey into the interior by Centering on one
point—a word or phrase, an image, a candle's flame, a physiological function like the heartbeat—in order to generate a concentrative state culminating in a phenomenon known variously as "the
sign of concentration," or "the Christ-eye."

Having reached this level of focused inner stability, adherents
of these schools, traditions or techniques then use widely different
methods to achieve their equally varied ultimate aims. Mystics

might at first seem to be most closely related to contemplatives because of our common faith, but their supercharged emotions and glowing visions are actually almost the exact antithesis of the inner state we need to achieve to reach the Silence within. In fact, our nearest methodological cousins are Buddhist *vipassana* practitioners; they too seek to erode the self by confronting it over and over again with the basic insubstantiality of its physical, emotional and intellectual/conceptual manifestations. Their goal, however, is to escape the cycle of *samsaric* existence by emptying the self, whereas for us *kenosis* is only the prelude to the indwelling of the I AM.

Dismantling the self by forcing it to recognize its own nothingness does not require deep levels of concentration at all, but only enough to maintain a sensitive alertness to, and heightened awareness of, the inner processes of the self. These processes are our target: the ability to focus is merely a tool to slow down that noisy torrent and to create a zone of relative quiet from which we can take aim undisturbed. Because our quarry is literally as fast as thought itself and devilishly tricky to boot, we need to be extraordinarily quick-witted and vigilant to keep it in our sights; that is what makes contemplation so challenging as well as satisfying. And just as a real hunter cannot afford to become so absorbed in his prize buck that he neglects wind direction, topography and other relevant factors, so too can excessive concentration become a hindrance for the contemplative.

The real danger is that truly intense focusing can easily turn into a form of grasping at or clinging to our Father. From the contemplative point of view, this is the basic mistake of both mystics and *yogis*: the former intensify their desire for God into an ecstatic passion, while the latter induce a trance state by obliterating the self through an act of will. Of course they are rewarded with magnificent visions in one case and profound absorption into the One in the other. But both of these means of reaching for the I AM still involve the self and its afflictive emotional wants—in this case, the otherwise quite laudable wish to be (re)united with God—and so long as that self remains active, the inner experience of the divine must remain temporary. As soon as the state of concentration ends, so does the self-willed state of union.

What contemplatives seek, on the other hand, is the permanent transformation of every waking and even sleeping moment into oneness with our Father and his will. Millennia of experience have shown that the only effective path to this goal is to open a space for the I AM to enter at *its* initiative, by clearing away the self's sensations, feelings and ideas. Thus we do not learn the skill of concentration to take hold of God with special intensity, but to focus on and evaporate away the flood of physical, emotional and intellectual/conceptual encumbrances that separate our soul from God.

As your own contemplative career progresses, you should become aware of how the inner space of silence expands both during prayer and subtly but increasingly in daily life. When you begin, you will feel yourself clinging to your prayer word like a drowning person hugging a life preserver in a storm-tossed ocean. Practice will soon stabilize your inner focus, as if your soul were perched one-legged on the narrowest of rocks amid the raging waves. Eventually that rock becomes an island and then a continent from whose beaches you can safely observe the sea. One day you will see the other side: the ocean has turned into a wide stream. At last it narrows to a river, then a brook, and finally a trickle or drip at your feet.

When the self's inner processes flow by at such a low rate, the transition from concentration to contemplation is so fluid as to be almost imperceptible. And even if we remain "only" in the concentration phase, we are doing essential spiritual construction work, expanding and stabilizing yet further the soul's base of assault on the self. Skillful Centering is the key to contemplation, so additional practice in holding focus is time very well spent indeed.

6—Centering Prayer—Concentration—Focal Point— Prayer Word

To calm the body, heart and mind during Centering Prayer, we need a focal point upon which our attention can rest and from which it can resist the pulls and pushes of the self. The traditional focus for silent inner prayer is a word or phrase, but novices may find the idea of "choosing" the "right" word a little intimidating. Since even secular transcendental meditation (TM) instruction includes the ceremonious transmission of an individual, secret mantra to each student there must be some special significance to this aspect of contemplative prayer as well—or so one might think.

While other traditions have their own teachings and techniques that deserve our respect, of course, I would advise you to attach no importance to the choice of prayer word and to select a word *without* meaning or emotional content. Methodologically, the prayer word is nothing more than a concentrative focal point, a tool we need to quiet the self and prepare the soul for contemplation. Whichever one we use, its meaning lies entirely in that letting go of our own concerns and turning to God. The word is a sign of our intent to surrender the grumbling stomach, the frustration at our coworker, and that clever idea for rearranging the furniture, and instead dedicate our time completely to the opening to the I AM.

Long before I realized that "Hallowed be your name" served nicely as a shorthand description of Centering Prayer, I thought of the different prayer words I tried out as being various names of God: Abba, Father, Jesus, *Christos*, One (as in the *Shema*), but also Mercy, Grace, Faith, Hope and Love. Most of the words I experimented with had two syllables because I prefer to "say" the first one on the in-breath and the second one on the out-breath, but "saying" the entire word on the out-breath is absolutely permissible too. In fact, there are no hard rules here at all, except that the word should hold as little significance as possible for the practitioner.

That last point seems counterintuitive only so long as you think of the prayer word as having some magic power of its own.

On a practical level, a word without special meaning is less likely to spark off one of the never-ending chains of thoughts, feelings, memories and associations that are the self's most potent weapon against prayerful quiet. "Mercy," for instance, can lead to "Sisters of Mercy Hospital . . . that's where they took my sister when she broke her leg when we were ten . . . the kid in the next room had the biggest teddy bear I'd ever seen . . . why didn't we see any bears when we visited Yellowstone National Park last year? . . . boy, I can still taste the burgers we grilled out there . . . that reminds me, I still have to check if my stock in Heinz Ketchup rose or dropped." All of that, as any novice with even five minutes of Centering experience knows, takes about two seconds during actual prayer! And, unfortunately, all prayer words carry the potential for similar mental digressions. Where were *you* when you heard that the pop group Abba broke up, for instance?

In the end I settled on "Yahweh" as "my" prayer word precisely because it has the least superficial significance of all. It also contains no plosive or sibilant consonants, which you too will probably find to be distracting, and the vowels are pleasingly low and sonorous. Most importantly, "Yahweh" *sounds* like the in- ("Yah-") and out-breath ("-weh") and thus blends beautifully into my primary focal point, the breath.

7—Centering Prayer—Concentration—Focal Point—Breath

After some experience in Centering Prayer, you will find that the prayer word fades and eventually even disappears as your concentration deepens. It becomes almost like a hum in the background, the tightrope you can feel under your feet without necessarily having to see it. Centering without an apparent Center is a sign that your practice as a whole and this prayer session in particular are progressing as they should be, since silent inner prayer really is meant to be wordless. When you encounter the great Silence within, you will *not* be hearing yourself chant "Yahweh, Yahweh, Yahweh" inside!

For this and several other reasons laid out below, I advocate using the breath as the primary focal point to build concentration and prepare for the transition to contemplation. While prayer words and even prayer phrases have their uses, as we shall see, they are not by any means required and in my opinion should not be the mainstay of this spiritual discipline. Praying completely without words is not some radical notion of my own but a practice specifically endorsed by virtually all Christian denominations. Below I quote the *Book of Common Prayer* as one example among many, only because I hope it has the broadest ecumenical appeal for readers of this volume:

Q: What is prayer?

A: Prayer is responding to God, by thought and by deeds, with or without words.

Q: What is adoration?

A: Adoration [one of the principal kinds of prayer] is the lifting up of the heart and mind to God, asking nothing but to enjoy God's presence.[20]

But even if we can agree that words are not necessary to "lift... up . . . the heart and mind to God . . . [and to] enjoy . . . [his] presence," why should the breath be our preferred point of focus? Why not a candle, an icon or statue, a mental visualization or even the heartbeat? All of these have indeed been used in Christian prayer and that of other religions, but I believe there are excellent scriptural, practical and—if you will forgive my presumption—personal "visionary" reasons to Center on the breath or spirit.

Scriptural. Anyone who has dipped his or her exegetical toe into the deep sea of New Testament Greek will realize that the preceding sentence contains an implicit error: the authors of the gospels, epistles and Revelation knew only *one* word for both "breath" and "spirit": *pneuma*. This fact has direct bearing on my argument for using the breath as the primary concentrative and, later, contemplative focal point, so I think it will be helpful to examine Strong's entry for *pneuma* in its entirety:

> 4151. Pneuma, *pnyoo'mah*; from [*pneo*, to breathe hard]; a current of air, i.e. breath (blast) or a breeze; by analogy or figuratively, a spirit, i.e. (*human*) the rational soul, (by implication) vital principle, mental disposition, etc., or (*superhuman*) an angel, daemon, or (*divine*) God, Christ's spirit, the Holy Spirit:—ghost, life, spirit (-ual, -ually), mind. Compare [*psuche*; . . . breath, i.e. (by implication) spirit, . . . the animal sentient principle only; thus distinguished from [*pneuma*] which is the rational and immortal soul].[21]

What strikes me as significant here is that the origin of *pneuma* lies in a verb exclusively devoted to breathing, *pneo*; that the primary definition of *pneuma* is breath; and that the three uses of *pneuma* associated with spiritual matters are all "by analogy or figuratively." My point is that, when the Greek-speaking authors of our holy scripture set down their texts, they did not think of the word "spirit" in anything like the way we understand that term but instead thought *pneuma*—a word that even sounded like "breath" to them because of its origin and certainly evoked all kinds of subconscious and conscious associations with the respiratory process.

Especially in contexts where *pneuma* is used figuratively, the cloud of breath-related connotations can bring us prospective and practicing contemplatives many new and interesting insights into what the authors of scripture "heard" or "thought" alongside the obvious surface, denotative meaning of the word. Here are some examples:

- "God is pneuma-breath, and his worshippers must worship in pneuma-breath and truth" (John 4:24).
- "And with that [Jesus] breathed on them and said, 'Receive the Holy Pneuma-Breath'" (John 20:22).

- "We do not know what we ought to pray for, but the Pneuma-Breath intercedes for us with groans that words cannot express" (Romans 8:26).
- "And pray in the Pneuma-Breath on all occasions with all kinds of prayers and requests" (Ephesians 6:18).
- "For the word of God is living and active. Sharper than any double-edged sword, it penetrates even to dividing psuche-soul and pneuma-breath" (Hebrews 4:12).

With only two exceptions (Matthew 14:26 and Mark 6:49, relating to possession by an evil spirit), every use of the English word "spirit" in our New Testament is based on the original Greek *pneuma,* so you can continue the above experiment at will without fear of failure.

Pneuma is translated as "breath" only twice in the New International Version, and in both cases "spirit" would serve just as well:

- "And [God] is not served by human hands, as if he needed anything, because he gives all men life and pneuma-breath and everything else" (Acts 17:25).
- "And then the lawless one will be revealed, whom the Lord Jesus will overthrow with the pneuma-breath of his mouth and destroy all the splendor of his coming" (2 Thessalonians 2:8).

Especially this second passage is a perfect example of how the original and primary meaning of *pneuma* clearly influenced the Greek-speaking authors in their metaphorical use of that term. In John 20:22 (Jesus "breathed on them . . . the Holy *Pneuma-Breath*"), we can still recognize the Judaic influence of Genesis 2:7 (God "breathed into [Adam] the breath of life"), but in 2 Thessalonians 2:8 the respiratory connotations of *pneuma* are so strong that translators commonly use "breath" here in spite of their

overwhelming preference for "spirit" everywhere else. Yet semanti-
cally—and, arguably, theologically too—it is the same *pneuma* that
Jesus used to bless the disciples in the upper room and will use
again at the Second Coming to destroy the lawless one.

(To complete and conclude this excursion into ancient Greek:
the New Testament uses another word for the verb forms
"breathed" or "breathing" only twice (John 20:22, Acts 9:1), and
neither one of these instances is relevant to our discussion here.)

All of the above serves nicely, I think, to support the use of the
pneuma as focal point in both Centering Prayer and contemplation. Scripture tells us to "worship in *pneuma*" and "pray in the
pneuma on all occasions," and by concentrating our prayerful
attention on the breath, we are doing just that. Only the "breath
of life" that God blew into Adam's nostrils separates us humans
from the lump of clay to which our bodies return upon death; only
the breath of his Son's spirit of faith saves us from eternal separation from the I AM. And with each inhalation and exhalation, I
connect with all of God's beautiful creation, literally taking into
myself the same sea of air that swirls through my friends' *and* my
enemies' lungs, that washes over my mother's grave in Germany,
and that sweeps up the tall Himalayas at the far end of the world.
Breath *is* life, just as is spirit. When I sit in contemplation and focus
on the *pneuma*, God gives me a foretaste of the future, when the
Breath and I shall be one.

Practical. Why do I argue so strongly for Centering on the
breath instead of on a prayer word? Above all because of the practical benefits this method will bring both to your formal prayers
and to the development of a contemplative state or attitude in
daily life. These subjects will be treated separately below and later,
but in this context a preview is necessary.

If a prayer word with little overt significance is preferable
because it is less likely to set in motion a chain of digressive emotions and thoughts, then a concentrative focal point with no
apparent meaning, the breath, is obviously even better for our pur-

poses. A non-verbal focus also allows us to dodge the primary tool and weapon of the intellectual/conceptual manifestations of the self, human language. Finally, the Centering technique I use involves a graduated "up-shifting" to increasingly subtle concentrative foci—word, breath, consciousness—so some intermediate step is necessary anyway.

Of course contemplative prayer is merely the school that teaches us to live contemplatively every moment of each day, and it is here that the breath as focal point yields its greatest fruits. If you are already used to it from your silent inner prayers, you can easily Center on the breath *while* you read scripture, or *as* you sing in church, or *during* a stressful encounter with someone looking to exchange the afflictive emotion of hatred with you, or *in the midst of* a bout of writer's block. All of the above work surprisingly well with the breath, but I at least have been unable to read or hold a conversation while simultaneously repeating "Yahweh" or any other word.

Personal or "Visionary." One and a half months after I began consistently practicing Centering Prayer, I felt ready to let go the life preserver that had carried me safely through the inner storms of those first six weeks, so I dropped my prayer word and Centered on the breath. The very next day I experienced one of those small promissory glimpses of "know[ing] fully, even as I am fully known" which most beginning contemplatives are granted as divine encouragement to continue on this difficult path (1 Corinthians 13:12). Since my little vision confirmed the rightness—at least for me—of Centering on the breath, I recount it here as the final, though admittedly subjective, support for using this particular concentrative focal point.

At some point during this prayer session, I experienced an almost physical sensation that, retrospectively, I can only compare to sliding down a children's playground slide: one moment I was sitting there peacefully, and then *whooooosh*—suddenly I was someplace else, someplace deeper. In fact, there was no more "place" at all. For the span of a few breaths, I *was* the universe and felt myself *breathed* by God, as if I—that is, the physical cosmos—were the lungs being filled with his *pneuma*. The "big bang" and the subsequent expansion of the universe felt like the inhalation of God's breath, while the exhalation seemed like the contraction and "big crunch" of all the galaxies that many physicists predict. Throughout those few seconds or endless eons, as many universes came and went as there were breaths; no "I" existed apart from the billions of stars that made up "me," nor was "I" doing the inhaling and exhaling. There was no breather, only the Breath, and the cosmos being breathed: "me."

Although this experience had a timeless quality, I believe it lasted only very, very briefly. In addition to confirming my decision to Center on the breath, I felt this vision—if that is the right word—also gave final, but somehow indefinable, corroboration to my views on the nature and purpose of good and evil, which I had previously arrived at intellectually but now came to know in my soul. (Briefly and no doubt platitudinously: just as the spirit-breath moves from inhalation to exhalation and back to inhalation, so too God "turns blackness into dawn and darkens dawn into night," only to let the sun rise again; life ends in death but becomes life eternal, and good requires evil "to make the riches of [God's] glory known to the objects of his mercy" (Amos 5:8, Romans 9:23).) Whether you are persuaded by this description of one unusual prayer session of mine, I do not know, but at least you now know why I believe so strongly in the use of the breath as focal point.

8—Centering Prayer—Concentration—Developing and Maintaining Focus

Here is the biggest dirty little secret of the Christian contemplative tradition: on the basic mechanics of how to concentrate, neither the ancient nor the modern masters' teaching texts are as practical and useful as some of their spiritual competitors, especially modern American *vipassana* Buddhists'. The reason for this relative deficiency may be the interrupted history of silent inner prayer in the West and the consequent lag in refining technique; another may be the tendency of all great teachers of meditative or contemplative practices, including most Buddhists, to forget just how difficult those long-ago days of learning concentration really were! In any case, the solution to this problem is simple: acquire and use the best Centering *methods* from all points of the globe, but employ them with the specifically Christian *intent* of freeing the soul of self and (re)uniting it with God.

Perhaps the most useful basic technique for developing and maintaining focus, not only as a novice but also later in each prayer session, is the use of a graduated series of several focal points to lead the practitioner step by step to ever deeper levels of concentration. Both at the beginning of your contemplative career *and* at the start of each prayer session, it clearly makes sense to use a strong, obvious Center, like a prayer word, to calm the body, heart and mind from the residual agitation of daily life. As noted earlier, I used nothing but a prayer word for the first month and a half of my own practice, but since everyone presumably progresses at a different rate, you must let yourself be guided by the spirit (or breath!) on the timing of your transition. Even nowadays I *begin* each of my three daily prayer sessions with a word and continue to use it until I feel ready to "shift up" to the breath, usually after two to seven minutes.

Virtually all practitioners of contemplation report that their prayer word eventually fades and disappears in the course of a session anyhow, but learning when to drop the word intentionally makes this phenomenon into an ally in the process of deepening concentration. Training yourself to sense the intensity of your focus helps you maintain your attention on, or "interest" in the prayer word and prepares you for the subtle alertness needed for contemplation. Finally, relinquishing your prayer word—and later, to some extent, the breath—is part of this discipline's general movement of surrendering *all* of the self's crutches and accoutrements, including the comfort of an obvious concentrative focal point.

As you Center on your prayer word, you will find yourself instinctively synchronizing it in some way with your breathing: one example cited earlier is my own "Yah-" (in-breath) and "-weh" (out-breath), but the modalities do not matter. Maintaining awareness of how your prayer word and breath interact and eventually fuse into one is an important first step toward dropping the word altogether; the transition should be smooth, almost imperceptible, a gentle letting go and lightening. (Later you will repeat this process when you abandon the breath and Center primarily on the third focal point, consciousness.) Thus, throughout your whole contemplative career as well as in each prayer session, the breath remains the constant, steady bridge or base that ties all three concentrative focal points together: first as a solid foundation for the word, then on its own, and finally as the hook from which consciousness swings freely in the breeze of the spirit.

Even as your attention rests on the prayer word or breath, the stream of physical sensations, emotions and ideas continues to flow through your consciousness, of course. But you stand apart from the rushing torrent of mental phenomena and simply observe their passing. You neither grasp at a pleasant memory from your youth nor reject a surge of frustration at your apparent failure to reach total inner silence immediately; you simply let all these potential distractions float past the rim of your nostril.

With a little patience, you can perceive the aching knee, the righteous anger and the new insight into a difficult scriptural passage as being events in your mind, temporary mental states that have no reality outside the unending, ever-changing stream of the self's three types of manifestations. *Observing* a thought (or feeling, or sensation) is an entirely different experience from *thinking* a thought while caught in "your" mental stream. In the former, the thought (or feeling, or sensation) feels light, airy and insubstantial, while in the latter it seems heavy and real because you are identifying with and attaching your self to it. Learning to recognize this distinction *during* prayer and maintaining your soul's distance from these fluctuating mental events are the twin purposes of the following techniques for staying on Center.

Filling the Mind. Occasionally the stream of mental phenomena becomes so obtrusive that your one- or two-syllable prayer word is overwhelmed; no matter how hard you try, you simply cannot maintain concentration on your Center. Modern *vipassana* masters advise beginners experiencing this problem to count their breaths *temporarily* until the body, heart and mind calm down again, in effect drowning out the interior noise with a neutral verbal substitute for the non-verbal focus of the breath. There are a wide variety of such techniques: counting "one" on the in-breath, "two" on the out-breath, etc., until you reach "ten"; counting rapidly "one" to "ten" when inhaling and again when exhaling; repeating "one, one, one" as many times as necessary on the in-breath, and "two, two, two" on the out-breath. All of these methods work by filling the mind with something other than the particular thought, emotion or sensation disturbing your concentration, so it hardly matters which one you use or invent for yourself. Of course you should stop using this crutch just as soon as you have reestablished some degree of inner quietude.

Noting the Pause Between Breaths. Keeping your attention on the breath is not easy at first because the cycle of inhalation and exhalation *seems* to remain monotonously the same. With only a little practice, however, you will soon discover that each in-breath and out-breath is slightly different, like waves lapping on a beach. Not only the "texture" changes constantly—sometimes smooth, sometimes rough—but the "shape" of each breath also differs from moment to moment, depending on the force and rate of the diaphragm's contraction. One way to start noticing these variations is to train yourself to focus on the minute, almost imperceptible pause between every inhalation and exhalation. Do *not* consciously stop the respiratory process at these points but simply observe that brief, continually recurrent instant, how subtle and evanescent and beautifully simple it is. If this method works for you, you can stay with it, or you can move on to the next few techniques and use them as a cycle or ascending ladder.

Connecting Breaths. Next you can try noting, not the pause between breaths, but the smoothness of the transition between inhalation and exhalation. Really, there are no individual in- and out-breaths at all, but only one long, flowing process of breathing. I experience the respiratory cycle very strongly as an oval or egg laid on its side: each inhalation rises slowly like a logarithmic curve on a graph paper, then levels off, and finally falls relatively steeply down again toward the imperceptible, imaginary dividing line between inhalation and exhalation, where the out-breath now turns to curve back toward its point of origin. This method is my personal favorite because, in addition to finding the continually changing shape of the breaths' "curves" inherently fascinating, I believe the process of noting or observing in itself subtly smooths out the respiratory process. As we shall see later, the transition from a relatively rough or gross breath to a silky, fine, subtle breath signals a sufficiently stable level of concentration to change one's focal point from the breath to consciousness and begin contemplation in the expansion phase.

Fixing. While you continue the "connecting" technique above, you will quite naturally begin to fix on one point in your respiratory tract where you can physically feel the tiny rush of air going in and out of your body. This touch or tingle is almost imperceptible, so maintaining your focus on so subtle a sensation is a great aid in staying on Center. Most people, including me, experience the flow of the breath at the rim of the nostrils, but I have also "fixed" on a point at the back of my nasal cavity and on a point in my throat. Once you select a spot, you should not change it during the course of one prayer session, since the purpose of Centering is to keep one's focus on *one* point. Merely stay with the single, simple sensation of air tickling the rim of your nostril; you will be surprised how sensuous and strangely delicious even such a basic physical experience can be. Who needs caviar when the *pneuma* tastes this good?

Listening. I have found that the principle of "fixing" on the *touch* of the breath on the rim of the nostril applies equally well to the *sound* produced by respiration. At the beginning of a prayer session, it is possible to actually hear the air pass through the lungs, throat and nose, but as the respiratory cycle becomes ever smoother and finer, all you can really feel is the subtle vibration in the inner ear—and only if you pay *very* close attention. I do not recommend switching between "fixing" and "listening" in a single session, to avoid the danger of "chasing the breath" from nostril-rim to throat to inner ear, but *either* "fixing" *or* "listening" can and should be done in conjunction with "connecting." The key to success in any of these techniques for stabilizing concentration is to dive as deeply as possible into one point, not to splash through a series of shallow focal puddles.

Noting the Decreasing Size of Breaths. This final method is really an extension of "connecting," but I have found it so useful that I think it is worth a paragraph of its own. While "connecting" inhalation to exhalation and noting the smooth roundness of the respiratory cycle, you will inevitably observe that every breath becomes just a tiny bit smaller and subtler than the preceding one as your body and mind relax. Making this continuous decrease in the size of your breaths an ancillary focal point is a wonderfully effective way of refining respiration and deepening concentration because it encourages progress toward the "subtle breath" transition point between Centering and contemplation. Simply stay focused on the ever-circling wheel of inhalation and exhalation and observe how, like a spiral, each pass around has a slightly smaller diameter. You are not *switching* Centers here but noting a specific new *aspect* of the same one point of the breath: its decreasing size, instead of (or in addition to) the tingle at the rim of the nostrils. As your breath becomes smaller and calmer, you will also observe it "sinking" down and settling in a quiet "spot" at your feet like a puppy taking a nap, and your attention will appear to "curl" over and around it almost protectively. When you have reached this point in a prayer session, you are ready for the transition to contemplation.

Both practicing contemplatives and biological scientists have noted the direct correlation between respiratory levels and mental activity.[22] Whether shallower breathing slows down a racing mind or inner quietude reduces the brain's need of oxygen from the lungs is not entirely clear, but this technique's effectiveness does not depend on the direction of the causal relationship. Please note that you are *not* making any attempt to control, shape or alter your breath, but *only* paying attention to the phenomenon of constant diminution. "Noting the decreasing size of breaths" merely takes advantage of the well-known scientific principle that the presence of an observer changes the outcome of an experiment.

As unlikely as it may seem, the few techniques presented here are all you will need to deepen concentration in preparation for contemplation. Their very simplicity is what makes them effective, an idea we find more objectionable the more sophisticated we consider ourselves to be. There *must* be some sort of secret to all this, right?

Fortunately or unfortunately, depending on your point of view, there really is no mystery here beyond the faith it takes to try Centering long enough for it to begin working on you. You cannot fail because your soul was *made* for this: your *pneuma*-spirit has been waiting for you to let go of all the nonsense of this world and focus on the *pneuma*-breath. At the rim of your nostrils, you will find God flowing in and out of you in endless smooth circles, if only you will pay attention.

That is why we Christian contemplatives, unlike Indian *pranayama* practitioners, do not attempt to control the breath, but let it control us. Through faith we can abandon ourselves completely to the Spirit-Breath and trust the I AM to wash through us without interference from us. Our discipline is to follow the *pneuma* in Centering Prayer, just as we follow Christ in Centering Practice.

9—Centering Prayer—Concentration—Dealing with Distractions

"Dealing with distractions" is, of course, the whole point and purpose of the concentration phase of contemplative prayer. Only by first doing this inner work of dismantling self-produced mental hindrances can we then progress to the expansion phase as John of the Cross described it in *Dark Night of the Soul*:

> What [practitioners of contemplation] must do is merely to leave the soul free and disencumbered and at rest from all knowledge and thought, troubling not themselves, in that state, about what they shall think or meditate upon, but contenting themselves with merely a peaceful and loving attention toward God, and in being without anxiety, without the ability, and without the desire to have experience of Him or to perceive Him.[23]

St. John makes it sound so easy "merely to leave the soul free and disencumbered," but if it were really that simple, neither he nor countless other contemplatives would have experienced those inner dark nights that gave his great book its title!

Fortunately, our spiritual forefathers and -mothers have developed useful, practical methods for coping with the self's counterattacks. The first of these techniques is knowing our enemy: through endlessly repeated direct experience during prayer, we come to recognize instinctively and instantaneously that *every* distraction from our concentrative focal point is *always* a manifestation of the self. And while the self's weapons may take innumerable outward forms, they are all at bottom either physical, emotional or intellectual/conceptual in nature.

Boredom, for instance, is a function of the intellect, which wants (or grasps at) facts to process, so the self can feel clever and important. By focusing our attention on a beautifully simple phenomenon like the breath or a short prayer word, we are denying the intellect the grist it needs to keep its noisy mill going, thereby forcing it to grind up not facts but . . . itself! Of course the self will protest against its gradual destruction by producing the feeling of boredom, for instance, but this *apparent* obstacle is *in fact* a sign that our contemplative work is meeting with success.

Every concentrative hindrance, seen in this light, is not only a new opportunity to study our opponent and a chance to dissect him again, but also a small crown of victory. All three of these are causes for gratitude, not self-chastisement for supposedly failing to concentrate properly. Discouragement and doubt are, of course, nothing more than the self's commando troops infiltrating behind our lines to sabotage our home base.

The alternative to catching a distraction as it develops is *not* recognizing our enemy's latest trick and, for example, drifting off into a pleasant sexual fantasy of the type Anthony of Egypt reported. This too happens to all contemplatives, apparently even after years and decades of practice. Withdraw, regroup, prepare to give battle again another day—that is all any of us can do.

Distractions can be broadly arranged in two classes: those characterized by inactivity or "sinking," and those distinguished by excitement or "scattering." Within these two classes each of the self's three manifestations develops ever-new obstacles in its desperate attempt to deflect the burning laser of one-pointed concentration:

- physical/inactive: e.g., sleepiness, floating sensations in the limbs, hands or feet "falling asleep";
- physical/active: e.g., restlessness, itchiness, nervous tics, hearing the pulse very loudly, grumbling stomach, sexual

fantasies, in my case also the ability to direct warmth or "energy" to different parts of my body;

- emotional/inactive: e.g., discouragement, frustration, doubt, worry;
- emotional/active: e.g., fear (with or without an apparent object such as a repressed memory), anger, desire, mystical visions;
- intellectual/inactive: e.g., lethargy, boredom, a heavy gray stupor completely unlike the clear light silence of contemplation; and
- intellectual/active: e.g., "brilliant" insights and ideas, agitated jumping from one concentrative focal point to another, pride at being so "successful" in your quest for inner quietude and God.

Of course this list is very incomplete, since your own self will develop weapons specially directed at your own weakest point. My self, for instance, loves nothing better than to disrupt my prayers with particularly clever ways of phrasing sentences for this book. And the annoyance I feel when this happens is yet another distraction!

Throughout your contemplative career, your self will gradually change its focus of attack on your Centering Prayer. The first few weeks are usually marked by primarily physical hindrances such as floating sensations; then, as the "unloading of the unconscious" unfolds, emotional obstacles come to the fore; and finally, intellectual/conceptual impediments like pride become the main distraction. In each of these phases we can of course only speak of a relative predominance, since all three types of distractions occur not only in each stage of the journey, but even in each individual prayer session. Father Keating in *Open Mind, Open Heart* uses the image of a spiral staircase to illustrate this point: though it may sometimes appear that we are getting nowhere because we keep encountering the same spiritual obstacles over and over, we are in fact rising continually by encountering ever-subtler forms of the same basic hindrances. Anthony of Egypt, as you will recall, spent *twenty years* fighting devils in his desert fort—*after* his amazing night of spiritual battle in the tombs!

So, what do you do with a spiritual hindrance once you have observed its arising? The anonymous author of *The Cloud of Unknowing* would have you "[t]read it down quickly with an impulse of love . . . [or] strike down every kind of thought . . . [with] your shield and your spear," his metaphor for the prayer word. A little later he adds:

> Try to look over [the disturbing thoughts'] shoulders, as it were, as though you were looking for something else; that something else is God, surrounded on all sides by the cloud of unknowing. . . . [Or] cower down under [these thoughts] like a poor wretch and a coward overcome in battle, and reckon it to be a waste of time for you to strive any longer against them, . . . and give yourself up to God.[24]

For reasons I shall elucidate shortly, I would advise you *not* to "[t]read down" or "strike down" mental obstacles in prayer, as our medieval author recommended at first, but instead to follow his subsequent advice to "reckon it a waste of time for you to strive any longer." I personally have not been able to make his two visualization techniques work in my own Centering Prayer, but they do capture the paramount quality of *gentleness* in dealing with distractions: as always and everywhere in contemplative practices, you simply let go. Softly release the mind's hold on the disturbance, and return your focus smoothly and calmly to your Center. The sensation, feeling or thought may remain for a little while even after you relinquish it, but your consciousness is no longer attached to, gripped by or identified with it. Once your self notices that your attention is back on the Spirit-Breath, this mental hindrance fades away and, inevitably, another arises.

Of course you may be tempted to "push" the disturbance away, but even this thrust of rejection is a form of attaching to it because you are investing it with the emotional energy of aversion. In effect you would be feeding your enemy even as you try to shoo him off; your self does not care whether you love or hate its manifestations, so long as you let yourself be persuaded of the self's reality! That is why the proper technique for dealing with mental obstacles is what Evagrius and John Climacus (525–605) called *apothesis*, meaning "shedding" or "putting aside" the distraction gently.

The less hard you try, the more successful your concentrative re-stabilization will be. Striving of any kind involves and therefore reinvigorates the self, so your emphasis here should be to develop effortlessness. You cannot become a "good" contemplative by force of will or by "applying your*self*."

Nor can you become a "good" contemplative by judging individual hindrances as "good" or "bad." In the first place, discernment is a function of the intellect and therefore, in this context, yet another obstacle created by the self to keep the gurgling stream of mental phenomena going. And in the second place, there *are* no "good" distractions! A mystical vision of the great I AM is just as much an impediment to developing inner silence as a long-repressed memory of childhood abuse; both may be important and valuable outside of prayer, but when the self drops either pearls or hand grenades in your lap *while Centering*, its purpose is only to stop you from emptying the self of its afflictive structures and processes.

Similarly, you are missing the point of contemplative practices and giving aid and comfort to your enemy, the self, if you judge any one prayer session as "good" because it had relatively few disturbing thoughts or "bad" because it had many. We call Centering Prayer a spiritual *practice* because that is what it is: a rehearsal, a gradual progress toward an ultimate perfection that we will only reach when our souls are reunited with the Spirit. The fruits of Centering Prayer and contemplation come outside your seated prayer sessions: in the way your inner Center of divine peace and silence expands even as you struggle through each day's chores, and in the way you begin seeing God's *pneuma* shining through the rainbow of a roadside oil slick or the wrinkles of an alcoholic's smile. Striving for these gifts of the spirit, and trying to measure your progress toward their achievement by supposedly objective measurements like the number of mental obstacles encountered during prayer, simply will not work.

Only very recently, after (at the time of this Book's writing) a year and a half of quite intensive Centering and contemplative prayer, am I finally beginning to know in the depths of my soul just how important this theme of surrender, of letting go and relinquishment, is to our spiritual discipline. I tried so long to "master" concentrative techniques, to perform them "well," and I suppose to a certain extent I did; but all my contemplative exertions and careful post-prayer analysis of *kenotic* advancement were nothing more than higher-level, subtler hindrances. Now my whole practice has been transformed by letting the *pneuma* master me and giving up all attempts at control. I sit down and close my eyes and let the Spirit-Breath carry me effortlessly to the ground of my being, simply trusting the *pneuma* to deliver me to my inner destination. Who could have guessed that the process of Centering could be so joyous, so easy?

10—Centering Prayer—A Novice's First Year

Every contemplative journey is unique, so yours may well differ in the order in which you experience stages like John of the Cross's "nights" or Teresa of Avila's "prayers." In my own case, something like John's "night of sense" actually *preceded* my contemplative practice and thus pushed me into committing myself to this spiritual discipline. I hope the following summary of progress during my first year of so of Centering Prayer will nevertheless give you some useful guidance as to what you might experience on your own spiritual path.

Month 1: *Despair* is actually an important first milestone. Tibetan Buddhists call this "attaining the cascading mind," when one feels bombarded and close to drowning beneath a roaring waterfall of thoughts, feelings and sensations. My interior seemed completely beyond my control, the task of overcoming the self appeared impossibly huge. Nevertheless, this feeling of despair is an achievement in itself because very few people ever bother to observe first-hand just how unruly their own minds are.

Month 2: By clinging fanatically to my prayer word, I was soon able to carve out what felt like a bubble of *comfort* in the torrent of mental phenomena, like sitting next to a window while a storm rages outside. It was also during this stage that I was granted an extremely brief glimpse of God's inner presence, no doubt to encourage me.

Months 3, 4, and 5: The comfort phase gave way to a long period of increasing *boredom*. The bubble of peace did not seem to be growing, and those noisy ideas and emotions kept repeating themselves in the same endless, monotonous circles. I was learning a very valuable lesson by direct experience: the self really does not consist of very much at all! The same old tired hungers, an amazingly small assortment of pet peeves and pleasures, and a handful of thought-loops repeating themselves over and over and over . . . yawn!

Month 6: Eventually boredom tipped over to *disgust*. I recall experiencing something like a vision: my thoughts seemed no longer like drops of a roaring waterfall, but like millions of flies circling a rancid, dead carcass: my self.

Month 7: Disgust became *self-hatred* when I entered an intense phase of "unloading of the unconscious," to use Father Thomas Keating's very useful term and concept. A great deal of emotional pain welled up both during and, most often, outside of my prayer sessions. If you give the self enough space and time to reveal its own hidden motivations even for supposedly good or noble acts, it appears not just boring and disgusting but downright ugly. Also, although I did not recognize this as a hopeful sign at the time, the number of mental phenomena arising during contemplation continuously decreased in number even as they increased in intensity.

Month 8: Self-hatred turned into a fairly dramatic *renunciation and intensification*. For a little over a month I went into a kind of retreat during which I wrote no letters, watched no television, ate only a minimum of food, and increased my Centering Prayer from two to three daily sessions totaling over one hour. My prayer life itself seemed particularly bleak and joyless throughout this period, but that suited my mood.

Month 9: After a month of intensified practice, I was occasionally able to sustain longer stretches of relative *silence* in prayer, during some of which I developed an *awareness of an inner Presence*. This silence was (and continues to be) relative because mental phenomena continued to arise, but during these periods they seemed to recede so far into the "background" that the overall sensation was one of great inner calm and focus. When the mental phenomena grew "louder" again and intruded into this quiet space, they were fewer in number and, more importantly, somehow felt less solid than before, almost soft and spongy; although I did not realize it then, I had begun to learn to *see through them*. At this point I felt confident enough to drop the form of Centering Prayer and move on to contemplation proper. (For the record, I also resumed contact with my family and again ate normally. I now watch an average of forty-five minutes worth of television news only per day because this frees up so much time for praying, reading and writing.)

Months 10, 11, and 12: The last quarter of my first year of Centering Prayer and contemplation was marked by a gradual but cumulatively dramatic intensification of the three changes of Month 9. The length of the periods of relative *silence* grew little if at all, but they occurred with greater frequency. The *awareness of a Presence* somehow became less opaque, sometimes almost translucent, and definitely more reliable. Mental phenomena no longer rushed in like a waterfall, as in the early months, but mostly came in single file, almost shyly. Where once they had been hard as hailstones, or by month 9 soft as rotten fruit, they now felt like continuously thinning clouds: from thick, puffy cumulus in month 10 to wispy, nearly transparent cirrus by month 12.

Months 13, 14, and 15 (up to the time of writing): The above trends continued, but with some new elements. During a (very) few of the periods of silence, my self became sufficiently quiet for the soul to begin to melt briefly into the Presence. On each of these occasions the self immediately pulled the soul back in fear, since the self definitely does not want to lose its increasingly tenuous existence! According to the contemplative literature, this reaction is fairly common at first and will eventually cease. Also, in month 14 I had what I suppose must be called a contemplative, as opposed to a mystical, experience outdoors, which I describe in Book II.

Again, your first year of Centering Prayer and contemplation will almost certainly differ in many details from mine. But the above description should give you some warning of the possible hazards along the way as well as some of the pleasures. Like other contemplatives, I too can confirm that access to God becomes much easier and more reliable once the soul (note: *not* "my" soul) is trained to expect three daily visits with its Source. Of course there are occasional setbacks and slipups, but they become fewer and fewer.

A sense of liberation and even excitement increasingly pervades our lives and contemplation: each day we get to remove another smudge of dirt from the lens of the soul and get a slightly clearer view of God. When prayer time approaches, I sometimes find myself rushing back to the quiet of my cell so I can have a few extra minutes with the Silence within. Even when the I AM is—or appears to be—unavailable, there are plenty of rocks for us to break out of the prison wall separating the soul from God until he returns.

11—Centering Prayer—The Golden Rule

Throughout your contemplative career you will find yourself applying general guidelines to situations simply not covered in any of
the relevant literature. Undoubtedly the most important of our
universal rules is this one: *Do not become attached to anything during
contemplation!* In this context, "attach" means to grasp or reject a
particular mental phenomenon instead of merely noting it.
Whatever arises in prayer, whether pleasant or unpleasant, the procedure is always the same: see through it to its lack of substance,
release it, and return to your point of focus.

Along with humdrum distractions and temptations, you will
encounter extremely painful memories of your childhood, overwhelmingly beautiful visions of God and much, much else. *All* are
simply states of the mind, heart or body, nothing more. They soon
vanish, bring no lasting joy (or pain!) and have no genuine existence because they are things of *this* world, not God's. "[D]o to others what you would have them do to you," the Golden Rule tells us
(Matthew 7:12). We can apply this rule even to our own thoughts
and desires, relinquishing our attachments to all mental phenomena, just as we would wish our lusts, wants and preconceptions to
relinquish their grip on our souls.

During each prayer session as well as our spiritual journey as a
whole, our two greatest dangers—the most devilish of all those
tempting mental phenomena—are mystical experiences and intellectual insights. I personally am not very susceptible to the former,
but even so I have on occasion felt or seen God as a warm, golden-
green, glowing light, for instance. Medieval mystical poets had
much more florid and expansive visions than mine, beautiful roadside flowers that seduce the contemplative into stopping his or her
progress down the interior path. Yet any *form* in which the Spirit
appears to our mind and heart is bound to be misleading because
the I AM is formless.

Apart from visions, the devil's other great weapon—the one to
which I am so susceptible—is the rational, reasoning mind, which

does not distinguish between understanding and knowing, between being informed and being wise. On a mundane level, this temptation takes the form of attractive thoughts during prayer that divert us from the real work of contemplation: sudden breakthroughs with personal or psychological difficulties, brilliant solutions to workplace problems, and all manner of insights about God and the world. Examined in the cold light of reason *after* prayer, these seemingly inspired ideas are inevitably revealed to be shallow, often to the point of embarrassment. Another form is the constant chatter of a commentator, explaining every mental process to itself as it occurs. But these manifestations of our clever-clever minds are fairly easily dealt with once we have gained some experience.

What is far more dangerous and insidious is the intellect's devilishly persuasive arguments against beginning the practice of contemplative prayer in the first place. I read countless books about meditation and related subjects for *eighteen years* before I finally started and maintained a continuous discipline of contemplation! Until then I acquired an enormous amount of facts and honestly believed I had learned the spiritual truths I had read about. And because in all those years I only practiced meditation or contemplative prayer for a few weeks at a time, I never realized the incomprehensibly vast difference between understanding something with my mind and knowing it in the very fabric of my soul.

If you have never engaged in contemplation, you *cannot* know what I mean and will have to trust the thousands of other contemplatives, even if you do not quite believe me. Meanwhile, your mind will do its utmost to persuade you to stick with its old, familiar ways of processing information, instead of soaking your soul in the Truth. I spent eighteen years in that trap of the intellect—time that perhaps was not entirely wasted, but certainly could have been better spent. To really absorb the central teachings of the contemplative tradition, we must saturate the self and the soul with them over and over again in prayer; there is no other way. Studying the walls of our prisons, measuring the size of the bricks, doing spectroscopic analy-

sis of each link of our chains, speaking or writing about them eloquently—none of these will free us. Instead, we must start chipping
away at the rocks, ropes and chains, one prayer session at a time.

12—Centering Practice—Making Peace with Our Pasts

One of the most interesting and beneficial effects of Centering
Prayer is that it subtly changes our thinking by heightening our
level of awareness even outside prayer. During contemplation we
train ourselves to note carefully the birth, life and death of the
most evanescent creatures in the universe: our sensations, feelings
and ideas. This delicate skill, once learned, naturally manifests
itself in all areas of life and thought.

On one level it makes us much more sensitive to even slight
changes and thus, in the words of one contemplative author, "more
intelligent." This new intelligence is really more like a greater clarity of mind: one can actually see reality itself as the buzz of inter-
fering thoughts diminishes.

Another this-worldly effect of learning the otherworldly skill
of contemplation is that it allows us to "see through" surface
appearances of things to the underlying, deeper realities and patterns much as we "see through" mental phenomena in prayer. I
believe this is one of the things medieval contemplative authors
meant when they wrote of seeing God's hand and presence in all
the processes of life. The world begins to make sense—admittedly
sometimes a very painful kind of sense—as one begins to really see
how everything hangs together, the unity beneath the diversity.

In the Centering Practice sessions of this volume I want to
share with you one of these underlying patterns I discovered in my
life during the "unloading of the unconscious" I experienced during my first months of silent prayer. What I found, as I worked back
through my biography again, was the process of *kenosis*. As I was
learning how to consciously empty the self of its attachments in
contemplation, it seemed to me that even in all the years before,
the events of my life had worked to crack, break down and clear

away my ego to prepare me for the discipline of Centering Prayer. Amazingly, this process had even followed the physical, emotional and intellectual/conceptual paradigm!

Another way to express this insight is to say that I finally recognized God's hand guiding me, by means of the crosses he gave me, to turn to his love and peace. This knowledge has given me not only comfort in some extraordinarily painful experiences, some of them still ongoing, but also a sense of gratitude for them. Especially in the case of my latest blows, which ended all hope of justice and freedom for me in this world, I am not at all sure I could have survived if I had not come to understand the purifying and spiritualizing effects of my suffering.

I believe this way of using our crosses as tools for spiritual progress can work for you, whatever your particular prison is. If there are any practical steps you can take to alleviate your anguish, by all means take them, for God surely finds needless suffering offensive. But whatever pain cannot be "fixed" with all of our modern, scientific tools and methods need not be meaningless. My hope is that describing the process of *kenosis* in my own life will encourage you in your contemplative practice to dig deeper and clear away even more rubble than I did.

13—Centering Practice—Stepping *toward* Our Crosses

Transforming pain into self-emptying *as you experience your life's tragedies* always requires the same basic attitude or approach: facing your suffering honestly, letting your self experience its very depths. As I noted earlier, this is the contemplative method of nonjudgmental noting, applied here to instances of pain instead of to mental phenomena.

The essence of Centering Prayer is facing the self. No matter what trick or diversion it deploys against us, we persist in confronting it with its own lack of substance until it finally admits that it does not exist and vanishes, leaving the soul free to be transformed in union with God. The key is to maintain focus, to continue looking at this figment of the body, heart and mind, to stare it down till it squeals—and it *will* squeal, believe me! The only way to break out of the prison of self is to force it to stop telling the lie, "*I* exist." Thus in some ways Centering Prayer is an exercise in absolute, almost fanatical truthfulness.

The same principle applies to Centering Practice. If we are to use the tragedies of our lives to break down the structures of the self and liberate our soul, we *must* confront our prisons, our chains, our crosses, and let them do their agonizing but necessary work on us. Only if we let ourselves fully experience all of our suffering can it grind down the self and liberate us. Nothing is harder, but nothing is truer to the model Christ gave us in his own final hours in Gethsemane and on Golgotha.

If he had chosen to do so, the son of God could surely have gone to his cross stoically, perhaps demonstrating by cool, calm demeanor that he was about to gain victory over death. That certainly would have given the Pharisees, the Romans and the jeering crowds something to think about! Instead, his "soul [was] overwhelmed with sorrow" to the point that he prayed for "this cup [to] be taken from" him and asked his Father, "My God, my God, why have you forsaken me?" (Matthew 26:38, 39; 27:46). Christ's mission was to *suffer* for us, so he let himself fully experience all the sadness, reluctance and despair that comes to us in our lives' tragedies.

With his tears of blood and forlorn, lonely cries, Jesus also gave us permission to scream out our agony, to voice our pain. False bravado is just another form of pride, one of the devil's first temptations. Confronting our own anguish also means not pretending to ourselves or others that it does not hurt.

The work we must do on our crosses is different from Christ's, of course, but we have to face our torment as squarely as he did. Our task is the same as that of the two thieves executed with him: allowing the pain to do its work of tearing down the structures of the self. If we try to escape our suffering—like the first thief, who gave in to the self's afflictive emotional need to vent anger and frustration on the nearest available object—then we gain nothing. But if, like the second thief, we let our anguish weaken our sense of self long enough for us to recognize our own mortality and need for salvation, then divine Love will find us in the moment of our greatest pain, right there on the cross alongside us.

No author has expressed more movingly the self-emptying effect of honestly experienced suffering than Jean-Pierre de Caussade, who captured the very heart of Centering Practice in his collected letters published as *Abandonment to Divine Providence*:

> We must offer ourselves to God like a clean, smooth canvas and not worry ourselves what God may choose to paint on it, for we have perfect trust in him, have abandoned ourselves and all our needs. . . . It is the same with a lump of stone. Each blow from the hammering of the sculptor's chisel makes it feel—if it could—as if it were being destroyed. As blow after blow descends, the stone knows nothing of how the sculptor is shaping it. All it feels is a chisel chopping away at it, cutting it and mutilating it. For example, let's take a piece of stone destined to be carved into a crucifix or a statue. We might ask of it: "What do you think is happening to you?" And it might answer: "Don't ask me. All I know is that I must stay immovable in the hands of the sculptor, and I must love him and endure all he inflicts on me to produce the figure he has in mind. . . . But what I do know is that his work is the best possible. It is perfect. I welcome each blow of his chisel as the best thing that could happen to me, although, if I'm to be truthful, I feel that every one of these blows is ruining me, destroying me and disfiguring me.[25]

That, I think, is how Christ must have felt on his cross—and how he wanted us to bear our crosses, too.

14—Centering Practice—A Case Study, Part 1

I think it might be helpful to begin our study of Centering
Practice's general principle as it applies to two educated, middle-
class, law-abiding, decent citizens anyone would want as neighbors:
my parents. Their prison or cross was their eldest son, of course,
and they responded in diametrically opposite ways to the terrible
anguish I inflicted on them. One of my parents was unable to face
this pain and was eventually killed by it. The other confronted the
suffering, felt it honestly, shouldered it, made both personal and
professional sacrifices for it—and became a gentler, freer person as
well as a genuine spiritual victor in the process.

So, let us meet my parents in their own, their generation's, and
their country's historical ground zero: 1945. At the end of World
War II my nine-year-old father, his mother and his baby brother
were part of the millions-strong German refugee columns fleeing
westward from the advancing Soviet armies. His own father was a
prisoner of war, his little family was homeless, and what few goods
they had rescued from years of Allied bombing were now being
taken by Cossack scouting units that strafed, robbed and raped
these exiles in revenge for the *Wehrmacht's* crimes in Russia.

Meanwhile, my ten-year-old mother had just survived the last
major city siege in the west, "Bloody Bremen" as the U.S. Army
called it, but her elderly father had not. Her young mother, used to
a life of servants and society balls, now found herself without protection or even shelter, since her house had not survived the war.
Thus both of my parents entered the brave new era of peace with
nothing more than their wits.

By the late 1950s their high intelligence and motivation had
secured them entry into the most exclusive of elites Germany then
had to offer young high flyers: the diplomatic service. After post-
ings in Belgium and Guinea (Africa), they had their first child in
1966 while stationed in Thailand and their second in Cyprus in
1968. My father earned promotions quickly and early, so a short
tour of duty in Germany was followed by the plum assignment of

Atlanta, Georgia. There we lived in a house that by American standards was impressive and by German standards nearly palatial, in order to accommodate the regular large cocktail parties at which diplomats try to spread good will for their country.

Much like first-generation immigrant parents in America, my father and mother invested all their hopes and energy in their children. They managed to enroll us at the socially more exclusive of Atlanta's two top private schools, and to send us to "rich kids' " summer camps. Yet my father and mother certainly did not spoil their heirs. It never occurred to my brother and me not to keep our bedrooms Germanically neat and organized, and one of my friends' mothers actually broke down in tears while asking my mother for advice on turning her sons into "perfect little gentlemen" like us. If there was anything slightly disquieting about my brother and me, it was that we never got into any trouble.

Both of us boys brought home awards by the bucketful to our encouraging but never demanding parents. Under my editorship my school's newspaper won first prize at a statewide student journalism competition; I never left the headmaster's list and became a National Merit finalist; and at my graduation in 1984 my teachers voted me both Best Art Student and Best English Student—with English as the *second* of my three languages.

What made my father and mother proudest, however, was that I was the first student at my school ever to win a full academic scholarship to the University of Virginia, Charlottesville, then one of the top ten colleges in the country. The scholarship program's sponsors, the university's Alumni Association, even arranged for special trips for the dozen or so Jefferson Scholars, as we were called. During one of these excursions, to the Alumni Association-Capitol Hill chapter's annual meeting in Washington, D.C., our little group of precocious "geniuses" was introduced to U.Va. alumni like Senator Ted Kennedy, then considered to be a likely future President of the United States.

Imagine, please, how my parents must have felt at that time

about their forty-year journey: from bombed-out homelessness in 1945 to their eldest son shaking hands with the most powerful men in the capital of the most powerful country in the world in 1985! They had achieved more than they could even have dreamed of as little children. What could possibly spoil this fabulous story?

15—Centering Practice—A Case Study, Part 2

I could: On April 30, 1986, I was arrested for and eventually convicted of double murder. My own journey will be discussed later, but I want to relate the very different ways in which my father and mother reacted to the unexpected agony I brought into their lives. Their hopes for me and for their own legacies had been shattered completely, but one of them turned this tragedy into a kind of triumph.

While growing up I had been closer to my mother than to my father. One of the greatest shocks of my life was to see him come through the prison visiting door first—and burst into tears at the sight of me. I had never, ever seen my father express emotion that strongly before, apart from verbal outbursts of anger during earlier domestic "disasters." Those tears of his were, I now believe, the first and most important step to saving my own soul, because they led me to suspect that perhaps I was not a hero after all. More importantly, my father's tears—his ability to cry, to recognize the full dimensions of the disaster his elder son had wrought—now seem to me the key to how he saved his soul.

My mother actually visited me a little more often than my father during the nearly four years of incarceration before my trial. She also appeared to be coping with the tragedy better: she was always chatty and cheerful and tried to give me hope. If anything bothered me at all about her attitude, it was her strange belief that I was somehow "safe" (her word) in prison.

My father, on the other hand, spent most of his visits on legal or practical subjects, which were inevitably gloomy. His personal comments were restricted to some version of the unanswerable question, *why?* Looking back, I now understand that he was grappling with the very heart of this tragedy and never stopped seeking its painful truth and meaning. Many years later I also came to recognize that much of his work in those early visits consisted of protecting me from the knowledge of how my mother suffered at home. Long after their 1990 divorce he dropped a few hints about a suicide attempt and repeated trips to hospitals.

At my trial in 1990 I naturally expected my mother to continue in her role as top cheerleader and emotional support. But only my father and brother came to court, while she was declared to be too "ill" to attend. "Illness" was one of our family's euphemisms for my mother's bouts of alcoholism, so I suspected nothing more than perhaps a severe form of stress-induced drinking.

But my mother's "illness" continued for the next seven years; the last time we were to see each other was in 1989. Until 1994 I was allowed to receive her telephone calls from Germany, during which she continued to try to spread good cheer even when she was obviously drunk. Her letters too were unfailingly upbeat. In 1997 emergency services personnel discovered her body in the litter- and bottle-strewn apartment that she had left only rarely in her last months.

This country's courts and I disagree on most things, except that I am indeed a killer. My mother, like millions of others, was a functional alcoholic for decades—until I tipped her over the edge and into death. But for me, she would be alive today.

With hindsight it is easy for me to see that my mother never really confronted or accepted just how catastrophic her older son's mistakes had been, how completely I had destroyed the dreams she had held for me. She sensed all this on some intuitive level, of course, but she could not allow herself to know it fully and consciously. So she chose to pretend that everything would be fine, that prison was "safe," and that she really was too "ill" to see me face-to-face in a visiting room. These lies required increasing quantities of alcohol to remain believable, so much that her poor body could take no more. That is the torture and death I inflicted on my own mother, whom I loved so very much.

16—Centering Practice—A Case Study, Part 3

Could my mother have survived the cross I forced on her if she had been able to take a more truthful view of my situation and her own? There is no way to be certain, but I do know that just such an existentially honest attitude helped my father live and in some ways prosper during these awful fifteen years. From his first prison visit until today, he has used his natural fighting instincts not just to try to help me practically, but also to maintain close and realistic contact with the actual situation he was struggling so hard to improve. I have inherited my father's combativeness and tenacity, however differently I may express them, so I know those qualities do indeed require one to "embrace" one's cross, albeit in a wrestling hold.

Because I have battled merely for *my own* sanity, *my* integrity, *my* truth, fighting in itself obviously had no self-emptying quality for me. My father, on the other hand, went to war for someone other than himself, going so far as to risk his life for me. Thus in his case combat could develop the effects of *kenosis* and can therefore be considered a Centering Practice technique.

As mentioned earlier in the context of Centering Prayer, each spiritual journey is unique and may not follow theories or systems precisely. While my own experiences matched our paradigm's sequence, my father's struggle for me emptied him of self intellectually/conceptually first, and only then physically and emotionally. His progress produced the same spiritual results despite the different order, demonstrating once again that reality aces theory every time.

1986–1990, Intellectual/Conceptual: Our mind's first and most important conceptual construct is that the pitiful collection of lusts, greeds and ideas between our ears actually amounts to a separate entity called self. Pride in that self—basking in the crowd's applause as we *stand on the highest point of the temple*—is one of the devil's great temptations. To crack this shell of pride, some medieval monks and nuns performed acts not just of humility but of intentional humiliation, thereby giving a dubious reputation to a genuine spiritual insight into the nature of self and *kenosis*.

My father did not seek humiliation; I forced it on him. My arrest in 1986 was reported on the front pages of three countries' newspapers, as well as on national television and radio. One tabloid publication actually claimed that I had danced naked in my victims' blood. This near-hysterical, constant media coverage lasted for at least the first five years and resurfaced occasionally thereafter. And *he* was unmistakably the father of the alleged monster with the unusual last name of Soering.

As far as public association with me is concerned, my mother and brother—and for a time even my stepmother—all suffered as much as my father did. While they could not possibly have escaped the reporters harassing them at home, they could have spared themselves some degradation by disowning me publicly. Yet all of them stood by me in an amazing display of loyalty and love for which I will always be grateful.

What makes my father special is that, in addition, he took that all-important step toward his cross. Throughout the first four years of my imprisonment he pressed, cajoled and persuaded his employer, the German diplomatic service, to help the least sympathetic and most embarrassing of all causes: me. I will never know even a small part of what he did then, but having grown up as a child of the service, I can guess at the hostility he brought on himself at work by drawing his superiors into the fight for me.

In the end, my father succeeded in saving my life: the death penalty charges were dropped. But the damage to his career and reputation was incalculable. No medieval monk flogged naked at the altar before his brethren endured even a fraction of the humiliation my father endured.

And there is no encouraging, uplifting end to this part of the story. It was pure agony, nothing more. Yet agony that is borne unwillingly almost always leads to resentment and certainly brings about no spiritual transformation. Because my father voluntarily took on an extra portion of pain that he could have spared himself, his humiliation worked to break down the structures of the self on the intellectual/conceptual level, where pride and reputation do their insidious work. My father shed his soul of those burdens and took giant steps toward inner freedom during those awful early years.

1990–1994, Physical: My 1990 trial resulted in my conviction and six-figure legal bills. As a result, my father asked the diplomatic service to transfer him to one of its special hardship posts, which paid additional danger money and other financial incentives to lure reluctant volunteers to embassies in underdeveloped countries or war zones. His request was granted: he was sent to Mauritania, which ranked just below Tehran, Iran, on the severity scale.

Mauritania is not fit for human habitation, but at least it does not pretend otherwise. An enormous desert territory on the west coast of Africa, it has virtually no natural or mineral resources, no agriculture, no industry, no tourism, and only a few primitive and warlike nomadic inhabitants. Until the mid-1980s slavery was officially still legal. Perhaps Mauritania's most endearing and attractive feature is the season of sandstorms, when drifts of gritty dust block building exits much as snowdrifts do in colder climes.

I recall my father sending me a special letter, with photographs, to announce the discovery in his walled "garden" of a turtle—in other words, something besides sun, rock or sand. The other lifeform he and my stepmother encountered was a dangerous stomach bacillus, for which no local treatment was available; medical facilities are yet another thing Mauritania lacks. For entertainment, they had the option of Sunday drives along either one of the country's two roads, one leading north and the other east. It is not too much to say that their lives became as empty as the endless desert that was their home.

Again, I know only a little of what my father and stepmother endured in their quite literal desert, but I too have experienced prolonged physical hardship—to be described later—and thus have some sense of how such conditions affect the soul. There is a real and immediate sense of liberation as one learns how very few physical things one really needs, and how satisfying even the smallest of pleasures like a turtle can be—or, in my case, how miraculous the sun seemed after two weeks spent underground. Because my father is a dedicated professional and very good at his work, he sought out the Mauritanian people and came to admire their simplicity and their country's stark beauty. His letters only hinted at this re-discovery of the joys of simplicity, and I wonder if those who live in the insanely busy and lavish culture of the West can even comprehend the spiritual benefits of losing some of one's attachments to the world and the senses.

1994–1998, Emotional: To finance the appeals against my conviction, my father requested another hardship post and was sent to the south Pacific half-island of Papua New Guinea. Throughout his long career he had always been a team member at an embassy or consulate, but here my father was the solitary chargé d'affaires of a one-man outpost, Germany's sole and official voice to what little government existed in this isolated spot of nowhere. This loneliness and responsibility were heavy burdens not only professionally but also personally, both for him and my stepmother.

During my father's tour of duty Papua New Guinea experienced a major volcanic eruption, an armed rebellion in the capital in which my father's embassy limousine was attacked, a low-intensity guerilla war and a record-breaking tsunami that killed five thousand people. Physically this country was as rich and tropical as Mauritania had been poor and barren, yet the amenities of civilization were perhaps even fewer here. Pigs were the common currency outside the capital. Not even milk was locally available, and—perhaps to compensate this dietary deficiency—some isolated mountain tribes still practiced cannibalism. Once again interesting and lethal diseases assaulted my father and stepmother, in each case requiring evacuation to the nearest doctor in Australia.

From my father's and stepmother's letters I learned a good deal about the toll their isolation took on both of them. Feeling completely alone and cut off even in crowds of people was and remains the essence of my penitentiary life, too. Sometimes, if our souls have been prepared by previous suffering, this form of emotional pain can lead us to confront the futile circling of our afflictive desires and hates, and thereby to penetrate to those spiritual depths where we discover what really matters. I believe both my father and my stepmother experienced such a deepening process during and as a result of their stay in the lonely jungles of Papua New Guinea.

Whether you believe that I was worthy of such sacrifices or not, my father certainly thought so and threw his self away for me in action—the Centering Practice version of *kenosis*. Out of love, he "la[id] down his life [his old way of living] for his friend," his son, and thus came closer to the truth of God than many a pious churchgoer. His kind of spiritual victory found its truest, most beautiful expression in the words of the author Henri Nouwen, a practitioner of silent, wordless prayer who abandoned a prestigious academic career at Harvard to serve the handicapped in a L'Arche residential community:

> My own pain in life has taught me that the first step to healing is not a step away from the pain, but a step toward it. . . . [W]e have to find the courage to embrace our own brokenness, to make our most feared enemy into a friend and to claim it as an intimate companion. . . .
>
> The deep truth is that our human suffering need not be an obstacle to the joy and peace we so desire, but can become, instead, the means to it. The great secret of the spiritual life, the life of the Beloved Sons and Daughters of God, is that everything we live, be it gladness or sadness, joy or pain, health or illness, can all be part of the journey toward full realization of our humanity.[26]

Notes

1. *Webster's II New Riverside Dictionary* (Boston: Houghton Mifflin, 1984).
2. Keating, Thomas, *The Method of Centering Prayer* (Butler, NJ: Contemplative Outreach, Ltd., 1986).
3. Jäger, Williges, excerpt trans. Soering, J., *Die Welle ist das Meer*, 1, A, 5, 6, 21 (Freiburg, Germany: Herder spectrum, 2000).
4. Keating, Thomas, *Invitation to Love* (New York: Continuum Publishing Co., 1992).
5. Strong, James, *A Concise Dictionary of the Words in the Greek Testament, with their Renderings in the Authorized English Version* (New York, Cincinnati: The Methodist Book Concern, 1890).
6. Sophocles, trans. Watling, E. F., *Oedipus Rex* (New York: Penguin Classics, 1947).
7. Strong, James, op. cit.
8. Ibid.
9. Ibid.
10. Ibid.
11. Pseudo-Dionysius, trans. Luibheid, C., and Rorem, P., *The Complete Works*, MT 1 (Mahwah, NJ: Paulist Press, 1987).
12. Meister Eckhart, ed. McGinn, B., *Meister Eckhart: Teacher and Preacher* (Mahwah, NJ: Paulist Press, 1986).
13. De Caussade, Jean-Pierre, trans. Beevers, J., *Abandonment to Divine Providence*, IV, 6 (New York: Image/Doubleday, 1975).
14. Meister Eckhart, op. cit.
15. *New American Bible, Revised New Testament* (Washington, D.C.: Confraternity of Christian Doctrine, 1986).
16. St. Thomas à Kempis, trans. Sherley-Price, L., *The Imitation of Christ*, II, 12 (New York: Penguin Books, 1952).
17. Bonhoeffer, Dietrich, *The Cost of Discipleship* (New York: Macmillan Publishing Co., 1963).
18. Those readers already familiar with the subtleties of Father Thomas Keating's method should note that my definition differs slightly from his; please see the Postscript on Centering Prayer terminology.
19. See for example Carrington, Patricia, *The Book of Meditation* (Boston: Element Books, 1977, 1998).
20. *Book of Common Prayer* (New York: Church Hymnal Corporation, 1979).
21. Strong, James, op. cit.
22. See Keating, Thomas, *Open Mind, Open Heart* (New York: Continuum, 1986, 1992), and Carrington, Patricia, op. cit.
23. St. John of the Cross, trans. Peers, A. E., *Dark Night of the Soul*, I, X, 4 (New York: Image/Doubleday, 1990.)
24. Anonymous, ed. Walsh, J., *The Cloud of Unknowing*, XXIII (Mahwah, NJ: Paulist Press, 1981).
25. De Caussade, *Abandonment*, I, 3, op.cit.
26. Nouwen, Henri, *Life of the Beloved* (New York: Crossroad Publishing, 1992).

INTERMEZZO

I S HENRI NOUWEN right, that truly *"everything* we live, be it gladness or sadness, joy or pain, health or illness, can all be part of the journey toward full realization of our humanity"? Is it true that "in *all* things God works for the good of those who love him" (Romans 8:28)? If so, then even the horrific crime in which I involved myself as an eighteen-year-old might be more than just a senseless tragedy. The Way of the Prisoner is in part an exploration of that possibility, that hope of light in all the darkness my sins helped bring about. But before we can examine that hope, you may wish to learn the plain and not-so-simple truth about the crime that put me in prison.

The four chapters of this Intermezzo will be markedly different in both content and tone from the rest of this book, because the time has come for me to recount the facts of my criminal case. This material will, I hope, allow you to use my admittedly extreme example as a model for a similar Centering Practice analysis of your own life and "prison" during the "unloading of the unconscious" phase of Centering Prayer, and to examine the existential situation out of which The Way of the Prisoner arose, to determine whether it is merely one man's iconoclastic spiritual palliative or a path others, like you, may tread with benefit too.

The next few chapters narrate the investigation, trial and appeal in a straightforward, fairly dry manner, while the Centering

Practice section of Book II analyzes this raw material in terms of our *kenotic* paradigm. If you are uninterested in this part of my past, please feel free to skip this Intermezzo and proceed to Book II. None of what follows is an integral part of this volume.

Describing my criminal case is fraught with dangers for me. There are those who, perhaps quite understandably, will view *The Way of the Prisoner* as nothing more than an elaborate attempt to manipulate my way out of prison, and they will scrutinize this section in particular for any hint of dishonesty or deceit. The slightest mistake, the smallest bias thus exposes this volume to condemnation in its entirety.

Since *The Way of the Prisoner* is the only child that I, as a "double-lifer," am likely to ever produce, I have worked very hard to protect it from such attacks by scrupulously checking and re-checking each statement of fact. Every individual sentence below is directly supported by a specific piece of evidence, document or transcript passage in the thousands of pages of court records. My appellate attorney, Ms. Gail Starling Marshall, has reviewed the chapters that pertain to the trial and "can report that they portray the evidence with accuracy and thoroughness." Fortunately—and somewhat strangely—there exists *no* dispute at all between prosecution and defense about what the facts of the case are; the *only* disagreements revolve around how the evidence should be weighed.

Lest I be accused of selecting facts so as to slant the following presentation of the case in my favor, I provide you below with *all* the prosecution evidence, no matter how minor, while skipping over some secondary defense evidence and arguments. Most likely you will nevertheless begin to suspect that I am leaving out some crucial damning information, because—apart from my "confession"—there is so very little substantive evidence against me. All I can tell you is that there really is no more; I have omitted nothing. To be fair, you should also take careful note that the defense's evidence is equally weak: I am unable to *prove* my innocence, nor can

I establish a third party's guilt beyond a reasonable doubt. Perhaps you will come to agree with me that, based on the facts alone, no one except the persons directly involved can know what actually happened on the evening of the crime.

To assure fairness I carefully avoid making statements in my narration of the case such as, "I did not murder Derek and Nancy Haysom," since that is a mere allegation which no court has accepted. Instead, I write, "*I testified at trial* that I did not murder Derek and Nancy Haysom," an undisputed matter of record.

> *[Also, whenever I provide background information about which there might be some difference in point of view, I indent the passage and set it in italics as here; or I may distinguish a certain phrase or sentence in a passage of regularly-set text by inserting the italicized words* "in my opinion."*]*

Because my purpose below is to lay out the evidence relevant to my criminal conviction, I describe neither my relationship with my co-defendant, Elizabeth Roxanne Haysom, nor the months we spent on the run in Europe and Asia. Readers interested in those aspects of the case must turn to my autobiography, *Mortal Thoughts*.[1]

1—The Investigation

On April 3, 1985, Bedford County, Virginia, sheriff's deputies entered the home of Derek and Nancy Haysom at the request of friends of the family who had been unable to contact the couple since March 30. Immediately upon opening the front door and stepping into the living room, the officers discovered the body of Derek Haysom, 71, lying across the door to the dining room to the left. His throat had been repeatedly slashed all the way to the spinal column, and later twenty-five stab wounds were found on his body.

Beyond the dining room in the kitchen lay Nancy Haysom, 52, with her throat cut and her body stabbed seventeen times. Oddly enough, almost all the stab wounds were extremely shallow, especially compared to the enormous injuries to the neck.

[The lack of depth of the wounds may indicate a physically weak and/or psychologically disturbed attacker.]

The floors of all three rooms were smeared with blood, and the furniture in the dining room had clearly been disturbed in a struggle. Eventually some blood would also be discovered in the master bedroom's bathroom to the right of the living room.

Derek and Nancy Haysom had met and married in southern Africa, where their youngest daughter Elizabeth, 20, was born. Between them they also had five other children from previous marriages, all of whom were successful professionals residing (with one exception) in Canada at the time of the crime. Derek Haysom had worked as a steel executive in Africa, Europe and Nova Scotia, Canada, and had recently retired to his wife's hometown of Lynchburg in southwestern Virginia. Their modest two-bedroom cottage lay just across the Lynchburg City / Bedford County line in the wealthy suburb of Boonsboro among far more extravagant residences.

Only one hour's car drive away, Elizabeth Haysom attended the prestigious University of Virginia in Charlottesville as a first year academic honors student. She had entered college two years late because she had run away from her English boarding school as a teen to travel through Europe with her girlfriend in pursuit of their heroin addiction. Lately, however, she appeared to have settled down, as evidenced by her latest love interest: a male academic scholarship winner and honors student from Germany who, though 18, had no sexual, narcotic or criminal experience.

Though our relationship was only four months old, Elizabeth and I went to the funeral services in Lynchburg together, stayed at the houses of family friends and then returned to college. Meanwhile, the sheriff's department's investigation produced no arrests in spite of massive regional police cooperation and even the assistance of Canadian law enforcement. Forensic test results from the crime scene were slowly returning from the state labs, however, and these seemed to confirm the police's initial theory that they were looking for more than one attacker.

All four blood types were found in the Haysoms' cottage: along with vast quantities of the victims' A and AB, there was also a very small drop of type O blood on the floor on the master bedroom, between the living room and the blood-smeared bathroom, as well as a small drop of type B blood on a damp rag on top of the clothes in the half-open washer immediately next to Nancy Haysom's body in the kitchen.

[The rag's dampness suggests that it had been left there recently.]

Only much later would deputies learn that I have type O blood—as does 45% of the population, since it is the most common type. But because police obtained physical samples from Elizabeth soon after the crime, they knew very early in their investigation that she had type B blood, shared by only ten percent of the population. (Both the type O and B blood drops were too small to allow subtyping, and, according to state lab reports, the type O blood was destroyed in testing—making later DNA analysis impossible.)

[After I confessed to committing the crime by myself, the prosecution understandably began to dispute its own expert's finding of Elizabeth's blood type at the crime scene.]

Not only were the authorities aware that Elizabeth's relatively rare blood type had been found near her mother's body, but they also retrieved her fingerprints from a vodka bottle in the front row of the Haysoms' living room liquor cabinet near her father's body. This location was potentially significant because both Derek and Nancy Haysom had blood alcohol levels of .22 when they died.

[Since these prints were at the very top and the very bottom of the bottle, with the middle wiped clean, their position may indi-

cate an attempt to clean up the crime scene similar to the smear-
ing of the bloody sock- and shoeprints, below.]

Interestingly, when scientists examined a used shot glass at the scene, they discovered Derek Haysom's prints next to another set that, in spite of very extensive testing of the victims' friends and acquaintances, police were never able to identify. Investigators would learn later that no fingerprints of mine were found at the Haysoms' residence.

From the bloody bathroom sink where the killers had clearly washed, scientists retrieved a human hair belonging to neither of the victims. Of course they compared it to a sample from my head at the earliest opportunity—but it did not belong to me, either. This hair was never compared to Elizabeth's, nor has its owner ever been found.

Most importantly and confusingly, *three* different types of bloody footprints were recovered from the crime scene. Outside the front door were smeared boot- or shoeprints significantly larg- er than any inside. Almost all the prints on the kitchen, dining room and living room floors had been wiped away in what must have been an extensive attempt to cover the killer's (or killers') tracks, but three very smeared impressions in the blood remained: two were sockprints corresponding to "a size 6½ to 7½ woman's shoe or a size 5 to 6 man's shoe," and the last one was a sneakerprint of a size that fit a "woman or small boy."[2] Elizabeth wore a size 8 to 8½ woman's shoe, and the very first of her sample ink prints resembled the sockprints both in shape as well as in size; but so smeared and indistinct were the bloody crime scene prints that even one of her Canadian half-brothers could not be eliminated as its possible owner. Almost five years would pass before police learned that I wore a size 8½ man's shoe, 2½ to 3½ sizes larger than the sockprints at the cottage.

In the summer of 1985, while cleaning the Haysoms' house with family and friends so that it could be sold, Elizabeth was observed removing her shoe and placing her foot over the prints on the bloody floor in the living room, as if to compare them.

Soon after classes resumed in the fall of 1985, Bedford County sheriff's deputies interviewed me about the mileage on the car Elizabeth and I had rented on the weekend of her parents' murders. Company records proved that the Chevrolet Chevette had not only been driven to Washington D.C. for a weekend of fun, as we claimed, but could easily have been driven from Washington to Lynchburg and back as well. I told police some feeble lies, stalled them on providing physical samples and soon afterwards fled the country with Elizabeth.

In a diary entry written by her and later recovered by investigators, she suggested that my fingerprints on a coffee mug I used during questioning might have given me away. Yet the same diary entry also stated that Elizabeth had undergone experimental laser brain surgery just before our departure, and that she had contacted a fictional IRA terrorist named Rover to obtain false passports. Surprisingly, Bedford County authorities issued no warrants for our arrest even after our flight.

After traveling around in the world in the false belief that we were being hotly pursued, Elizabeth and I were eventually arrested for check fraud in London, England, on April 30, 1986. Among our possessions British police found letters we had exchanged over the Christmas 1984–85 vacation shortly after we had fallen in love. Elizabeth wrote me, among other things, "My mother begins her sixth gin (I pray she'll use the poker on my cold, goading father). Would it be possible to hypnotize my parents, do voodoo on them; will them to death? . . . It seems my concentration on their deaths is causing them problems." I replied, "Voodoo is possible. . . . Love [is the] ultimate weapon [that could cause her parents] to lose their wits, get heart attacks, or become lovers in an *agape* kind of way of the rest of the world."[3] These letters led English police to contact Bedford County authorities in Virginia, who then traveled to London to question us.

A British judge ordered that Elizabeth and I could be interrogated by an American officer, with the help of two English detectives, from June 5 to 8, 1986. The first day's police station log entry for me—but not for Elizabeth—read that I was "to be held *incommunicado*," and I was indeed never allowed to talk to our attorney.[4] Although he came to the station repeatedly to see both of us, he was permitted to speak only with Elizabeth. I asked for a lawyer numerous times during the many hours of seven taped and untaped interrogations over four days, but the English detectives told me this was "impossible."[5] Although one of the British officers briefly relented on June 6 and promised "to get that attorney now," my lawyer was again denied contact when he came to the station shortly afterwards.[6] The next day's question and answer session consisted almost entirely of my asking my interrogators for legal advice about different points of police and court procedure. Finally, in two untaped interrogations on June 8, I confessed to killing Derek and Nancy Haysom by myself while Elizabeth remained in Washington D.C.

Later that night, Elizabeth gave a statement substantially corroborating my account.

Many elements of my statement matched details of the crime scene:

- The Haysoms had indeed been drinking.
- The struggle began in the dining room and then spread in two directions, to the living room in Derek Haysom's case and the kitchen in Nancy's.
- The murder weapon was a knife.
- Both victims suffered neck wounds and stab wounds to their bodies.
- Some attempt was made to wipe away footprints in the blood.
- I showed detectives two small scars on my fingers to explain the presence of type O blood at the crime scene.

However, other elements of my confession did not match the evidence at the cottage:

- I claimed I sat to Derek Haysom's *right* at the dining room table, but police photographs show the second place setting to his *left*. This makes impossible my description of the beginning of the struggle, which revolved around having to step around Derek Haysom to leave but then being pushed by him against a wall to his *right*.

- In a sketch I made for investigators, I drew Derek Haysom's body lying in the dining room with his legs protruding into the living room, whereas he was found entirely in the living room. I placed Nancy Haysom's body correctly in the kitchen, but in two different positions.

- I told police that I threw away the murder weapon in a dumpster down the road from the Haysoms' cottage, but luminol testing revealed traces of blood on a single steak knife in the drawer of the dining room table where the struggle began. The knife had apparently been washed in the bloodstained kitchen sink and then "hidden in plain sight"—perhaps like the vodka bottle. At my trial four years later, this steak knife was passed around the jury box while Elizabeth testifed that I had told her how I had used it on her parents. Another six years later, at a *habeas corpus* evidentiary hearing, the Chief Medical Examiner of North Carolina testified that this knife was inconsistent with the wounds found on the Haysoms' bodies.

- I said Nancy Haysom wore jeans, but she was dressed in a flowered housecoat.

Finally, my confession contained several basic implausibilities:

- I described in detail what Derek Haysom supposedly shouted at me *after* I had allegedly cut his throat.

- I claimed to have killed two people by myself with a small knife in two different, widely separated rooms as part of one act.
- In spite of supposedly eating with the Haysoms, killing them and then cleaning up the crime scene, I allegedly left no forensic evidence linking me directly to the cottage—except for one tiny drop of type O blood shared by nearly half the population.
- Both Elizabeth and I told detectives that our motive had been her parents' opposition to our relationship. Not only was there no independent corroboration for this claim, but most fathers and mothers would have considered me a refreshing change from the lesbians and drug addicts to whom their daughter had been attracted in the past. The prosecution made no attempt to provide another motive at trial.

Shortly after my lengthy unrecorded statements admitting to the crime, Elizabeth confessed to police on tape, "I did it myself. . . . I got off on it." The detectives refused to believe her, in spite of the forensic evidence supporting this admission, and she quickly claimed she was only "being facetious."[7]

When American law enforcement officials returned to Virginia, they indicted me for capital murder, which carried the death penalty, and Elizabeth for first degree murder. Only after this development was announced did an acquaintance of Derek and Nancy Haysom come forward to tell police that he had observed a bruise on my face and bandages on my hand while I stood next to Elizabeth's college roommate at her parents' funeral service. Although numerous other acquaintances, friends, relatives and even children of the Haysoms had spent much more time with me during those days than had this gentleman, not one of them could corroborate his allegation. Elizabeth's roommate was also unable to remember any injuries on me.

*[At my trial I showed the jury the same scars on my fingers that
I had displayed to police in England to flesh out my confession.
One of them is clearly a wart or similar protuberance, and the
other a triangular ridge most likely not caused by a knife blade.]*

Toward the end of 1986, I repeated my confession to a German
prosecutor to provide him with a legal basis for an extradition
request from my own country. In Germany I could have been tried
on the American murder charges without the threat of execution.
Unfortunately, the British government did not cooperate with this
humanitarian effort by the German government to save my life and
instead gave preference to the American extradition request.

In 1987 Elizabeth returned to Virginia, pled guilty to first
degree murder "as an accomplice before the fact" and was sentenced to ninety years in prison. At least for a while, her sentencing hearing appeared to reveal a more plausible motive than
parental opposition to her affair with me: she claimed that her
mother had sexually abused her. Nancy Haysom's best friend testified that Elizabeth's mother had indeed shown friends nude photographs she had taken of her daughter, but that these pictures had
been part of her hobby of painting.

*[In some of the many informal, unrecorded interrogations in
London the year before, detectives had also asked me about
these photos, which they had found at the Haysoms' cottage. I
confirmed that Elizabeth had shown them to me during a visit
we had made there several weeks before the murders, although
she had not been willing or able to discuss details of her abuse
with me.]*

Sexual abuse could also explain an otherwise cryptic comment
in a letter Elizabeth wrote me shortly after the murders: "I thought
we did this so I could be free."[8] Free of *what*?

But in 1987 sexual abuse was still a subject not fit for public
discussion in America; only during the early 1990s was this taboo
finally broken. So, under cross-examination that *in my opinion*

could be described as aggressive, Elizabeth withdrew her allegation in court. An alternative explanation for the claim of sexual abuse was presented when a psychiatrist testified that Elizabeth had a borderline personality disorder and was a pathological liar.

> [Researchers have meanwhile established that many victims of abuse develop symptoms like a borderline personality disorder (formerly known as borderline psychosis), pathological lying, substance abuse and ambivalent sexuality.
>
> I was, incidentally, quite aware of Elizabeth's penchant for exaggeration. Police recovered letters we had exchanged before the murders in which I gave her lies the humorously intended acronym "p.o.t.'s," meaning "perversions of truth." I saw this character trait as merely another expression of her exuberantly creative artistic genius, which sometimes slipped out of her control.]

One other possible motive for the murders, not necessarily incompatible with the one above, emerged during Elizabeth's sentencing hearing: she admitted stealing some of her mother's jewelry during a visit to her parents' home one week before the crime. At my trial three years later, my attorney suggested that Derek and Nancy Haysom discovered the theft and died during a subsequent confrontation over this matter. One police photograph of Elizabeth's bedroom, upstairs from the crime scene at the cottage, shows a dresser with one drawer pulled out and a necklace lying on the floor in front of it.

> [It seems more likely that the drawer was opened and the necklace dropped there on the night of the murders as opposed to one week earlier, during Elizabeth's previous visit to her parents' house.]

Meanwhile, my extradition proceedings from England to Virginia lasted until 1990 because Bedford County authorities were unwilling to drop the death penalty charges against me. To its great credit, the German government joined my British lawyers as co-plaintiffs before the European Court of Human Rights, which ultimately condemned the so-called "death row phenomenon" in Virginia as inhumane. The Bedford County prosecutor reluctantly withdrew the capital murder indictment and, four and three quarters years after the crime and three and two thirds years after my arrest, I finally returned to America on New Year's Day, 1990.

2—The Trial

My trial was held in Bedford City, the small seat of a large, mostly rural county of the same name lying between southwestern Virginia's two main towns of Lynchburg and Roanoke. It is now home to the national D-Day Memorial because Bedford lost a greater percentage of its soldiers during the storming of the Normandy beaches than any other city in the U.S.: twenty-three out of thirty-five young men died fighting Nazi Germany that day, the equivalent of forty-five thousand fatal casualties from New York City. However, I did not notice any lingering anti-German resentment during my stay in the town's jail.

The Commonwealth of Virginia was represented by an eloquent orator who preferred dressing in all-white suits and boasted of one of the highest conviction rates in the entire state—especially in his many death penalty prosecutions, such as mine had very nearly been. My defense lawyer was a former prosecutor from Detroit whom my father had retained while posted at the German Consulate-General there in the late 1980s.

One of the first pre-trial hearings was a defense request for the town's only circuit judge to recuse himself because of his association with the victims' family. The judge admitted attending a retirement party for Derek and Nancy Haysom as well as knowing her brother for forty years, ever since their days as "rats" at the Virginia Military Institute. During pre-trial hearings and the trial itself, he repeatedly addressed the victim's brother in the gallery by his first name. And on the day the trial began, the local *Albemarle*

Magazine published an article in which the judge expressed an opinion that I was guilty: "As far as the acts themselves, I don't think [Elizabeth] planned all that out. It was like double-dare-you. I think she was shocked he took the dare." Nevertheless, the judge ruled that he could be impartial, and under Virginia's laws only the trial judge himself decides the issue of his own bias.

Another pre-trial hearing concerned the defense's motion to change venue. Because of the unusual gruesomeness of the crime, the high social position of the victims, the family and international connections of the two suspects, and the nearly four-year-long, precedent-setting extradition battle, the Haysom murders had already received far more media coverage than any previous case in the history of southwestern Virginia. Even before my trial began, a "quickie" true crime book went on sale in which the author imaginatively described how I had committed the crime—*not* "allegedly." Television, radio and newspaper reporting had been uniformly hostile, especially when the European Court of Human Rights was perceived to interfere with my apparently inevitable execution. If American media did not quite accuse me of dancing naked in my victims' blood, as had one British national tabloid, they were not far behind.

Transferring the trial to northern Virginia, where few people had heard of the case, would have meant that the proceedings could not be televised, however. In 1990 Bedford County was one of only two Virginia circuit courts participating in a "cameras in the courtroom" experiment, and my trial was to be the first truly high-profile test of this new practice. So the judge denied the motion to change venue but granted a motion to change *venire* to Amherst County: jurors would be bused to Bedford. Unfortunately, Amherst County also bordered on Lynchburg and extended toward Charlottesville, thus exposing its residents to exactly the same prejudicial publicity that, in the judge's own opinion, would have biased Bedford County jurors.

In the end, fifteen of the thirty-eight members of the jury pool—an unusually high percentage—declared that they were unable to judge the case impartially. Those twelve jurors and two alternates who were eventually seated made the *in my opinion* not altogether comforting claim that they could lay aside their previously formed opinions on my guilt.

In a third pre-trial hearing the judge denied the defense's motion to suppress my confessions because I had not been allowed to speak to my lawyer during the interrogations in England. He ruled that I had initiated contact with police by asking to be interrogated, and he refused to believe my claim that this request resulted from a British detective's implicit threat in the holding cells to harm Elizabeth if I did not drop my demands for an attorney.

[*My lawyer was not permitted to enter evidence that it was common practice until the early 1980s for English police to use coercive tactics during questioning of suspects. Only the infamous case of the Guildford Four, later made into the movie* In the Name of the Father, *finally forced British authorities to reform police procedure and release literally dozens of wrongly convicted inmates serving long sentences.*

I think it is fair to say that any request by a suspect asking to be interrogated without his or her attorney should be viewed with suspicion. In this case, it is also worth noting that I did not actually confess to the murders until three days after I supposedly expressed a desire to discuss the case with detectives. Finally, it seems strange that only six minutes passed between my allegedly voluntary request at 7:59 p.m. and the beginning of questioning at 8:05 p.m.]

The final major pre-trial hearing focused on the status and testimony of the prosecution's new footprint witness. Since the original state crime lab reports clearly excluded me as a possible owner of the bloody sockprints at the cottage—they corresponded to "a size 5 to 6 man's shoe," while I had a size 8½ foot—the

Commonwealth's Attorney needed a new forensic expert to testify at my trial. Instead of choosing one of the many state or private experts on foot- and shoeprints, he selected a former FBI lab technician (*not* a scientist) who had specialized in car tire and belt impressions and only recently had done some consulting work on footprints for the police department of a Caribbean island.

The trial judge ruled that this witness could not be qualified as an expert witness but allowed him to take the stand as a lay witness. Normally, non-expert witnesses testifying about forensic samples merely identify the item in question without commenting on it, but at my trial the judge permitted the former FBI lab tech to describe his "credentials," to use scientific-sounding terms like "double hit" and "correspondences" to explain at great length the size difference, to make markings and point out features on an "overlay" he had created, and generally to "designat[e] this [sockprint] as his," meaning mine. "It matches and it fits like a glove," the prosecutor summarized this witness's testimony about the sockprints in his closing speech at trial.[9]

The *top half* of one of the sample footprints I gave police did indeed resemble the bloody crime scene sockprint strongly, and the large difference in *length* seemed to have been resolved by the non-expert's "double hit" theory. On its own, the sockprint appeared quite damning.

When my actual trial began, the prosecutor and my defense attorney laid out the facts of the case much as I have done here, with three important omissions:

• The jury never saw the sample ink footprint of Elizabeth's that, at least to the untrained eye, resembled the bloody sockprint at the cottage as closely as did mine. Instead, the prosecution's lay witness selected another of her samples which strongly differed, thus leading jurors to believe she could not have left the crime scene print. Especially in combination with the strong resemblance between my sample and the bloody sockprint, the non-expert's choice of comparison for Elizabeth made a very powerful impression on the jury, as we shall see. Oddly enough, it was the very first of her ink footprints that so closely matched the crime scene print, so the lay witness could hardly have missed the resemblance. Unfortunately, my own attorney did not compare the bloody sockprint to all of Elizabeth's sample footprints until after the trial.

- My lawyer also did not call to the stand the state's original footprint expert, who had prepared the lab report *before* my arrest that found the sockprint corresponded to a man's size 5 to 6 shoe.

- Neither prosecution nor defense brought up Elizabeth's allegations of sexual abuse at her sentencing hearing, nor did either side submit her mother's nude photographs of her as evidence at these proceedings. This possible motive was therefore never properly investigated and explored, much less presented to the jury for consideration.

Elizabeth's testimony against me at trial was one of the highlights of the prosecution, though it did not go quite as smoothly as anticipated. On the day before she was to take the stand, a Virginia attorney with whom my father had discussed the case years earlier sent the prosecutor a photocopy of some items my father had shown him: movie ticket stubs from Washington D.C. theaters, purchased on the night of the Haysoms' murders. At this point Elizabeth had already given approximately half a dozen different accounts of what she had or had not supposedly done in Washington while I allegedly killed her parents in Bedford County, the most recent of which quite definitely did *not* include a purchase of movie tickets. The timely arrival of these—*in my opinion* confidential—photocopies of the ticket stubs in the prosecutor's office allowed her to fashion a new version of events for trial: she now claimed to have attended the movies *Witness* at 1:00 p.m., *Stranger than Paradise* at 4:00 p.m. and *The Rocky Horror Picture Show* at midnight of March 30, 1986.

Under cross-examination my attorney confronted Elizabeth with the original movie ticket stubs, which my father had found in my college dorm room after our flight in the fall of 1985. The original stubs showed the movies' starting times clearly, whereas the photocopies sent to the prosecution the day before were too indistinct to be read. Contrary to Elizabeth's sworn testimony, the tickets were for the 5:05 p.m. showing of *Witness*, the 10:15 p.m. performance of *Stranger than Paradise*, and the midnight showing of *The Rocky Horror Picture Show*.

> *[The tickets for* Stranger than Paradise *could not have been bought before 7:30 p.m. Since the drive from Washington to Bedford County took three and a half hours under the 55 m.p.h. speed limit of 1985, those ticket stubs did in fact provide an ironclad alibi for the purchaser, as the prosecution agreed.]*

When I took the stand in my own defense, I gave the following testimony, which no trial or appellate court has accepted:

> *[On the afternoon of the murders, Elizabeth revealed to me that she needed to meet a drug dealer in Washington to perform a favor that would finally free her of her Charlottesville drug dealer, a fellow honors student. She asked me to purchase movie tickets as an "alibi" for her parents, in case her college drug dealer—whose parents also lived in Lynchburg and were acquainted with the Haysoms—threatened to tell her mother and father of her continuing drug abuse and her trip to Washington.*
>
> *When Elizabeth returned many hours later than expected and told me she had killed her parents, she asked for my help to avoid execution. In shock, in love, in trouble already as the accomplice who had bought the alibi movie tickets, in full expectation of almost immediate arrest, in the false belief that my father's diplomatic status meant I would be tried in Germany as*

a juvenile, subject to no more than ten years incarceration, in the grip of romantic ideals like Sidney Carton sacrificing his life for his love on the guillotine in Charles Dickens' A Tale of Two Cities ("It is a far, far better thing that I do, than I have ever done . . .") . . . I volunteered to take the blame for Elizabeth's crime to save her from the electric chair. We spent the rest of the night arranging our lies on the model of Shakespeare's Macbeth and thereafter never discussed the events of March 30 again.]

I could produce only one piece of corroborative evidence for my account: on June 7, 1986, two days *before* I confessed, a British detective asked me, "Would you consider . . . pleading guilty to something you didn't do?" "I can see it happening, yes," I replied, adding that I believed such things happened "in real life."[10] The officer told me he disagreed and quickly changed subjects.

[All of the dozens of inmates released in England in the early 1990s were freed solely because their confessions were no longer considered "safe," and many of the inmates exonerated by DNA evidence in the U.S. over the past decade also confessed falsely.]

On June 21, 1990, the twelve Amherst County jurors convicted me of two counts of first degree murder after only four hours of deliberations and recommended a sentence (later adopted by the trial judge) of two consecutive life terms. The jury was split six-six when it began considering my case, but, according to one panel member's statement to a Charlottesville newspaper (and later in affidavit form to my attorney), a closer examination of the bloody sockprint quickly convinced the twelve men and women of my guilt. "Had it not been for the sockprint and the testimony concerning it [by the prosecution's non-expert witness], I for one would have found it more difficult, if not impossible, to place him at the scene of the crime," the juror said. "If it had not been for that footprint, I would have found him innocent."[11]

3—The Appeal

The media circus surrounding my case reached a new level in the months following the verdict, with a two-hour documentary on regional prime time TV as well as segments on *Larry King Live*, *Inside Edition*, *Hard Copy* and *Geraldo Rivera*. The wife of one of the senior members of the law enforcement/prosecution team printed and distributed yellow T-shirts with the logo, "I Survived the Soering Trial—Local Yokel," many of which sheriff's deputies smuggled into the jail with requests for my autograph. ("Local Yokel" referred to a letter of mine that Elizabeth had turned over to police, in which I called Bedford County policemen "yokels"— something the prosecutor, perhaps understandably, would not let jurors forget.) I also received over three hundred letters of support from Roanoke, Bedford and Lynchburg residents, as well as two pieces of hate mail.

One of my correspondents showed considerable initiative and intelligence by visiting E. C. Glass High School in Lynchburg to examine graduating class yearbooks from the late 1940s. There she found photographs of my trial judge and Nancy Haysom's brother in several extracurricular clubs together and, at least apparently, arm-in-arm in a separate picture of their own. At the pre-trial hearing on recusal, of course, my judge had only admitted to knowing the victim's brother at the Virginia Military Institute.

My trial attorney, meanwhile, finally compared the crime scene sockprint to all of Elizabeth's sample ink footprints and discovered, as explained above, that the very first of her ink samples resembled the bloody impression from the cottage *in shape* as closely as did mine and *in length* much more closely.

Also, my lawyer at last examined the standard forensic textbook on foot- and shoeprint analysis and found in its pages the definitive study on sneakerprints made by shoes manufactured in the 1980s. According to this study's fully credentialed expert author, the sneakerprint at the Haysom cottage corresponded to a size 7½ or smaller man's shoe—whereas I wore a size 8½. This scientist later provided an affidavit to my new appellate attorney during later *habeas corpus* proceedings.

Both the Court of Appeals and Supreme Court of Virginia denied my trial lawyer's direct appeals. Then, in 1995, I filed charges against him before the Michigan Attorney Discipline Board, which eventually found him guilty of:

- failing to competently handle my appeal; and
- misappropriating $5,000 of my funds, lying about witnesses, and creating phony affidavits;
- refusing to turn over files to me once I decided to drop him as my lawyer.

In his defense, my trial attorney wrote that his "ability to practice law was materially impaired by an emotional or mental disability" from January, 1989, to November, 1992, a period encompassing my entire trial and both direct appeals. The board suspended his license but, to his considerable credit, my former lawyer continued to maintain my innocence in newspaper interviews even after these proceedings.

The lives and careers of other major figures in my case also took sometimes strange turns in the years following my trial. Shortly after his retirement, Bedford's sheriff was sued by the county for allegedly misappropriating department funds to buy himself a pickup truck; this suit was settled out of court with a repayment of the monies in question. All of the policemen were promoted— except for the chief detective, who left the sheriff's department after an investigation into his conduct at a capital murder crime scene. Using a videotape of his cross-examination of me, my prosecutor sought but failed to obtain his party's nomination for the 1993 election of the state's Attorney General; he has meanwhile taken over the seat of my trial judge, who retired. And finally, Elizabeth went up for an unusually early parole hearing with public praise from the prosecutor for helping to convict me, but she was not released because—*so I am told*—friends and members of her family wrote the parole board that they believed she had physically been present at the murders.

In 1995 a new lawyer took over my *habeas corpus* proceedings: a former Deputy Attorney General of Virginia, now a University of Virginia law professor, who represented me first at a reduced rate and later without charge, because she believes in my innocence. One of the first things she did was to obtain affidavits by a retired Special Agent from the FBI's Crime Lab and a retired New Jersey state police forensic scientist specializing in finger- and footprints, both of whom found that the bloody sockprint at the crime scene had more likely been left by Elizabeth than by me. According to these genuine experts, the prosecution's non-expert's testimony about "correspondences" and "double hits" was "quite misleading." The smeared print at the cottage was of such poor quality that it "provides no evidence whatsoever that Mr. Soering was at the scene of crime. . . . I can state that the crime scene print matches in size only with Ms. Haysom's print. . . . There too, however, the evidence does not prove 100 percent that the blood impression print on the floor belonged to Ms. Haysom."[12]

The state never contested these scientists' findings during the lengthy subsequent appellate proceedings and eventually even admitted in its own legal briefs that the bloody sockprints "could not be sized with precision."[13] This newest and latest position by the state directly contradicted the original and offical 1985 state lab report ("size 5 to 6"), the prosecutor's claim at trial ("fits like a glove" on my 8½ feet) and at least one juror's opinion immediately after the verdict ("If it had not been for that footprint, I would have found him innocent.").

In 1996 a former Bedford County sheriff's deputy told my appellate lawyer that, only a few days after the Haysom homicides, he had stopped and searched two drifters on a highway near the victims' residence. While frisking one of the men, the deputy locked the other in the back of his patrol car, where the vagrant apparently hid a Buck 110 knife—which the deputy still had and now gave to my attorney! The men told him they had gone to Lynchburg "to see a girl," and since they were not otherwise suspicious, he released them. Only a few days later they murdered a man in the next town, Roanoke, by stabbing him twenty-six times in the body and throat and cutting off his penis, a crime for which they were now both serving life sentences.

As soon as he heard of the two men's arrest for murder in 1985, the deputy repeatedly urged his superiors to investigate the drifters more closely as suspects in the Haysom homicides, but his suggestions were ignored. And five years later, in the months before my trial, the prosecution also neglected to inform the defense of this potentially exculpatory evidence. Now, after another six years had passed, the Virginia Supreme Court granted my lawyer an evidentiary hearing to examine this matter and sent the case . . . straight back to my original trial judge, whose lack of complete candor about his relationship with the victim's family had been one of the main points of the last six years of legal appeals!

At this hearing the state's own expert confirmed that the two vagrants' Buck 110 knife could have inflicted the Haysoms' slash and stab wounds, and that the Haysom homicides and the third murder in Roanoke revealed a similar *modus operandi*. But after eleven years in a drawer in the deputy's home, the knife no longer carried any detectable traces of blood, nor did the two drifters' fingerprints match any of the still-unidentified crime scene prints. Still, a past president of the Richmond Bar Association, accepted as an expert in law by both sides, testified that this evidence created so much doubt that it would have led to a different verdict, had it not been suppressed by the prosecution.

Although Virginia's laws normally made such uncontested expert opinion binding on the fact finder, my trial and now appellate judge nevertheless refused to overturn my conviction. Later a federal district court ruled that I would have been convicted even if the jury had heard about the two drifters who had been "to see a girl" in Lynchburg and only days later stabbed another victim over twenty times.

(The same expert in law who testified at the above evidentiary hearing had earlier studied the entire three-week trial transcript as well as the direct appeals and concluded, as an entirely separate matter, that I would not have been convicted but for the unconstitutionally inadequate representation of my trial attorney, especially in regard to the foot- and shoeprint evidence. No appellate court showed any interest in this finding by a recognized expert in criminal defense advocacy, even though his professional judgement in other cases has meanwhile earned him promotion to a federal magistrateship.)

In 1996 the Charlottesville *Daily Progress*, the Richmond *Times-Dispatch*, the Roanoke *Times* and the smaller Charlottesville *C'ville Weekly* published major front-page articles implicitly questioning my conviction. The first of these articles, "Trial and Error?" by Ian Zack, eventually won a statewide prize for investigative journalism. That year and the next, German TV and major newspapers also carried stories sympathetic to my defense.

But in January 2001, the United States Supreme Court denied *certiorari* to my appellate lawyer's final petition for writ of *habeas corpus*; without further comment, the court refused to hear my case. This decision concluded all legal appeals and effectively ended any hopes of my ever being released.[14]

4—Questions, No Answers, One Solution

Now that the strictly factual presentation of my case is complete, let me add by way of commentary that I did not murder Derek and Nancy Haysom, either by myself or with one or more other person(s). I was not in the state of Virginia at the time of the crime, and I did not even know about it until afterward. While I am certainly not completely innocent either legally or especially morally, I am also quite definitely not guilty of the crime of which I was convicted.

Since my story evokes the same standard reactions from virtually everyone who has read or otherwise heard about it, I have put
together a series of questions and answers that will, I hope, address
any issues left unresolved in the preceding three chapters.

This can't be true; what aren't you telling me? Unfortunately, the
above account of my case is indeed true and as balanced and complete as I can make it. I left out no piece of prosecution evidence
or testimony of which I am aware; there is simply so little of it that,
according to several lawyers, I could not even have been indicted,
much less convicted, without my so-called confessions. On the
other hand, I have left out several pieces of evidence helpful to my
defense because of lack of space and relative unimportance.

My story is not so unusual or, compared with many other
inmates', even particularly egregious or tragic. Certainly during my
extradition and *habeas corpus* proceedings, I had the best lawyers
anyone could wish, and I did not end on death row. Nor should one
forget that I voluntarily involved myself in a gruesome double murder instead of phoning the police on the night of the crime.

That miscarriages of justice occur even in America's vaunted
judicial system is simply a consequence of humankind's fallible
nature. At the time of this writing over two million people are
either on probation, on parole or in prison in this country; if the
court system's error rate were as unbelievably and indeed impossibly low as one half of one percent, that would still leave *ten thousand* innocent people behind bars. And since the pressure to convict increases exponentially the more heinous and high profile a
particular case is, one is more likely to find those ten thousand
"mistakes" serving life sentences or awaiting execution. Any war,
including the "war on crime," inevitably produces collateral damage and "friendly fire" casualties.

*Why didn't the federal courts order a new trial after the state admit-
ted that the bloody sockprints "could not be sized with precision"?* No
court has ever considered the evidentiary and exculpatory weight
of the sockprints or shoeprints *by themselves* because America's

legal system provides no avenue for doing so. The only context in which the foot- and sneakerprints were ever discussed was on the question of whether my trial lawyer's failure to properly research and present this evidence rose to the level of unconstitutionally ineffective assistance of counsel—and that is a very different matter indeed. Practically no appellant is granted a new trial based on his or her attorney's decision not to call forensic experts to testify for the defense, because appeal courts are required by law to defer to the lawyer's judgment on the most appropriate trial strategy—even when the attorney is suffering from an "emotional or mental disability." Virginia has the additional legal hurdle of its infamous "twenty-one day rule," forbidding the introduction of newly discovered evidence on appeal if it comes to light more than twenty-one days after sentencing.

But haven't you proved your innocence? No. All I can prove, by means of the bloody sneakerprint at the crime scene, is that my so-called confession—and therefore the whole basis of the prosecution's case—definitely cannot be true: someone other than myself, someone wearing a smaller tennis shoe than mine, was at the Haysoms' cottage on the night of March 30, 1985. But theoretically I could have been there *with* that person, though that hypothesis would require a third member of a conspiracy to have purchased the movie tickets in Washington, D.C. (You will recall that the prosecution conceded that those tickets provide an alibi for whoever bought them.) Unlike feet, which are flexible, the soles of shoes do not stretch but produce the same print every time, so the sneakerprints provide comparatively "hard," uncontroversial and essentially incontrovertible evidence that the murders could not have been committed as I initially claimed during interrogation.

The "new" facts surrounding the sockprints that emerged after my trial merely destroyed the one piece of evidence that, according to the jury, convicted me. But that does not positively prove my innocence, of course. Although one of the defense's two recognized experts concluded that my foot is too long to have created the bloody sock impression at the crime scene, this print is so smeared that I really do think it is fairer and safer to say that it "could not be sized with precision."

I have no idea whether the two drifters with the knife were involved in Derek and Nancy Haysom's murders, nor am I able to perform the appellate judges' feat of retroactively reading jurors' minds to know if this information would have led to a different verdict. Again, all this *proves* nothing but only raises doubts.

Would an impartial judge, a mentally competent defense attorney and a jury unprejudiced by five years of intensive prior media exposure have provided me with a fairer trial? Of course. But these factors have no direct bearing on the question of my guilt or innocence in the murders of Derek and Nancy Haysom.

It is worth noting, too, that I bear some responsibility for their deaths: there is no doubt in my mind that I could have prevented the Haysoms' murders by obtaining professional help for Elizabeth much earlier. Thus I do not claim to be, nor do I consider myself "innocent," except perhaps in the restricted sense of being not guilty of the crime of which I was convicted.

Isn't there anything I can do to help? No. In any case, I did not write this book to solicit your or anyone else's help, but to help others in "prisons" of their own to find meaning in their suffering through contemplative spiritual practices. My death—for that is what a double life sentence means, in effect—would be a pointless waste if my experiences could not be put to use by people like you in bearing your cross. So, if you want to "help" me, you might drop me a note to let me know, *not* whether you enjoyed this book (that would merely be a temporary reaction by the emotional and possibly intellectual component of your self), but whether your Centering Prayer is slowly bringing you into direct contact with the Silence within.[15]

Since you've served seventeen years in prison already (at the time of this writing), won't you be released on parole soon? I become eligible for parole consideration in 2003, after seventeen years of incarceration. However, in 1995 Virginia abolished parole for all new incoming inmates and is now *in effect* applying the same policy retroactively to several thousand prisoners still serving sentences imposed under the old, pre-parole-abolition law. Since parole is purely discretionary, this procedure is not only legal but also very popular with voters. Thus I can expect never to leave prison.

Should parole ever be reinstated in Virginia, I still cannot be freed because the primary criterion for release has always been the inmate's willingness to accept responsibility for his or her crime— in my case, for a crime I did not commit. The "smart" course of action under these circumstances would be for me to keep my mouth shut, serve another ten to fifteen years behind bars, and then hope to convince some young parole board interviewer that I did indeed murder Derek and Nancy Haysom and now feel heartily sorry for "my" misdeeds. But while I deeply regret my illegal and immoral acts and omissions, as well as the terrible suffering I needlessly inflicted on the Haysom and Soering families, I refuse to "plead . . . guilty to something [I] didn't do" one more time.

Thus *The Way of the Prisoner* comes very close to being a suicide note, since its publication and the resulting public controversy very effectively nails shut a prison door that in my case was never very likely to open anyway. I follow this path, this *Way*, because I believe it is what Christ's example calls me to do. If this volume is true and Centering Prayer does indeed lead to Centering Practice—from contemplation of God's Presence within to truly self-giving service—then I *must* sacrifice my small remaining hope of freedom and parole for the greater good of passing on my insights to readers who may benefit from contemplative spiritual practices.

This is what I meant by the "logic of the cross" in the *meditatio* section of Book I. To empty the self completely means giving *all* of it away—even one's life—and following Jesus not only in words or prayers, but in deeds and in death. Only by "sharing in [Christ's] sufferings, becoming like him in his death," can we come "to know Christ and the power of his resurrection," so he can "transform our

lowly bodies so that they will be like his glorious body"
(Philippians 3:10, 21).

Such scriptural ideas and ideals are not mere theory for me, but
a living and breathing and dying reality. The fact that you are holding this volume in your hands right now proves my sincerity; its
physical existence draws unwelcome attention to the more unap-
petizing aspects of the criminal justice system and thus has almost
certainly sealed my fate with a possible future parole board.
(Incidentally, I also fully expect to be transferred to a much harsher prison for making such a nuisance of myself.) My great hope is
that your being able to *touch* the courage of my convictions, in the
form of these printed pages, will persuade you to try Centering
Prayer and Centering Practice yourself as you struggle with your
cross. If I, a convict serving double life sentences, can be transformed, then surely, surely so can you!

Of course I do not want to die behind bars; my cross hurts terribly and, like Christ and any Christian, I would much rather for
this cup to pass me by. I dream of being paroled and living again in
Germany, of meditating among adepts in a mountain monastery,
even of working as a janitor in one of Germany's great medieval
cathedrals, since prison life has made me a master of the mop and
toilet brush. But the essence of *kenosis* is letting go, even of modest
dreams like that one, and I have already done so—*for you*.

Now go and do likewise. Go and do likewise.

Notes
1.   Available at http://lucy.ukc.ac.uk/Soering/Contents.html.
2.   State lab or sheriff's department's reports, available from trial court file and in
     appendix to petition for writ of *habeas corpus* in *Soering v. Deeds*.
3.   Letters, read into trial transcript and appended to petition for writ of *habeas cor-
     pus*. At trial, the prosecution also made much of a reference to my having "the
     dinner scene all planned out." However, police found the dinner dishes stacked
     away in the dishwasher; the Haysoms died during a late-night snack of ice
     cream, not during dinner. Another letter of mine contains the line, "I have yet
     to kill, possibly the ultimate act of crushing." But this letter does not refer to the
     Haysoms in any way. Instead, it was my reaction to a TV documentary on the

Holocaust and George Orwell's *1984*; I questioned whether even I could have succumbed to the temptation of totalitarian violence.

4. Police station log, read into trial transcript and appended to petition op. cit.
5. Transcript of June 6, 1986, interrogation, read into trial transcript and appended to petition op. cit.
6. Ibid.
7. Ibid.
8. Letter, read into trial transcript and appended to petition op. cit.
9. Prosecutor's closing comment, trial transcript.
10. Interrogation of June 7, 1986, read into trial transcript and appended to petition op. cit.
11. Newspaper reports and affidavit in *Soering v. Deeds*.
12. Expert affidavits filed with petition for writ of *habeas corpus* in *Soering v. Deeds*.
13. Commonwealth's brief in *Soering v. Deeds*, March 10, 1997.
14. After completing *The Way of the Prisoner*, I filed a new petition for writ of *habeas corpus*, based on an arcane legal theory with only a minimal possibility of success. I am acting as my own lawyer in this proceeding, further reducing my chances.
15. You may obtain my current address from the Virginia Department of Corrections hotline at 800-467-4943. All incoming letters will be returned unless they conform to prison mail regulations: no more than one first class stamp per incoming envelope, no more than five pages, no money or stamps enclosed. My inmate ID number is 179212.

BOOK II

Lectio

Your kingdom come,
Your will be done,
   on earth as it is in heaven.

(Matthew 6:10)

[T]he kingdom of God is within [*and*] among you.

(Luke 17:21)

Two men went to the temple to pray. . . . [T]he tax
collector . . . would not even look up to heaven,
but beat his breast and said, "God, have mercy on
me, a sinner." I tell you that this man, rather than
the other, went home justified before God. For
everyone who exalts himself will be humbled, and
he who humbles himself will be exalted.

(Luke 18:10, 13–14)

Your attitude should be the same as that of Christ Jesus:
Who, being in the very nature God,
did not consider equality with God some
thing to be grasped,
but made himself nothing [*or:* emptied himself,
NAB],
taking the very nature of a servant,
being made in human likeness.
And being found in appearance as a man,
he humbled himself
and became obedient to death—even
death on a cross!
Therefore God exalted him to the highest place. . . .
(Philippians 2:5–9)

Meditatio

1—Divine Union

If you have taken the Way of the Prisoner and traveled this far
down the path of inner quietude, then your soul should be stirring
and resounding from the echoes evoked by the passages above. We
have arrived at the deep center, the very heart of silent wordless
prayer! All the concentrative Centering techniques covered in
Book I are merely the tools we need to progress onward to true contemplation and, ultimately, divine union: bringing about God's
"kingdom . . . *on earth*"—in this case, "within us," during prayer—
"as it is in heaven."

To help us reach this goal Christ provided us with a specific
spiritual technique for emptying the soul of false pride before its
Creator: the humble tax collector's prayer, "God, have mercy on
me, a sinner," which later inspired the Eastern Orthodox *hesychast*
prayer of the heart. Humility to the point of inner emptiness is also

what Paul had in mind when he wrote in Philippians that Christ "made himself nothing [*or*: emptied himself, NAB]": there Paul combined *tapeinoo*, meaning "to humble," with *kenoo*, meaning "empty," whence our term *kenosis*.[1] And just as "equality with God" was not "something to be grasped" by Jesus, so must we "receive the kingdom of God like a little child," without the old afflictive emotional mechanism of grasping/rejecting (Mark 10:15).

Since our "attitude should be the same as that of Christ Jesus," we must do more than merely free the self of its physical, emotional and intellectual/conceptual attachments to the world through concentrative prayer practices. In the following pages we will:

- explore the need to free the soul of conscious awareness of the self itself, so God's "will [not ours] be done";
- study specific, advanced techniques of contemplative prayer that can lead to direct, self-less encounters with the I AM—what St. Teresa of Avila called the "prayer of union" and modern academics term a "pure consciousness event"; and
- examine one teenager's truly disastrous attempt to overcome his self without our Father's help, on a long-ago night when his girlfriend's parents were murdered.

Traditionally, the subjects covered in this Book are considered to be the apex of the contemplative path, but, as you know from Book I, I maintain a different position. Like Teresa of Avila and Father Thomas Keating, I believe that the "prayer of union" is merely the prerequisite to consciously living every waking and sleeping moment in God's spirit in the "prayer of *full* union." Centering Prayer must lead to Centering Practice; we must work toward Christ's kingdom not only "within" but also "among" us, which is why Luke used the preposition *entos*, meaning both, only in this verse. In Book III we shall see that full, permanent union with God means becoming "obedient to death . . . on a cross," self-sacrificially serving all who live and breathe through the I AM's *pneuma*.

At the time of this writing, I have not yet myself reached Teresa's "prayer of union"—much less the permanent restructuring of personality that comes through the later "prayer of *full* union"— so some of the following information will necessarily be second-hand. But as I related in Book I, I have repeatedly reached a place of inner stillness where I became aware of an emerging Presence and felt myself beginning to melt into an infinite pool of Silence or "no-thing." Thus there is *no* doubt in my mind of the reality and achievability of union with the I AM.

2—Terms and Definitions—Contemplation (Prayer of Quiet)

One of the great hazards of discussing or writing about silent inner prayer is that every practitioner experiences it differently, depending on a wide variety of personal, cultural and historical factors. St. Anthony of third-century Egypt and Father Thomas Merton of twentieth-century America were indeed traveling on the same inner path, but you would hardly have known that by the disparate descriptions they left behind. What neophytes like you and I need, then, is a common vocabulary and comparative conceptual framework that allows us to make sense of our spiritual forefathers' and - mothers' writings, so we can follow in their footsteps.

To begin our task of clarifying terms and definitions, let us quickly review the concentration phase of silent prayer from Book I: its **purpose** is to free the practitioner of the self's physical, emotional and intellectual/conceptual attachments to the world, and its **method** consists of maintaining focus on a single point such as a word, the breath or an image. Our **scriptural model** is the tax collector's prayer quoted at the beginning of this Book, though below we will be more interested in his self-emptying humility than his rudimentary technique. **Historical guidance** on prayerful concentration can be found in the writings of Eastern Orthodox *hesychasts* like Symeon the New Theologian or the English author of *The*

Cloud of Unknowing, while **modern instruction** in the method is provided by Thomas Keating and his collaborators or the Irish Benedictine monk John Main, for instance. John of the Cross's "night of sense," Teresa of Avila's "prayer of recollection," the *hesychast* "Jesus Prayer" and "Centering Prayer" are only some of the **names** given to this initial stage of the interior journey.

The subject of this Book, the expansion phase of silent prayer, actually has three subordinate phases of its own, summarized here by the author of *The Cloud of Unknowing* in his later *Book of Privy Counseling*:

> If you begin to analyze thoroughly any or all of man's refined faculties and exalted qualities (for he is the noblest of all God's creatures), you will come at length to the farthest reaches and ultimate frontiers of thought, only to find yourself face to face with naked Being itself.[2]

Phase 1. "[T]o analyze thoroughly any or all of man's refined faculties" in order to break down and see through the basic structures of the self, as opposed to the self's three forms of attachments, is the **purpose** of true contemplation. In Book I we took a brief advance look at our **method** for achieving this lofty aim: after slowing down the stream of mental phenomena to a trickle through concentrative prayer, we then:

- dispassionately note each obstacle to inner silence as it arises;
- note its impermanence, unsatisfactoriness and lack of an inherent self; and
- gently let it disappear or "self-liberate."

The **scriptural model** for this prayer method is Christ's desert battle with the devil, but useful **historical guidance** on its proper performance is almost entirely absent from our tradition's classic teaching texts.

Almost all the contemplative masters of the past stress the need to relinquish the evanescent, fickle and insubstantial mental phenomena cluttering up our souls, but almost none of them bothered to provide useful, practical advice on the proper technique for doing so. The best discussion of methodology that I have been able to find is the following woefully brief paragraph from John Climacus' *The Ladder of Divine Ascent*:

> The spirit of despondency is your companion. Watch him every hour. Note his stirrings and his movements, his inclinations and his changes of face. Note their character and the direction they take. Someone with the gift of calm from the Holy Spirit well understands what I have in view.[3]

And the ones who do not have this "gift of calm" are apparently out of luck!

Even **modern instruction** by masters like Thomas Keating lacks details, though Keating repeatedly alludes to this first phase of true contemplation in *Open Mind, Open Heart*:

> If you fully accept [mental phenomena], they will begin to fade into insignificance . . . [like the] constant hum of traffic from the street. . . . Emotional swings are gradually dissolved by complete acceptance of them. To put this into practice, you must first recognize and identify the emotion. . . . When a thought is not disturbing, letting go means paying no attention to it. When a thought is disturbing, it won't go away so easily, so you have to . . . let it go [by] sink[ing] into it and identify[ing] with it, out of love for God. . . . The principle discipline of contemplative prayer is letting go.[4]

Unfortunately, that is virtually all the specific advice Keating gives on this subject.

But you need not despair: through my years of studying, though not consistently performing, Buddhist *vipassana* meditation, I am able to provide you with a variety of detailed, practical methods in this Book's *contemplatio* section that will allow you to battle the devil just as Jesus did in the desert. I have been using these techniques successfully every day, and so can you. This initial phase of contemplative prayer is neither as difficult nor as vague and flighty as some of the historical **names** given to it might imply: "spiritual sorrow," "dark contemplation," "prayer of quiet" or "the gift of calm from the Holy Spirit."

Phase 2. "[T]he farthest reaches and frontiers of thought" is how the author of *The Book of Privy Counseling* described the second phase of contemplation in the passage quoted at the beginning of this chapter. At this point in my own spiritual journey, I have progressed no further than here, nor do the majority of my prayer sessions reach these heights or depths. This seems to me to be a transitional step at best, with no inherent **purpose**, no specific **method** of its own, nor any direct **scriptural model**.

The distinguishing feature of this stage is a near-total absence of mental phenomena, a profound inner stillness or quiet, which is occasionally punctuated by a partial emergence of a felt Presence within. Of course this silence does not last very long, only until the subconscious burps up another sensation, feeling or thought. But it is sometimes possible to sense the imminent birth of a mental phenomenon *before* it actually arises, and this act of recognition seems to stop its intrusion into the quiet interior space.

Throughout this phase of contemplative prayer, there is a continuing awareness of a self that is experiencing the stillness within, though this self is temporarily inactive and devoid of content. To use *vipassana* terminology: there is Breathing *and* a Breather, Watching *and* a Watcher, but nothing else—nothing that is watched. Technically, then, the consciousness is not truly empty, for even the awareness of no thoughts is, itself, a thought. By contrast, in the "prayer of union" or the "pure consciousness event" of "phase 3," the practitioner is conscious but *unaware* of his self, and only later recognizes that he has just passed into and out of this interior state.

Since all authorities agree that the "prayer of union" is of very brief duration indeed, the first and the second phase of contemplation must be considered the normal or baseline mode of silent inner prayer. That has certainly been my own experience, with the additional proviso that even this second phase of self-aware, near-total quiet never lasts very long, as Teresa of Avila also noted: "If what [the soul] feels within itself absorbs it, well and good. . . . I know that often the intellect will be suspended, even though only for a very brief moment."[5] She views this suspension of the intellect as a passing phase of the "prayer of quiet," not as a separate stage as I do here, and I too see no hard and fast distinctions. But since it was during some of these occasions of experiencing the complete silence within that I felt myself begin to melt into a great pool of clearly divine Silence—in what I took to be a foretaste of the "prayer of union"—I thought it wise to draw attention to this transitional stage by distinguishing it as "phase 2."

3—Terms and Definitions—Pure Consciousness Event (Prayer of Union)

Phase 3. "[F]inding yourself face to face with naked Being itself" seems to me to be an admirably concise and accurate description of temporary union with the I AM, although I have not personally reached this third and final stage of contemplative prayer. In spite of their wide variety of backgrounds and approaches, all of our tradition's masters agree on the key features of what modern academics charmlessly term a "pure consciousness event" and Teresa of Avila called the "prayer of union":

- Perhaps most importantly, this spiritual state is involuntary and passive: you "find yourself" in the presence of God, since "however great the effort we make . . . we cannot enter of our own will," according to Teresa.
- With the phrase "face to face" the author of *The Book of Privy Counseling* alluded to the unmediated intimacy with divine Love that Paul described to the Corinthians: "Now we see but a poor reflection as in a mirror; then we shall see face to face. Now I know in part; then I shall know fully, even as I am known" (1 Corinthians 13:12).
- To be "made one with the dazzling rays" is how Pseudo-Dionysius expressed this ultimate closeness to the I AM in *The Divine Names*:

> But again, the most divine knowledge of God, that which comes through unknowing, is achieved in a union far beyond the mind, when mind turns away from all things, even from itself, and when it is made one with the dazzling rays, being then and there enlightened by the inscrutable depth of wisdom.[6]

- Finally, the words "naked Being" suggest that the I AM is to be known without internal or external means, whether they be creatures, emotions, thoughts or even (partially) self-induced spiritual states like raptures or visions.

The **purpose** of the "prayer of union" seems almost self-evident, but at least some contemplatives appear to have been misled on this point. Instead of loving God for himself, they came to love the spiritual pleasure of this experience—thereby re-engaging the self's afflictive emotional grasping/rejecting mechanism and, inevitably, losing contact with the divine presence within. In one of his most frequently quoted passages, from Sermon 16–b, Meister Eckhart wrote:

Some people want to see God with their own eyes, just as they see a cow; and they want to love God just as they love a cow. You love a cow because of the milk and cheese and because of your own advantage. This is how all these people act who love God because of external riches or because of internal consolations. . . . Everything which you make the object of your intention which is not God in himself— that can never be so good that it will not be an impediment to the highest truth.[7]

Note that Eckhart does not dispute that a temporary experience of divine union is "good"; only the desire for it, "mak[ing it] the object of your intention," makes it an "impediment to highest truth."

What is this "highest truth," the real purpose of the "prayer of union?" It is the "prayer of *full* union" or "transforming union," the permanent restructuring of personality in which "one breaks up the inwardness into reality and leads reality into inwardness," according to Eckhart. Teresa of Avila tells us that temporary union during prayer is only meant as an encouragement "that we strive always to advance" on the interior path toward this ultimate goal.

To ask after **method** misses the point, of course. We can merely till the ground of the soul, trust the *pneuma* to pull out the weeds of the self's mental phenomena during the harvest of contemplation, and thus let the small seed of the prayer word grow into the largest of spiritual trees—whether that be the tree of knowledge or of eternal life, who can know? Patience and endless repetition are the only "methods" available to us, and perhaps John of the Cross was not so wrong to describe the long wait as a dark, frustrating night: "purging the soul, annihilating it, emptying it or consuming in it (even as fire consumes the mouldiness and rust of metal) all the affections and imperfect habits which it contracted in its whole life" simply takes *time*.

Our **scriptural model** is the three apostles' experience of
Christ's transfiguration, cited above by Pseudo-Dionysius and discussed at length in Book I. When Peter, John and James "entered
the cloud" of God's presence, they briefly enjoyed the divine union
which Jesus later promised all believers (Luke 9:34):

> [Y]ou will realize that I am in my Father, and you are in me,
> and I am in you. . . . My Father will love [you], and we will
> come to [you] and make our home with [or: dwelling in]
> you. . . . I pray also for those who will believe . . . that all
> of them may be one, Father, just as you are in me and I am
> in you. May they also be in us . . ., that they may be one as
> we are one.
>
> (John 14:20, 23; 17:20, 21, 23)

Historical guidance as well as **modern instruction** on this
phase of contemplation is available from any of our tradition's masters, all of whom refer to their experiences with similar **names** con-
taining some reference to union. Teresa of Avila described it in *The
Interior Castle* thus:

> [D]uring the time of this union [the soul] neither sees, nor
> hears, nor understands, because the union is always short
> and seems to the soul even much shorter than it probably
> is. . . . God so places Himself in the interior of the soul that
> when it returns to itself it can in no way doubt that it was
> in God and God was in it. This truth remains with it so
> firmly that even though years go by without God granting
> that favor again, the soul can neither forget nor doubt. . . .
> I don't say that it *then* saw the truth, but *afterward* it sees
> the truth clearly, not because of a vision but because of a
> certitude remaining in the soul that only God can place
> there.[8]

4—Terms and Definitions—Teresa's Sixth Dwelling Place

Between the "prayer of union" in the fifth dwelling place of her *Interior Castle* and the "prayer of full union" in its seventh dwelling place, Teresa inserted a sixth dwelling place whose architectural (or developmental) location requires further explanation. This suite of rooms in the divine palace, by far the longest chapter of the *Castle*, contains detailed descriptions of the many different types of visions she experienced as well as analyses of their benefits and dangers. Though both fascinating in itself and useful on a practical level, the sixth dwelling place's position between "union" and "full union" should in my view—and, I will argue, also Teresa's—be seen more as a stylistic device, not an indication of when to expect such spiritual delights and consolations on the interior path.

In fact, John of the Cross tells us that visions are especially common among "beginners . . . lured by the sweetness and pleasure they find in such exercises, [who then] strive more after spiritual sweetness than after spiritual purity and discretion." All of the contemplative masters give similar warnings, including Teresa, and even I experienced what she would have called a combined "flight of the spirit" and "imaginative vision" at a very early point, immediately after switching from a prayer word to the *pneuma* as my concentrative focal point. Finally, Teresa herself affirms twice (in V.2.7 and VI.4.5) that there is "no closed door" between the various higher dwelling places in her castle, thus countering the possible—but incorrect—inference by non-practitioners that the so-called mystical graces are somehow a separate step of their own on a hypothetical neat, orderly spiritual staircase.

Although she obviously experienced visions in enormous variety and frequency, Teresa constantly expressed her ambivalence about them: "this path may seem to you very good, . . . [but] desiring it is inappropriate [because] imagination itself, when there is great desire, makes a person think that he sees what he desires." Even if the visions are of genuinely divine origin, they may easily lead the contemplative into the sins of spiritual gluttony for more such consolations, or pride at having been blessed by God with these gifts, or blackest despair when they are temporarily withdrawn. No wonder Teresa called her visions "trials" almost as frequently as she called them "favors!" And no wonder they all fall neatly into our familiar categories of physical, emotional and intellectual/conceptual temptations, as I demonstrated in Book I.

For our present purpose of developing a useful, shared contemplative vocabulary, then, we must understand visions as a special category of *mental phenomena*—that is, one more type of content of the mind. Thus the mystical graces are really just another distraction from the interior quiet, the silent space in the soul which we prepare in prayer in order to receive the I AM.

5—Terms and Definitions—*Theosis*

Most contemplatives agree that the ultimate, though distant, **purpose** of their practice is *theosis*, or divinization: full, permanent union with the I AM not only during but also outside of prayer, to the extent of being "transformed into [Christ's] likeness with ever-increasing glory" (2 Corinthians 3:18). Yet only a very few of our tradition's teaching texts clearly distinguish the *unaware* and *temporary* experience of union during contemplation from this *conscious* and *constant* existential state, perhaps because they confuse the after-glow of the former with the new, steady flame of the latter. So, as usual, we beginners are faced with a wilderness of contradictory terms and definitions liable to confuse even experts.

Not surprisingly, we are further impeded by the complete absence of any discussion of **method** in the contemplative classics, though for once we may excuse this lack: the only route to *theosis* is the patient practice of self-emptying silent prayer over years and, some say, even decades. Our **scriptural model** for permanent union is Christ, of course, who first prayed in the desert and then returned to the world to serve his fellow man self-sacrificially. Finally, **historical guidance** and **modern instruction**—or, if not instruction, at least discussion—are offered by Teresa of Avila, Meister Eckhart and Thomas Keating, who refer to this state by **names** like the "prayer of full union," "being-at-home" and "transforming union."

Perhaps the most beautiful expression of the *theotic* view of reality was left to us by the twentieth-century American monk and author Thomas Merton:

> Life is this simple.
> We are living in a world that is absolutely transparent
>   and God is shining through it all the time.
> This is not just a fable or a nice story.
> It is true.
> If we abandon ourselves to God
>   and forget ourselves,
>   we see it sometimes
>   and we see it maybe frequently.
> God shows Godself everywhere,
>   in everything,
>   in people and in things and in nature and in events.
> It becomes very obvious that God is everywhere and
>   in everything and we cannot be without God.
> It is impossible.
> The only thing is that we don't see it.[9]

While I can only gaze at these Himalayan spiritual heights from the distant foothills—perhaps only anthills—that I have scaled until now, I believe I have detected three distinguishing characteristics of divinization that may help you recognize this concept when you delve into our tradition's literary *corpus* yourself:

- it is a permanent mode of being instead of a temporary experience;
- it appears to have a conceptual content related to the ultimate unity of the Trinity; and

- it compels the practitioner to enter a life of radically self-giving and inevitably suffering service, combining in one the two traditional religious paths of Martha (active) and Mary (contemplative) (Luke 10:38–41).

In *The Interior Castle* Teresa of Avila compared the short-lived "prayer of union" with the permanent "prayer of full union" on the basis of the first of the above characteristics, continuity:

> The favor of [the prayer of] union with the Lord passes quickly, and afterward the soul remains without that company; I mean, without awareness of it. In this other favor from the Lord [i.e., *full* union], no. The soul always remains with its God in that center . . . like the joining of two wax candles to such an extent that the flame coming from them is but one, . . . [o]r when a little stream enters the sea. . . . [I]n this His dwelling place, He alone and the soul rejoice together in the deepest silence.[10]

While Teresa claims her *theosis* was precipitated during prayer by a visionary self-revelation of God, others appear to conceive of divinization as a gradual process. Meister Eckhart, for instance, tells us that "the more a person lays himself bare, the more he is like God; and the more he is like God, the more he *becomes* united with him" (emphasis added). By writing of our transformation into Christ's "likeness with *ever-increasing* glory," Paul also seems to suggest a progressive change rather than a sudden shift (2 Corinthians 3:18, emphasis added). Finally, Thomas Keating considers both models of change equally possible, with the gradualist approach perhaps being the more common.

Perhaps the best way to state the purpose of our discipline is that we are not trying to "produce" divine indwelling; rather, we are breaking down and trying to forget the lie that we ever left our Father's loving embrace. According to Meister Eckhart, "God is *always* present to . . . and within" the ground of our soul, and remembering or re-learning this truth does not *necessarily* require a sudden, convulsive insight; it seems perfectly plausible for our awareness of his inner presence to dawn within us gradually, just as it took a two-steps-forward-one-step-back approach for the apostles to understand who exactly their *rabboni* was. Certainly John of the Cross does not seem to have undergone the "rapture" of union or the "intellectual vision" of full union, and modern masters like Ruth Burroughs and Thomas Keating report that several contemplatives of their acquaintance have been transformed without ever encountering pure consciousness, blinding lights or the flutter of angels' wings.

Being a good German, I would compare the *kenotic* process to the marinading and pickling of my mother's magnificent *Eisbein und Sauerkraut*. Slowly, slowly the vinegar of divine light works its way into every pore, every fiber, penetrating into every last crevice. Then life adds some external heat or cooking, in the form of seemingly pointless suffering. And what emerges is the food of the gods, though one can never point to a particular moment and say, "Aha! *That's* when the ham became the *Eisbein*, the cabbage turned into *Sauerkraut* and the soul 'achieved' union!"

The second distinguishing characteristic of *theosis*, its monistic conceptual content, may have some relation to the *Shema* ("Hear, O Israel: The Lord our God, the Lord is one" [Deuteronomy 6:4]) and finds its clearest expression in Teresa's *Interior Castle*:

> [T]hrough an admirable knowledge the soul understands as a most profound truth that all three Persons . . . of the Most Blessed Trinity . . . are one substance and one power and one knowledge and one God alone. . . . What we hold by faith, it [now] understands, we can say, through sight— although the sight is not with bodily eyes, nor with the eyes of the soul, because we are not dealing with an imaginative vision.[11]

Like Teresa, Meister Eckhart also discovered that "in the ground of divine being . . . the three Persons are one being, [and] the soul is one according to the ground," though it is far from clear to me that God showed him this truth during a transforming visionary experience comparable to Teresa's.

The third, final and perhaps most interesting characteristic of *theosis* is the resulting irresistible impulse to serve our fellow humans and especially to suffer for them in the name of God. "This is the reason for prayer," Teresa of Avila wrote: "the birth always of good works, good works. . . . Martha and Mary must join together to show hospitality to the Lord and have him always present." Using the same scriptural metaphor, Meister Eckhart wrote in Sermons 88 and 12:

> "Mary sat at the feet of the Lord and listened to his words," and learned. . . . But afterwards, when she had learned . . . then she really for the first time began to serve. Then she crossed the sea, preached, taught and became the servant and washerwoman of the disciples [*according to medieval folklore*]. Thus do the saints become saints; not until then do they really begin to practice virtue. . . .
>
> It is a oneness and a pure union. In this state, a person is a true human being, and such a man experiences no suffering, just as the divine being cannot experience it. . . . In regard to this St. Paul says, "I would be willing to be eternally separated from God for my friend's sake and for God" [cf. Romans 9:3]. . . . The noblest and ultimate thing that a person can forsake is that he forsakes God for God's sake.[12]

Many contemplatives indeed forsook the comfortable peace of their cloisters to "share in [Christ's] sufferings in order . . . [to] also share in his glory," offering their very lives in service (Romans 8:17):

- Meister Eckhart rose high in the hierarchy of the Dominican Order, holding senior posts both in his native Germany and in France—but was tried and convicted of heresy and died, somewhat conveniently, before the Pope heard the final appeal of his case.
- In complete violation of her age's gender roles and against much ecclesiastical opposition, Teresa of Avila spent her later years founding convents and reforming the Carmelite Order throughout Spain, until her already weakened health collapsed completely.
- John of the Cross, her younger collaborator in these efforts, was jailed by enemies of reform, escaped from prison, returned to high office and finally was banished.
- A modern-day practitioner of silent inner prayer as well as a popular spiritual author, Henri Nouwen left his prestigious academic post at Harvard University to live in a L'Arche community for the mentally handicapped, befriending and serving some of society's least wanted members.

Oh, my! A condemned heretic, a proto-feminist revolutionary, an escaped jailbird and some odd fellow who prefers "nut cases" to "normal" people! Into what disreputable company have we fallen here? Could it be that contemplative prayer is not some dreamy escape from the messiness of ordinary life, but that the Way of the Prisoner leads you straight back to the real problems of the real world—except now it is not you, but God inside you, who deals with all the turmoil?

6—*Anicca, Dukkha* and *Anatta*
The real problems of the real world, the messiness of ordinary life—we nearly forgot all about those during our brief excursion to the dizzying heights of union, visions and *theosis*. But our everyday existence, with its chains and prisons in their infinite variety, will

still be there when we put down books like *The Interior Castle*, and after half an hour of rattling around our cages, we will have forgotten all the fine, high-flown feelings evoked by Meister Eckhart's sermons. In my view this is one of the greatest dangers of reading the classics of contemplative literature: so dazzled are we by the stunning spiritual sights Pseudo-Dionysius describes that we forget to begin our thousand-mile journey with that unavoidable first step. Or we fool ourselves into believing that the quick emotional high of reading about the "prayer of union" is in fact the same as experiencing that state, as John of the Cross warned in *Dark Night of the Soul*:

> [Some] persons expend all their effort in seeking spiritual pleasure and consolation; they never tire, therefore, of reading books . . . in their pursuit of this pleasure . . . in the things of God.[13]

Yet our souls, our lives and our prisons can only change if we practice what the masters preach and enter the inner desert to battle the devil in silent prayer.

Before studying the actual techniques of contemplation, however, we must learn how to use these new spiritual tools effectively, from the carpenter who invented them. Fortunately, he left us clear instructions: just as forgiveness is the key quality of the petitionary Lord's Prayer, so is total reliance on God the essence of a *kenotic* prayer:

> [D]o not worry about your life, what you will eat or drink; . . . [f]or your heavenly Father knows that you need . . . [food and water]. But seek first his kingdom . . . and all these things will be given to you as well. (Matthew 6:25, 32, 33; cf. 7:9–11)

Buddhist *vipassana* meditators would say that "all these [world-ly] things" that we "worry about" are marked by impermanence (*anicca*), unsatisfactoriness (*dukkha*) and a lack of a permanent sub-stance or self (*anatta*). None of them last; even when they please us momentarily, they soon leave us craving more; and they exist, not because of some inherent eternal essence of their own, but only as a product of innumerable causes and conditions external to themselves. Christ would have added that those causes and condi-tions can all be traced back to the First Cause, the Prime Mover, his Father, but otherwise he would have applauded this Buddhist analysis of worldly existence and possibly added some scriptural citations of his own.

I think it is worthwhile to examine more closely what our Bible has to say about the world's impermanence, unsatisfactoriness and essential insubstantiality, because a profound understanding of these factors of existence is the key to developing the child-like humility or dependence Jesus advocated. After all, it is much easi-er not to "worry about" food, clothes and pride if we truly *know* such things to be mere wisps in the winds of eternity. And, as we have seen, the techniques of contemplation involve a holistic or visual noting of the impermanent, unsatisfactory and insubstantial quality of all mental hindrances, until they fade into (near-) noth-ingness. That process is not nearly as complicated as it may sound here, but we do need to prepare ourselves for the *contemplatio* with some *meditatio* on God's word.

My purpose in introducing terms like *anicca*, *dukkha* and *anatta* in this chapter is not to mix the two age-old religions of Christianity and Buddhism into a New Age pseudo-philosophy, but to draw attention to certain specifics of Jesus' own teachings by borrowing useful conceptual tools from another meditative or con-templative tradition. Unfortunately, we have read and heard the Sermon on the Mount far too many times to really *listen* to what Jesus told us about "treasures on earth" versus "treasures in heav-en," or to his instruction "not [to] worry about" the world's physi-

cal, emotional and intellectual temptations; familiarity has bred
inattention bordering on contempt, because we pass over the
implications of Christ's discourses for our lives and our contemplative practice. Re-examining both the New and the Old Testament
through the fresh, somewhat exotic lens of *anicca*, *dukkha* and *anatta* will, I hope, let us see more clearly how deep a change Jesus
wanted us to make.

I think it is also important to note that the quotations below
are not jerked out of context to illustrate doctrines foreign to our
scriptures. The evanescence of worldly things and the need to focus
on the eternal truths of God are major Biblical themes from
Genesis to Revelation. In fact, some of the most moving and lyri-
cal passages in both the Old and the New Testaments are medita-
tions on the *impermanence* of life, that "mist that appears for a
while and then vanishes" (James 4:14):

> You have made my days a mere handbreadth;
>> the span of my years is as nothing before you.
>> Each man's life is but a breath. *Selah*.
> Man is a mere phantom as he goes to and fro:
>> He bustles about, but only in vain;
>> he heaps up wealth, not knowing who will get it.
>>>> (Psalm 39:5, 6)

See also 1 Chronicles 29:15; Job 14:1; Psalm 62:10; Psalm
90:4–6, 9, 10; Proverbs 27:1, Ecclesiastes 6:12, Isaiah 40:8, 65:17.

Scripture is equally eloquent on the basic *unsatisfactoriness* of
worldly things, the "vanity of vanities" of Ecclesiastes, which only
set off the afflictive emotional grasping mechanism that wants
more, more, more:

> Do not love the world or anything in the world. . . . For
> everything in the world—the cravings of sinful man, the
> lust of his eyes and the boasting of what he has and does

[N.B.: *gluttony, avarice and vainglory*]—comes not from the Father but from the world. The world and its desires pass away, but the man who does the will of God lives forever.

(1 John 2:15–17)

See also Ecclesiastes 1:8, 2:11; Proverbs 27:20; James 4:1, 2.

Finally, our whole Bible is one long revelation of God's continuous creative action, sustaining the whole universe through his will and his *pneuma.* "He is before all things and in him all things hold together"; they are in the truest sense of the word *insubstantial,* because all depend on him for their existence (Colossians 1:17):

> When you hide your face,
>   they are terrified;
> when you take away their [spirit-]breath,
>   they die and return to the dust.
> When you send your Spirit[-Breath],
>   they are created,
> and you renew the face of the earth.

(Psalm 104:29, 30)

See also John 1:3, Romans 11:36.

None of the foregoing should be interpreted to mean that the physical world, our emotional responses to it or even our thoughts and our concept of a "self" are not real. All of these do indeed have a genuine existence—but one that depends completely on God, not ourselves. Recognizing the essential impermanence, unsatisfactoriness and insubstantiality of all created things is a conceptual tool that we use to break the self's attachments to the "treasures on earth"—including our greatest treasure, the illusion of a separate self. Once freed of those chains, we can then approach both worldly and divine realities directly and truly unselfconsciously—and that, after all, is the goal of our practice.

Of course we can all consciously assent to metaphysical propositions like the above, but making such concepts part of our automatic thought processes, our basic approach to life, requires contemplative prayer. We must soak our minds in the truths of *anicca*, *dukkha* and *annatta* in order to absorb in the depths of our soul that we are "aliens on earth . . . looking for a country of . . . [our] own . . . a heavenly one" (Hebrews 11:13, 14, 16). In the actual performance of contemplation this means not just letting go of mental hindrances, as in concentrative Centering Prayer, but deliberately "seeing through" each of the mental phenomena that arise, to remind and teach ourselves over and over again just how impermanent, unsatisfactory and insubstantial such disturbances really are. The inner clarity we develop through this silent work in the cloud of unknowing carries over into our daily lives more quickly than one might think, and soon each day's little triumphs and tragedies no longer seem quite so earth-shattering.

Through this new way of interacting with reality, even apparently terminal or fatal catastrophes can become opportunities for making progress, as a relative beginner like me can attest. It was only one year after starting my contemplative journey that the United States Supreme Court informed me that I would have to die in prison for a crime I did not commit. Of course I suffered from that blow, but it did not destroy me, nor did it lead me to seek comfort in the usual convict palliatives: signing up for free "state" psychotropic medication, acquiring a juicy young punk, escaping into the fantasy lands of Dungeons & Dragons or television, or deluding myself with hopes of parole "*next* year for sure." Instead, within two weeks of receiving my *de facto* death sentence, I began writing *The Way of the Prisoner* to help others deal with (hopefully less severe) prisons and problems of their own.

My purpose in reminding you now of this background is not to solicit a pat on the back from you, my reader, but to point out that this volume's very existence is proof that Centering Prayer and

Centering Practice really do work. If I did not truly believe in the ground of my being:

- that my life and its suffering are only ripples on the ocean of time;
- that the fulfillment of my old dreams—exoneration by the courts, release from prison, a return to college and law school so I could free others like me, a wife and children of my own—would have carried within them the same virus of unsatisfactoriness that infects even the greatest of life's inevitably fleeting pleasures; and
- that this "self" called Jens Soering, who is experiencing this bizarrely tragic fate, has no real, inherent substance, apart from the *pneuma* in whom I live and move and have my being,

then I would not have worked so long and hard to write *The Way of the Prisoner*. My hope is that you will take courage from my story to shed your old self in prayer and draw closer to God.

7—The Death of Self and the Abandonment of the Will

Shedding your old self in prayer is, of course, a kind of death—and that is a frightening idea indeed. Yet Paul told the Philippians in the passage from this Book's *lectio* section that our "attitude must be the same as that of Christ Jesus, [w]ho . . . became obedient to death . . . on a cross," and Christ himself demanded of his followers a commitment so total that it amounted to a dying to one's entire past and present life:

> If anyone comes to me and does not *hate* his father and mother, his wife and children, his brothers and sisters—yes, *even his own life*—he cannot be my disciple. . . . In the same

way, any of you who does not give up *everything* he has cannot be my disciple.

(Luke 14:26, 33, emphasis added)

"Go, sell *everything* you have," Jesus told the rich young man, and the man seeking the hidden treasure and the pearl also "sold *all* . . . [and] *everything* he had" (Mark 10:21, Matthew 13:44, 45, emphasis added). No wonder Christ's own "disciples turned back and no longer followed him" when he promised that "[w]hoever eats my flesh and drinks my blood remains in me, and I in him"; the price of this divine indwelling was simply too high (John 6:56, 66)!

In some cases that price could rise as high as martyrdom, as Jesus explicitly and repeatedly warned his followers, but even if we do not join him on a literal cross, we must still share his dying fate on a sacramental and spiritual level in order to be "united with him . . . in his death" (Romans 6:25):

We were . . . buried with him through baptism into death in order that, just as Christ was raised from the dead through the glory of the Father, we too may live a new life. . . . [O]ur old self was crucified with him so that the body of sin might be done away with; that we should no longer be slaves to sin. . . .

(Romans 6:46)

As the preceding sentence implies ("*might* be done away with," emphasis added), baptism and the entry into this "new life" as a Christian does *not* mean our contemplative task of self-emptying is miraculously accomplished in one easy step. It is certainly true that, upon conversion, "you died, and your life is now hidden with Christ in God," Paul wrote the Colossians; and it is equally true that "you have taken off the old self with its practices and put on the new self" (Colossians 3:3, 9, 10). But that "new self . . . is *being renewed* in knowledge in the image of its Creator," *in a still-ongoing process*, which is why the Colossians must continue to "[p]ut to death . . . whatever belongs to your earthly nature" (Colossians 3:10, 5, emphasis added). In his letter to the Romans, Paul made the same point: although "we died with Christ" in baptism, our efforts "not [to] let sin reign in . . . [our] mortal body" are far from over (Romans 6:8, 12). Throughout our lives as Christians, we never stop burning away the remnants of self and "offer[ing our] bodies as living sacrifices, holy and pleasing to God" (Romans 12:1).

It is against this scriptural background that we must read and understand the contemplative tradition's emphasis on the death of self, summed up nicely here by Thomas à Kempis in *The Imitation of Christ*:

> And the more completely a man renounces worldly things, the more perfectly he dies to self by the conquest of self, the sooner will grace be given, the more richly will it be infused, and the nearer to God will it raise the heart set free from the world.[14]

Of course "renounc[ing] worldly things" through Centering Prayer is comparatively easy because we know our enemies: gluttony, avarice and vainglory, the bread, splendor and pride with which the devil tempted Jesus. But once those physical, emotional and intellectual/conceptual manifestations have been attenuated, how do we recognize our foe in the "conquest of self" during contemplation? What does the bare, naked self actually look like?

The contemplative and indeed Christian answer to that question is *the will*, the mental agency that chooses between good and evil—or at least appears to do so. When the self dies in silent prayer, the human will becomes aligned with God's, as John of the Cross explained in *Dark Night of the Soul*:

> In this way God makes [the soul] die to all that is not naturally God, so that, once it is stripped and denuded of its

former skin, He may begin to clothe it anew. . . . This is naught else but His illumination of the understanding with supernatural light, so that it is no more human understanding but becomes Divine through union with the Divine. In the same way the will is informed [*or:* enkindled] with Divine love, so that it is a will that is now no less than Divine, nor does it love otherwise than Divinely, for it is made and united in one with the Divine will and love.[15]

In *The Interior Castle* Teresa of Avila conveyed the same concept through the metaphor of a silkworm of self that must die inside the cocoon of divine grandeur in prayer, only to be reborn as a transformed butterfly of the soul:

It is necessary for the silkworm to die, and, moreover, at a cost to yourselves. . . . [I]n the [prayer of union] it is necessary that, while living in this life, we ourselves put this silkworm to death. . . . [T]his death will require a great deal of effort. But there is no reason to doubt the possibility of this death any more than that of a true union with the will of God. . . . Oh, how desirable is this union with God's will![16]

None of this is unique to contemplative thinking, of course; as mainstream a Christian writer as C. S. Lewis wrote that true repentance "means killing part of yourself, undergoing a kind of death, . . . unlearning all the self-conceit and self-will."[17] Contemplation is merely a highly effective way of accomplishing this death of self and alignment of the human and divine wills—in other words, "not merely listen[ing] to the word . . . [but doing] what it says" (James 1:22).

That God's, not man's "will be done on earth as it is in heaven" is, after all, not just the *leitmotif* of this Book but the purpose of the Christian life. "Whoever does *God's* will is my brother and sister and mother," Jesus told the crowd, and those of us who follow his example must also strive "not to do my will but the will of" our Father (Mark 3:35, John 6:38). Even when our own "soul is over-whelmed with sorrow to the point of death," we Christians should be able to echo our older brother's famous prayer, "Yet not as I will, but as you will" (Matthew 26:38, 39).

So far, so good—but when we try to apply this theory in prac-tice, does not aligning our will with God's mean losing the freedom of our own human will? How then can Christ, "the way and the truth and the life," tell us that "the truth will set you free," if we are to become divinely controlled robots (John 14:6, 8:32)? And is it not much less trouble to leave the union of the human and divine wills to monks and nuns in their cloisters while we sensible men and women of the world continue to exercise our own, God-given free choice?

Such questions rest upon a whole series of misunderstandings of the scriptural concepts of freedom and will that have caused controversies, schisms and even religious wars for two thousand years. By far the safest course for me and for this Book would be to gloss over this dangerous subject for fear of offending you, my read-er, but unfortunately contemplative prayer depends upon overcom-ing the illusion that there is a self able to choose freely. Fortunately, the contemplative approach actually *resolves* some of the most dif-ficult problems associated with this thorny issue.

Let us begin, then, by recalling that the New Testament's con-cept of freedom is very relative indeed: "When you were slaves to sin, you were free from the control of righteousness. . . . But now you have been set free from sin and have become slaves to God…" (Romans 6:20, 22). Of course Paul did not invent this metaphor of two kinds of slavery himself but borrowed it from Christ's teaching that "[n]o one can serve two masters, . . . both God and Money"—the point being that there is only a choice of masters, not absolute freedom, whatever *that* might be (Matthew 6:24).

As far as choosing between "God and Money," salvation and damnation, is concerned, Jesus stated quite clearly that these are dependent upon divine initiative: "[y]ou did not choose me, but I chose you," for "[n]o one can come to me unless the Father who sent me draws him" (John 15:16, 6:44). Paul too emphasized that "it is by grace you have been saved, through faith—and this is *not from yourselves*, it is the gift of God," "who *works in you to will and to act* according to his good purpose" (Ephesians 2:8, Philippians 2:13, emphasis added). Asking rhetorically, "Then why does God still blame us? For who resists his will?" Paul explained that it was *precisely in order to demonstrate his total sovereignty*—"to make the riches of his glory known to the objects of his mercy"—that God saves only some while damning others (Romans 9:19, 23). Just like a potter he has the absolute right to "make out of the same lump of clay some pottery for noble purposes and some for common use," if only to reveal his holiness in contrast to unholiness (Romans 9:21).

What so much Christian blood has been spilled over is the question of how freely, if at all, we can respond to God's call. If "we were . . . chosen, having been predestined according to the plan of him who works out *everything* in conformity with the purpose of his will," do we ourselves really *choose* to follow his Son (Ephesians 1:11, emphasis added)? St. Augustine replied in *The Enchiridion* that, through Adam's fall, "the freedom of [man's] will was lost" forever; Martin Luther's *Commentary on Romans* explains in detail why "[m]an's free will without grace . . . is totally corrupt"; and John Calvin declared in his *Institutes* that human beings are "deprived of freedom of choice and bound over to miserable servitude" to sin. Only St. Thomas Aquinas relativized this absolute position in his own *Commentary on Romans* by arguing that our "will is [merely] *inclined* to desire what is contrary to the law . . . but grace makes men fulfill the law freely" (emphasis added).

Grace is indeed the key, though perhaps not in the manner Aquinas explained in *De Veritate*. There he described grace as a divine external force that "works in the free will by causing it to spring into action, by expediting the carrying out of the external act, and by achieving perseverance." Presumably the contemplative masters would not have dared to disagree openly with Aquinas, but as we have seen, they all experienced the I AM as an *inner* presence, not an *outside* power that "changes the will . . . by impressing a form on the will . . . by the addition of . . . a grace or a virtue" (Aquinas, *De Veritate*). Toward the end of his life Aquinas underwent a mystical experience that made all his prior writings seem to him like "so much straw," so perhaps he too eventually encountered the divine spark within that requires no compulsion to do the will of our Father.

That divine spark each of us carries is what responds freely to God's call; of course it wants nothing more than to rejoin its Source, so it can manifest in deeds that silent union with the I AM that it has always had and eternally will have. Only the prison of self, Paul's "earthly nature," Teresa's "silkworm"—only *this* can hinder and in some cases stop us from doing God's will. And it does so under the treacherous guise of offering us a putative freedom of choice, as if choosing anything but the good could ever be other than evil.

Our selfish desires thus actually *limit* the soul's freedom to exercise the only right choice, (re)union with God. Those who perceive a conflict between human free will and divine sovereignty are, from the contemplative point of view, wedded to a devilish deception that exploits the lust, greed and pride separating us from God. The sooner we lose the silkworm's illusion that these attachments to the world are worthwhile options, the sooner our butterfly is liberated and can fly home, as Meister Eckhart explained in Sermon 29:

> The person who is established in God's will and God's love finds it delightful to do all the things that are pleasing to God and to avoid doing those that are against God. . . . God does not force the will, but places it in freedom in such a way that it wills nothing but what God himself is and what freedom itself is. And the spirit can will nothing

but what God wills. This is not a deficiency in freedom; it is true freedom.[18]

And it is also true life. These are the great, glorious paradoxes that nourish our faith: we can only gain eternal life by letting our old selves die, only win real freedom by abandoning the self's will to choose its own corrupt desires over God's purpose.

Not only Christ's, but our own resurrection must be preceded by a crucifixion; not only Israel's, but our own return to Canaan requires leaving behind the fleshpots of Egypt. Contemplative prayer is our three-day stay in the tomb, our forty years in the desert—a necessary part of the process, but not the end in itself. *That*, of course, is *theosis*, "God giv[ing] birth to his Son in us" until we are "conformed to the likeness of his Son" (Meister Eckhart, Romans 8:29).

Oratio

Of the two prayers in this *oratio* section, the former is by me and the latter by David. Mine was composed during the dark night of the soul that precipitated my journey into the interior, and it now seems to me to be so perfect a bad example that it cannot help but teach you how *not* to overcome the self in prayer. Hating the self, as I did in this written petition to God, only feeds that little devil, whereas contemplation effectively dissolves the self in the acid bath of his own evanescence, insipidity and emptiness. By contrast, the psalm of David that follows my prayer flawlessly captures the essence of abandonment to divine providence: *this* is the spirit in which all of us should enter the inner silence.

> They have set a trap for my feet; . . . they have dug
> a pit before me . . .
>
> (Psalm 57:7)

Falling for fourteen years
into a trap I dug
    myself,

I see my enemy
each time a mirror shows
    my face.

Avenging my own sins
of youth upon myself,
    I am

Hunter and hunted, both.
No mercy do I seek
    or give:

Each day I drink my blood,
each night I gnaw and tear
    my flesh.

You said that you would save
me from the hunter's trap,
    my past

All gone, the "old man" dead,
wiped clean—if only I
    would drink

Your blood and eat your flesh
and take the spirit of
    your love

And love my neighbor as
… my *self*? The self I hate?
    I can-

not! But, God, if you love
all sinners who repent,
    then please

Teach me to slip the snare,
escape the trap, and love
    my self,
      your child.

My heart is not proud, O Lord,
    my eyes are not haughty;
I do not concern myself with great matters
    or things too wonderful for me.
But I have stilled and quieted my soul;
    like a weaned child with its mother,
    like a weaned child is my soul within me.
O Israel, put your hope in the Lord
    both now and forevermore.

(Psalm 131)

Contemplatio

1—Contemplative Prayer—Approach

Pure consciousness events and union, *theosis* and divinization, *anic-ca* and *dukkha* and *anatta*, the death of self and the abandonment of the will—who would have thought that together we could cover so much dangerous and difficult ground without having our heads spin in two different directions at once? Congratulations are in order, as is some good news as a reward, brought to us by the author of *The Cloud of Unknowing*:

> For though [silent inner prayer] is hard and constraining in the beginning . . . afterwards, when you have devotion, it shall become very restful and very easy for you, though it was so hard before. Then you shall have very little labor, or none at all. For then God will work sometimes all by himself. . . .[19]

As I related in Book I, that has also been my own experience, and if you follow the guidance of our spiritual forefathers and - mothers, you too will find that the gentle, effortless process of contemplation is actually easier to learn and to put into practice than the initially quite strenuous taming of the untrained mind through concentrative techniques.

Remember that silent inner prayer is meant for "*all* who have with a sincere will forsaken the world and who give themselves not to the active life but to . . . the contemplative," according to the author of *The Cloud of Unknowing* (emphasis added). Those of us who are imprisoned in some way—by physical pain, by emotional suffering or by a terminal blow to our former concept of self—have already been forced to forsake the world as we knew it, so a new, detached, contemplative approach simply makes more sense than trying to re-entangle ourselves in the old, breathless, active life we lost. If, in addition, we are sinners who bear at least partial responsibility for our imprisonment—as is certainly the case with me— then the author of *The Cloud* has even better news for us:

> [S]ome who have been wicked and habitual sinners come more quickly to the perfection of this exercise than those who are not. This is a miracle of mercy. . . .
>
> And I believe that our Lord will deign to effect this work [of divine aid in contemplation] . . . even more particularly and more often in those who have been habitual sinners than in others who, comparatively speaking, have never caused him great grief.[20]

Finally, recall that when Christ battled the devil in the desert, he practiced contemplative prayer, not Centering prayer. Nowhere does Luke describe Jesus repeating a word or phrase like the tax collector's, nor do we see the Son of Man fixing his attention on the *pneuma*'s flow past the nostril rim—presumably because he needed no such concentrative techniques to focus on his adversary.

Instead, as we saw in Book I, Christ observed each temptation arise; noted its basic impermanence, unsatisfactoriness and insubstantiality; and always returned to his contemplative object, God. If we want to follow Jesus into the desert, then we too must perform this (in practice nonverbal and instantaneous) deconstruction of mental phenomena, not merely coast along in the pleasant bliss of a Centered, quieted mind.

In fact, the self, though relatively silent, is still very active during Centering Prayer. Concentrating on a focal point is an act of the will and therefore the self, and the resulting sense of peace can very easily become yet another "treasure on earth" that we mistake for or desire instead of God. "[S]trive to free yourselves from this error and avoid such absorption with all your strength," Teresa of Avila warned relative newcomers to the practice; for it is precisely "when a person begins to experience the prayer of quiet and to relish the enjoyment and spiritual delights given by the Lord"—that is, when he or she learns to induce inner stillness at will—that the practitioner may wrongly conclude that "the important thing is to remain always in that state of delight."

Here we have reached the profound difference in approach between Centering Prayer and contemplation. To develop the necessary ability to maintain focus, concentrative techniques use the self to intentionally (or willingly) attenuate the self's sensations, feelings and ideas for the limited duration of the prayer session. These meditative skills can be and, in the East, have been developed much further in order to generate deep states of absorption—but always for a relatively brief time only, and always at the cost of subtly strengthening the self. True contemplation, on the other hand, seeks no temporary, self-induced spiritual experiences, but instead uses each prayer session as a training ground for transforming our way of relating to God and the world at *all* times. For contemplatives, the *real* prayer is not the time spent seated with eyes closed, but our ever-clearer view of the I AM working through champagne and chains, friends and seeming enemies, and even ourselves.

To sharpen our divine eyesight, we note the impermanence, unsatisfactoriness and lack of inherent substance of all the mental phenomena that flow through our minds. The various burps of our bodies, hearts and heads are the test cases that teach us and prepare us, through endless repetition, for "seeing through" *others'* bodies, hearts and heads to the *pneuma* flowing through all creation. So, can you spot the irony here?

Yes, it is true: in contemplation, as opposed to Centering, we actually *need* physical, emotional and intellectual/conceptual manifestations to arise, so we can continue to hone our vision of the evanescence of life and the eternal beauty of God! In *The Ladder of Divine Ascent* John Climacus conveyed this counterintuitive principle through one of his wonderfully enigmatic aphorisms, so reminiscent of Zen *koans*:

> The start of stillness is the rejection of all noisiness as something that will trouble the depths of the soul. The final point is when one has no longer a fear of noisy disturbance, when one is immune to it.
>
> The cat keeps hold of the mouse. The thought of the *hesychast* keeps hold of his spiritual mouse. Do not mock the analogy. Indeed, if you do, it shows you still do not understand the meaning of stillness.[21]

If you "do not understand the meaning of stillness" completely yet, then ask yourself: what is the "spiritual mouse" we are trying to kill in prayer, just as the cat kills its mouse?

This is *not* to say, of course, that we will go looking for, much less trying to generate sensations, feelings and thoughts during prayer, just to have something on which to practice our contemplative skill! In fact, no matter how far we advance on the inner path, we will never be in any danger of running out of mental phenomena, as the author of *The Cloud of Unknowing* makes clear:

As long as man lives in this mortal flesh, he will always see and feel this thick cloud of unknowing between himself and God. And not only that, but it is one of the painful results of original sin that we will always see and feel that some of the many creatures that God made . . . will always be inserting themselves in [our] awareness, between [our]sel[ves] and God.[22]

Even a "simple awareness and experience of your own being" is a mental phenomenon between our souls and God; and, yes, even the awareness of *no* thoughts is just another form of content of the mind, since that awareness is impermanent, therefore unsatisfactory, and certainly insubstantial.

Of course you "may suddenly lose and forget all awareness and experience of [your] own being, so that [your soul] takes no account of its [own] holiness or its wretchedness," *The Cloud of Unknowing*'s author tells us in his own description of temporary divine union. But because such an "experience lasts only a very short while," it can neither truly satisfy us nor claim to have an inherent essence or genuine substance. And so we return to our "simple and direct reaching out to God for himself," "treading down . . . the awareness of all the creatures that God ever made, and . . . keeping them under the cloud of forgetting." So long as we continue forgetting the creature and remembering the Creator, our gradual transformation into the image of his Son continues.

2—Contemplative Prayer—Preparation

Perhaps the greatest key to successful contemplative prayer, as opposed to Centering prayer, is making sure one is truly ready, both in terms of one's overall inner development and of each individual prayer session. Although I realize I sound suspiciously like John of the Cross, it really is necessary to purge ourselves of our more obvious attachments to the world in a "night of sense" *first*, so we can reach out to God for his sake instead of ours. If you are in any doubt at all whether you have passed through your "night," your "unloading of the unconscious" yet, then you have not. It is unmistakable and unforgettable, both painful and liberating. For some people this process apparently involves the emergence of some distressing memories during prayer itself, while many others merely experience boredom and disgust at the endless repetition of the same old thought patterns. My "night of sense" took this latter form—what John of the Cross called "aridity"—and it culminated in the written analysis of my past that you will find in this Book's Centering Practice section.

Whether you experience anguish and tears or boredom and disgust during your "unloading of the unconscious," you will of course treat these mental phenomena just like any other sensation, emotion or thought that arises during prayer. *All* perceptions in the mind are impermanent, unsatisfactory and insubstantial, and you *can* let them go and return to the *pneuma*. Sometimes you may need to stay with a particular memory and focus on it, instead of the breath, until it fades—though you should not make a habit of this, lest you attach to and thereby feed this particular manifestation of your self. Stay only long enough with such a particularly troublesome mental phenomenon to note how it constantly changes, waxes and wanes; how it can neither truly please nor really harm you; and how it lacks any reality of its own outside of the brief flicker of neurons that presents it to your consciousness.

Once you have passed through your "night of sense," I think you will discover a continuity between that first injury all of us suffer as children, the prisons that trapped us many years later, the crisis that precipitated our practice of Centering Prayer and finally the focus of the "unloading of the unconscious." There really are no accidents: "all the days ordained for me / were written in your book / before one of them came to be. . . . I know, O Lord, that a man's life is not his own; it is not for man to direct his steps" (Psalm 139:16, Jeremiah 10:23).

Life itself jams the forbidden fruit of knowledge down each of our throats at a very early age, and ever after the apple's sharp stem stays lodged in our throat and makes us bleed internally. Over the years debris collects around that obstruction, festers in the wound and steals our freedom bit by bit as our breath gets shorter each day. At last we strangle, choke and faint—and many of us never recover from this second fall, preferring to stay dead in a pill-induced pretense of happiness rather than to be reborn.

Only a few are blessed by providence to receive mouth-to-mouth resuscitation from our Father: the Spirit-Breath of Centering Prayer, a blast of *pneuma* to our lungs and heart. As fresh and clear as this divine wind feels to our soul, however, the apple stem still stuck in our throat feels God's gale tearing at it, working it loose, stripping it bare of all the covers and camouflages it once used to make us think it was somehow part of us. And then one day it all comes out—the apple stem, the vomit and the blood, like some satanic fishbone! Of course it hurts like hell and smells of decades-old pus and corruption, but every mother knows that birth means pain as well as joy.

And just as with a baby's delivery, the *kenotic* rebirth of the "night of sense" requires courage. Some of us may have to face our own responsibility for the cross to which we have been nailed, in spite of our natural preference for thinking of ourselves as innocent victims. The truth is, of course, that "I was sinful at birth, sinful from the time my mother conceived me," so I cannot "say, 'God is tempting me.' For God . . . does [not] tempt anyone; but each one of us is tempted . . . by his own evil desire" (Psalm 51:5; James 1:13, 14). Others of us may have to accept that, no matter what we might have done differently, we could not have avoided the fate our Father chose for us for his own reasons. No one likes to admit that however "many are the plans in a man's heart, . . . it is the Lord's purpose that prevails" (Proverbs 19:21; cf. 16:9, 16:33, 20:24). Our inclination is to seek explanations and to assign blame, even when "[n]either this man [born blind] nor his parents sinned . . . but this happened so that the work of God might be displayed in his life" (John 9:13; cf. 11:4). That is a hard truth to hear when *we* are that man born blind.

After I emerged from my "unloading of the unconscious," I felt a strong need to test whether I really had the courage to face my own guilt and powerlessness—and to let that guilty, powerless self go. I thus went into a one-month retreat of renunciation and intensification, as described in Book I, from which I surfaced with the strength to try contemplative prayer and, not much later, to survive the living death sentence the U.S. Supreme Court imposed on me. You too may be moved to step back from your life at this point in your inner journey, and I strongly advise you to regroup and recover properly before moving on.

Aside from attempting contemplative prayer too early on their inner journey, beginners also frequently try to rush past the concentration phase and into the expansion phase too quickly during any given prayer session. Here I can speak from personal experience, because I must have made this mistake a hundred times. Developing real competence at Centering is *so* seductive: within a minute or two of sitting down to pray, I could induce fairly profound states of concentration without fail, so I naturally felt a little pride at "getting it right." But whenever I then tried to move from this near-instantaneous concentration to true contemplation, which requires some loosening of focus, I soon lost my way amid all the resurgent mental phenomena I had crushed only temporarily by my act of will. The resulting hailstorm of sensations, emotions and ideas reminded me of my earliest days of Centering Prayer—a quick cure for my pride!

Sometimes I coped with such failures by persuading myself that the forced truce of concentration was as good as the real peace of contemplation, because I knew *I* could produce the former, whereas the latter meant having to trust the *pneuma*. Falling into this particular trap is especially easy for people like me, who are used to "achieving" their way out of any problem. But the self-induced calm of concentration has a heavy, almost sterile feel that eventually becomes boring, whereas contemplative stillness is *alive* with the Spirit-Breath.

Of course all this seems terribly obvious now, but subtle pride in one's own spiritual skills can easily masquerade as an ally if the inner battle with the devil grows hot. Whenever you experience a dry spell during your journey into the desert within, you may find as I did that a speedy return to the basics of non-striving Centering will break open the rock and water your soul. Such a step backward takes humility, of course; but if a simple concentrative prayer was good enough to justify the tax collector before God, then it surely cannot be too insignificant for us.

3—Contemplative Prayer—Technique, Part 1

So how do you determine during any given prayer session whether you are ready to progress from concentration to contemplation? You watch for the emergence of a specific signal, the "subtle breath" that develops each time you have "stilled and quieted . . . [your] soul like a weaned child with its mother" (Psalm 131, *oratio*). Nothing could be easier to recognize than this so-called "sign of concentration": just think of the silky-smooth, fine breathing of a baby as it naps in its mother's lap after a good drink. With body, heart and mind at rest, the *pneuma* flows without obstruction, gently, softly, eternally.

As you practice the Centering techniques explained in Book I, you will soon make at least fleeting contact with the "subtle breath" and then learn to find your way back to this oasis in the inner desert. It is, in fact, nothing more than the final stage of the gradual smoothing of the respiratory process and the concomitant progressive quieting of mental phenomena that takes place throughout the concentration phase of prayer. When you are finally well Centered your breathing resembles a mere sipping of the *pneuma* in the tiniest quantities, and your faculties are collected and drawn within like "a hedgehog curling up or a turtle drawing into its shell," in Teresa of Avila's metaphor. Most likely you will also learn to identify a secondary physiological indicator of solid concentration in addition to the "subtle breath": in my case, my hands seem to grow heavy in my lap, but your body and mind may send you an entirely different signal.

The continuing presence of some thoughts at this stage is not necessarily a measure of the depth of concentration and thus need not concern you. Even if you do continue to hear an occasional murmur of the commentator's voice or Father Thomas Keating's "constant hum of traffic from the street," all that matters is that you are not drawn off Center—and, when you do inevitably lose focus, that you return to your one point effortlessly and without self-recrimination. In any case, developing anxiety about or pride in the ability to produce relatively total inner silence at will is the quickest way I know to *lose* focus.

And now comes the scary part: switching your attention from the *pneuma* at the nostril rim to . . . nothing! *No-thing* is, of course, the essence both of "the invisible God" whom "[n]o one has seen," as we learned in Book I, and of the self-emptied soul that has died to the world, as we saw earlier in this Book (Colossians 1:15, John 6:46). What is more, human nothingness is every child of God's avenue to union with the divine no-thing, according to the passage on *kenosis* from this Book's *lectio* section: it was *because* Christ "made himself nothing . . . and became obedient to death . . .[that] God exalted him" (Philippians 2:7–9).

"Since it is in God's nature that he is like no one," Meister Eckhart pointed out in his Sermon 76, "we must of necessity come to the point that we are nothing in order to be placed into the same being that he is himself." Unfortunately, the good Meister gave us no specific method for transforming ourselves into nothing, and the author of *The Cloud of Unknowing* does only marginally better on the subject of technique:

> Do not leave off, but press earnestly into that nothing with
> an alert desire in your will to have God. . . . This nothing
> is better felt than seen; it is most obscure and dark to those
> who have been looking at it only for a short while. Yet to
> speak more truly, a soul is more blinded in experiencing it
> because of the abundance of spiritual light. . . . [23]

Oh, how I wish just one of our tradition's masters had worn
spiritual sunglasses occasionally, so he would *not* have been "blind-
ed [by] . . . spiritual light" and could have given us more precise
directions for our own interior journey! But never fear: at least the
Buddha and his disciples left us some useful techniques for access-
ing what they called *sunyata*, the emptiness or void.

By developing *vipassana* or insight into the processes and
nature of consciousness instead of its overt content, practitioners
of these Eastern meditative methods are able to reach a state of
pure, unconstructed awareness of "the indescribability of things,"
according to the Indian sage Asanga. And those of us who have, in
addition, been granted the eyes of faith will not only see but even
join the I AM when it emerges into this no-thing. I have been
there myself—only to the point of seeing, just before joining—so
you can go there, too.

When you form the intent to switch focus from the *pneuma* to
the nothing, this intent itself is a thought to which you have
"attached" by drawing it out of the quiet hum of background chatter (or the relative silence). Therefore you are already off Center,
since your attention is no longer concentrated on your nostril rim
but on the idea "switch focus." And of course you treat this mental
phenomenon just like any other, by gently letting it go.

But instead of directing your attention back *within* to the eternal flow of baby-smooth breathing as you normally would in
Centering, you now focus on a point *outside* that island of stillness
and calm that you have so carefully constructed within: the spot on
the blank screen of your consciousness where the thought "switch

focus" just vanished. This change of direction of your awareness is crucial, for you are turning *away* from those last, highly spiritualized vestiges of the self—the willed sense of peace, the silent watcher who notes every mental phenomenon—and *toward* that empty space, that nothing where we can find God. To return to Teresa of Avila's image, your inner hedgehog is no longer completely curled up, and your turtle's nose is peeking out of its shell just a little.

This "simple and direct reaching out *to* God" should not, however, be confused with, much less degenerate into an afflictive emotional grasping *for* the divinity, according to the author of *The Cloud of Unknowing*. Instead of directing the "desire . . . to have God" at our Father himself, we must "press . . . into that nothing" which is the means to our end of transformation. "To arrive at being all, desire to be nothing," John of the Cross explained the all-important distinction between our aiming point and our actual target; "to come to the knowledge of all, desire the knowledge of nothing." Though God is indeed no-thing, he is not actually nothing at all: thus Meister Eckhart wrote in Sermon 71 that "in this nothing [within a man's awareness] God was born; he was the fruit of nothing," but *not* identical to it.

Maintaining focus on a blank spot of nothing is nearly impossible in practice, so this phase of prayer requires that you actually split your attention between the *pneuma* and the nothing. The challenge here lies in constantly readjusting the relative balance between, on the one hand, reaching outside your safe little island of selfish silence and, on the other hand, stabilizing your Center to prevent your mind from wandering off the nothing. Like learning to ride a bicycle, this interior balancing act can only be mastered through experience, but there is one technique I have found very helpful in this regard:

Directing the Breath. Whereas in Centering the breath appears to circle in ever-smaller ovals *within*, during contemplation you can send each exhalation streaming out *to* the nothing and experience every inhalation flowing back *from* that distant spot to your nostril. Of course this change of direction should not lead to any increase in the depth or rate of respiration; effortlessness continues to be the *sine qua non* of inner prayer, and even the tiniest sip or puff of *pneuma* easily carries all the way out to God's hiding place. Nor should you visualize the breath as some sort of golden stream going in and out, since you are trying to leave behind all mental phenomena no matter how "spiritual." "One must think neither of creatures, nor of angels, nor of the Trinity," the French Carthusian prior Hugo de Balma wrote in the fourteenth century. The only purpose of this technique of "directing the breath" is to establish an experiential link, neither visual nor conceptual, between the *pneuma* and the nothing in order to facilitate shifting between the two, "leaning" now more to the one, now more to the other. Like two poles on opposite sides of the river bank—breath here, nothing over there—you now have a frame of reference that allows you to note and observe the passing stream of mental and, as we shall see, henceforth mostly visual phenomena.

Under no circumstances should you attach any meaning or significance to the dark spot in your awareness, for the same reason your prayer word during Centering should be as neutral as possible. This is *not* your "vanishing point," where you disappear and the I AM materializes, nor does it somehow resemble God by being simultaneously infinitely distant and close by. Do not sense, do not love, do not think the nothing—just keep looking at it, as simple as that sounds and as difficult as it is in practice.

When you first focus on the spot of nothing where the thought "switch focus" just vanished, you will experience for a few seconds a consciousness of only the self itself without any sensations, emotions or ideas. Of course this calm, dispassionate watcher will eventually have to go as well, since he or she is just a particularly subtle form of mental phenomenon, but long before you have the opportunity to note the watcher's impermanence, unsatisfactoriness and lack of an inherent self, the seductively quiet, blank inner screen of your mind will be deluged by a flood of primarily visual distractions. That change in the nature of mental phenomena is, in fact, another indicator of the transition from concentrative to contemplative prayer: in the former, most of the inner distractions were auditory—the infamous commentator's voice—whereas now they are above all some kind of "eye candy" intended to knock you off Center with a variety of spiritual fireworks. Naturally, there are always plenty of exceptions to this rule in both phases of prayer, but it is surely no coincidence that *all* travelers on the interior path, both Western and Eastern, speak of the silence and the light(s) they encounter as contemplation deepens.

Virtually all newcomers and, as far as I can tell, even some experienced practitioners may mistake the very first inner twinkle or dawning glow as the great ray of divine light. But visual phenomena arise spontaneously as a by-product of deepening concentration even without any conscious intent to reach out to God, and they are definitely not an indicator of spiritual illumination. These balls, disks, eggs, bars, lines or circles of light are known variously as the "sign of meditation" or the "Christ eye," the latter term based on a misreading of Matthew 6:22 ("The eye is the lamp of the body").

What is important to note about all of these is that they are mere creatures of the mind—with a little effort you can easily make them change color, direction and shape—and thus they come between you and God. In my opinion and experience, the "Christ eye" does not even take on the appearance of a distinct, shining *form* against the black backdrop of the consciousness *unless* you make the methodological mistake of focusing on it. If, on the other hand, you "look through" it to the spot of nothing it is trying to cover up, the "sign of meditation" stays at the level of a hazy, flickering, translucent mist of light. Try "listening" for the *pneuma* at this time, as described in Book I; this tones down but does not eliminate this visual phenomenon.

Focusing directly on this initial "sign of meditation" not only gives it more substance than it should have, but also treats it as simply another concentrative Center. Some Eastern meditation schools actually advocate this practice as a technique for deepening absorption still further, but our purpose, as you will recall, is to train our perceptual apparatus to view the inner and outer worlds in a new, detached, *pneumatic* vision. For a while I too clung to my "Christ eye" as a concentrative anchor and wasted my time diving into a light of my own creation—in other words, my same old self. Instead, I should have followed Meister Eckhart's advice in Sermon 76 to "form myself into nothing and form nothing into myself and . . . remove and throw out *whatever* is in me" (emphasis added). For "the consciousness of any angel or any saint that is in heaven . . . is more of a hindrance than a help," the author of *The Cloud of Unknowing* tells us; "for in the end [this thought] will increase its chattering more and more until . . . your concentration is gone, scattered about you know not where." Our purpose, according to Pseudo-Dionysius's *Celestial Hierarchies*, must be "to get behind the material show, to get accustomed to the idea of going beyond appearances to those upliftings which are not of this world."

4—Contemplative Prayer—Technique, Part 2

Instead of using my methods for noting the essential emptiness of all the "material show" of inner visions, you can easily develop some of your own to suit your personal perceptual preferences. Not the tool itself, but its dual purpose matters here:

- stepping back from the visual phenomenon so it can be seen in its entirety; and
- noting the mental hindrance's impermanence, unsatisfactoriness and lack of an inherent self.

In practice this means temporarily switching your contemplative focus from the *pneuma*-nothing to the phenomenon itself—

just long enough to note its three-faceted insubstantiality—and then returning your attention back to the two poles of your frame of reference, the breath and the spot of darkness. As we shall see, that is nowhere near as complicated as it sounds!

The Bubble. The standard technique is a simple visualization: you take the "vision" of yourself and John of the Cross and Donald Duck playing beach volleyball together, stick it inside a child's soap bubble, and let it float away! Believe it or not, this works amazingly well and is in fact much subtler than it may seem at first. Not only does the visual image of a soap bubble break the emotional spell of the visual phenomenon by putting some conceptual distance between it and you, but a bubble also represents perfectly the three factors of existence: few things are more short-lived, it certainly does not taste very good (what, you never tried licking a soap bubble as a child?), and its essence is empty air.

Mental Noting. If visualizations do not suit you, you can train yourself to note mentally any visual phenomenon's impermanence, unsatisfactoriness and lack of inherent self *in one step*: holistically, nonconceptually, wordlessly and instantaneously. At first you will need to use a triple set of clumsy and slow questions: *what is it, how strong is it, how long did it last?* These queries require no answer, since simply the asking forces you to step back from the mental hindrance and—in reverse order—notice the three factors of existence. However, you must be sure to make the transition to *wordless* noting fairly soon, lest this method degenerate into a game of mentally tagging or labeling every phenomenon that arises in the mind. While some *vipassana* schools actually advocate this practice, most see it as an error of technique that adds a layer of concepts to a mind trying to empty itself of mental content.

Seeing Through. This method, as you know by now, is the one I use—and oddly enough, it is the one I find hardest to describe! By the time I switched from concentrative to contemplative prayer, all phenomena arising in my mind were already relatively soft and spongy, and I discovered that simply staring at them thinned them out still further until I could see the dark spot of nothing behind them once more. I knew that whatever appeared in front of my mind's eye was merely an illusion anyway, so I just *saw* it for the nothing it was. As in Centering Prayer, a thought or "vision" that is *observed* with this inner distance immediately feels much lighter, more insubstantial than when it is experienced directly from within the grip of the thinking or imagining process.

When you begin to use these techniques, they will of course seem a little awkward and cumbersome, and you will have to deal with one mental or visual phenomenon at a time. But as your practice deepens, you will gradually progress from content to process, from individual hindrances to a simple awareness of flow past the perceptual frame of *pneuma* and nothing. This is in part what I mean by the hazy, flickering, translucent mist of light I described earlier; the temptation to "attach" to images or figures or cobwebs ceases almost entirely, leaving only a mildly distracting, general glow. Eventually that too fades and darkens, because it simply is not very interesting compared with the infinite depth of the bright darkness beyond.

Some time after you have made this transition from the content of individual mental phenomena to the process of consciousness itself, you will reach a place beyond method, beyond all those aspects of technique that seem so difficult now: Centering and focal points and choiceless awareness and mental noting and all the rest. Of course you will need such techniques and—at least in my case—years of practice to reach this place; you must rehearse and perfect each step before the tango can dance itself. Once you have arrived, however, it is often simply a matter of sitting and letting the silence descend on you. No need to reach, it will come to you.

You will find yourself in a space that is airy and open and profoundly still, yet somehow intensely alive—as if you were standing on a circus high wire, alone in the bright light, but aware of the crowd in the seats all around. Though you sometimes hear a whis-

pered voice or two, some children throwing popcorn, such "distractions" do not bother you because you know in the depth of your
being that you are *at home* in this place. And you can go there any
time you wish: in the middle of the day, in the middle of writing
this sentence, any time.

Even that is only one step on a much longer journey, of course,
but the trip is worth taking. Oh, yes. Nor is it difficult: if I can do
it, you can, too.

The Desert Fathers and Mothers used the term *apatheia* to refer
to this state of quietude and ease in prayer. To develop this mind-
set ourselves, it may help to think of *apatheia* as having six attrib-
utes: it is present to the moment, non-judgmental, effortless,
detached, unselfconscious and trusting in God. Consciously foster-
ing these qualities in your prayer life deepens the transformative
process of contemplation, so let us examine these six qualities one
by one:

Present to the Moment. In Centering you had to use force to
bring yourself out of the rushing torrent of ideas, feelings and sensations into the eternal now; in early contemplation you were at
rest but still busy sticking visions into bubbles; in later contemplation, however—once you have permanently lost interest in what
your unconscious burps up, and simply note the burping process
continuing in some corner of your consciousness—you are finally
free simply to sit with the nothing, genuinely relaxed and at peace
in the present. The past has stopped chasing you, the future has
stopped pulling at you and there is nothing you are required to do
now to get from some here to some other there. At last you have
permission: your former master, the self, is at least temporarily
absent, and you are at liberty to sit by the riverbank with a fishing
pole in your hand. Of course the water still gurgles at your feet
(and, yes, occasionally still splashes you), but your eyes are fixed on
your Abba, your dad, who has been waiting for his beloved child to
come fishing with him all this time.

Non-judgmental. In Centering you did not discriminate between "good" prayer sessions and "bad" ones, nor between "good" mental phenomena and "bad," yet you still judged all manifestations of the self as hindrances to the development of a stabilized focal point; in early contemplation you experienced visions or "spiritualized" emotions as coming between you and the nothing; but in later contemplation, you realize in some new, profound way that getting your feet wet in the flowing stream is simply part of the process of going fishing with Dad. So you stop worrying about maintaining perfect stillness and "make friends with your [inner] noise," the splash of mental "distubances" soaking your rolled-up pant legs.

Effortless. In Centering you worked hard in hopes of earning a day off; in early contemplation you were like one of those frantic vacationers who spends every moment of his holiday practicing how to cast lines, reading books on angling technique and shopping for sonar equipment to track fish; in later contemplation, however, you realize that landing the biggest catch or emptying the river of all sea life is *not* the point of going fishing. Two or three times a day, you come down to the riverside for no other reason than just to be with your Father, so you cannot "fail" even if you catch nothing (or no-thing?).

Detached. In Centering you let go the three types of manifestations of self; in early contemplation you relinquished such subtle forms of self as a willed sense of peace or the silent watcher; but in later contemplation you release the urge to bleach the self out of the fabric of your personality, as if it were a bad stain. After all, God is the one who gave you your self, the river where the two of you now fish and pray together, and he did so for a reason: the two of you needed *some* place to meet! So why not on the banks of *this* little brook? In the end—watch for this!—you will even develop some fondness for your inner stream, the whole thing, not just the scenic spots but also the mud and the rocks.

(Of course this more *detached* approach to the process of self-emptying only becomes possible after you have progressed far enough in contemplation to experience some freedom from the self's iron rule. That is why I believe this to be a milestone as significant as the earlier shift from content to process during prayer: more and more, you can actually choose when to lay down your self and take it back up again. To let go of such extremely subtle forms of self as the urgent desire (!) for *kenosis* requires both vigilance and, in my experience, a sense of irony or humor regarding the whole process of living and dying and living again.)

Unselfconscious. In Centering, in early contemplation and even in later contemplation you remain conscious of your self even as you reach out to that nothing where you end and your Father begins. But on some days—not all, mind you, but some—your dad will take you down to the old fishing hole above the beaver dam, that oval of still, deep water where the river catches its breath before rushing on down below. Here there are no waves on the surface nor currents below; all the biggest catfish hide in this place, so the old men in the feed store will tell you, and no one has ever touched bottom. To have any hope of landing a catch, though, they say you must cast your lines at night.

When you and your dad reach the great rock that only lovers and anglers know, the sky above and the water below are already full of stars. Sliding over the moss and up to the edge, you lie flat on your stomach and stare down into the deep to try to see those ancient, enormous fish the old men talk about. But the water is too muddy: all you see is your own reflection looking back at you from the dark, opaque surface.

Slowly, the water changes from cloudy and obscure to transparent and limpid, until at last you feel yourself suspended above or before a vast empty space, a Milky Way deep both in front of you in the starlit fishing hole and behind you in the reaches of night sky. Dark, so dark is this space—and yet filled with a light whose presence you sense instead of see. "For darkness is as light to you . . . the night . . . shine[s] like the day" (Psalm 139:12). And though you hang there between eternity and infinity, simply looking, you are never scared, for you not only know but feel your Father right there on the rock next to you. His arm is wrapped around your shoulder, his breath is on your cheek, his scent is in your nose—you are safe.

Then something changes, you know not what: something is *moving*, either you going down or the water coming up or the night sky falling through. You feel slightly dizzy and clutch and . . .

. . . and that is as far as I have gone down the inner path, the Way of the Prisoner. I can guide you no further, at least not by personal experience. Too much of my self remains: every time I reach this point, I feel afraid, not of God but of losing that simple sense of being and awareness that was *just about* to melt into the pool of illumined dark. Such a very little thing, and yet it kept my soul from joining its Source.

Of course I always feel just a little sad after one of these close encounters, but I do not become discouraged. My Father so very clearly wants me to come to him, to become one with him, that I *know* I will let go and return home eventually. "If God is for us, who can be against us" (Romans 8:31)?

Trusting in God. That is the last and most important of the six facets of genuine *apatheia*, and I believe it is the one whose fullness I still lack. But my Father has shown me just where to go to mature my faith in him, to bring it to ripeness through direct experience of his love: I must keep returning to the banks of that internal river to cast lines with my dad, "reelin' 'em in and throwin' 'em back." This process of fishing, of contemplating the subtlest manifestations of self against the black backdrop of nothing, this is how my Abba and I will grow closer and closer.

5—Contemplative Prayer—A Fruit of Prayer

Such high-flown paeans on union with God in prayer need not remain pretty words printed on this page, however: "All these things come true in *you* in a mystical way," Origen wrote in the third century. As evidence to support that claim, I offer the following account of one of my own Centering Prayer sessions in the hope that this will persuade you that literally anyone—even a "lifer" in prison, and even you—can reap real fruits as you travel on the interior path.

Fourteen months after setting out on my journey into the interior, I decided on a whim to pray outdoors on a bench in a relatively quiet corner of the prison recreation yard. Normally I practice contemplation in a darkened room with earplugs, to facilitate my concentration on the mental phenomena generated through the three facets of the "self," so this session was a quite radical change for me. Since at that time my prayer life was in one of its fruitful, generally easy periods, I was able to relax and concentrate fairly quickly, and then moved on to the expansion phase.

The specific prayer method I used was precisely the one briefly described in Book I, based on Christ's desert battle with the devil: I observed each mental phenomenon arise, noted its insubstantiality (its impermanence, unsatisfactoriness and lack of independent existence or "self"), watched it "self-liberate" or vanish and returned to my point of focus, the breath or spirit. Some Eastern traditions call their form of this technique—without the distinguishing Christian element of the interior encounter with the divine, of course—the state of *choiceless awareness*, since the practitioner constantly and continuously switches his focus onto each new sensory perception, emotion or thought without judging, grasping or rejecting any of them. All such mental phenomena are equal anyway, in that they are only products of the self; the only true, eternal reality is God, onto whom I return my focus after each phenomenon melts away.

What I immediately became aware of during this session on the prison yard was the beauty of the various sounds around me. The earplugs I always wear during contemplation in my cell had habituated me to almost total silence, so I suppose some physical or sensory unfamiliarity raised still further the already heightened sensitivity of the contemplative state. The caw-caw of a seagull above me, the silvery tinkle of a water cooler leaking onto the concrete behind me, the wave-like murmur of conversation in the distance, even the wind rushing around and curling behind my ears—each of these sounds seemed glorious, unique, precious and somehow truly, deeply *interesting* to me.

Most importantly, they all initially struck my consciousness as sensory perceptions pleasurable in and of themselves, *before* I identified that particular tickling of my auditory nerve as having been caused by a seagull, for instance. Since I was familiar with contemplative literature, I knew that the nearly automatic mental labeling mechanism of the intellect would destroy this direct, unmediated experience of my environment, and in each case I was able to prolong a little longer that period of pure consciousness of sound. Once the mind tagged a specific noise with the words "leaky water cooler" and reduced it to a mental product, I let it go and returned to my original focal point without waiting for or expecting—that is, grasping at—the next magic tingle in my ear. Inevitably, I was rewarded straight away, almost without interruption, with another beautiful sound.

Although this experience was in the truest sense of the word "wonderful," it was perhaps a little too rich, like eating a mountain of chocolate mousse at one sitting. How long it lasted I could not tell, as is common with deeper contemplative states, but when I emerged I felt slightly dazed and exhausted. To shake off this effect, I stood up, looked around me and enjoyed the continuing sense of inner peace and silence.

It was at this point that I saw Hop-along.[24] Or rather, I saw the hunter's orange acrylic knit hat on his head and the golden reflection of sunlight on his very black forehead. What I mean to say is that I really *saw* these two colors in all their glorious vividness, as if for the very first time—the visual equivalent of the previous direct experiences of sound. That knit hat glowed orange as if it were the Platonic ideal of its color, the true, original Orange that

existed in God's mind before the world was formed. And the gold-
en light on Hop-along's forehead was so rich and warm that it
seemed to draw me in, to invite me to jump into its Goldenness.
The effect was quite overwhelming, and I am sure I must have
stood there like a nitwit, staring openmouthed at a fellow prisoner's head.

Now, Hop-along is . . . *Hop-along*, about as low as one can sink
in the penitentiary caste system. Nick-named for a deformed leg
and hip joint, he is also known for stealing from other inmates, as
well as for collecting feathers and bits of paper in the various pockets of his incredibly dirty clothes. When he noticed me looking at
him, he turned toward me and grabbed his crotch with gusto and a
suggestive leer; presumably he earns money for his nicotine addiction by turning tricks, like so many physically or mentally handicapped prisoners.

Hop-along will never know how close he came to getting a hug
from me that day. At that moment I felt so thankful to him for
being in my world and showing me the beauty of God's creation
that the only word for my emotions toward him was love.
Gratitude almost to the point of tears was in fact my immediate
response to the entire experience on the prison recreation yard.
What a blessing, to be allowed to hear and see such glory!

But it was only months later, while writing about the transfiguration, that I finally understood what God had shown me that
.day: not just the wonders to be found even in his humblest creatures, but the Christ in my fellow man. Luke wrote that in the presence of Peter, John and James "the appearance of [Jesus'] face
changed, and his clothes became as bright as a flash of lightning"—
a *perfect* description of what I experienced with Hop-along. Like
Peter, who "did not know what he was saying" on the mount of
transfiguration, I too did not understand at the time just what I had
seen (Luke 9:33).

Of course I realize that, at least initially, some readers may be
shocked by this comparison of the two visions, the three disciples'

of Christ and mine of Hop-along. That no doubt is why Mother Teresa spoke of discovering Jesus "in another *distressing* disguise" when she encountered one of her lepers (emphasis added). But if the first and only begotten son "is the atoning sacrifice for our sins, and not only for ours, but also for the sins of the *whole world*," then we are *all* potential sons and daughters of God, including the lepers and the Hop-alongs of this world (1 John 2:2, emphasis added).

Those who restrict this basic equality before the Father only to believers must still admit Hop-along's provisional or presumptive sonship, since he sometimes attends church, carries a well-thumbed Bible, and professes his faith as far as he is able. As for me, the light I saw shining through that sad, broken man profoundly confirmed my previously held belief that the Creator, who "saw *all* that he had made, and it was *very* good," must love each of his creatures, without exception, like a Father (Genesis 1:31, emphasis added). Whether such universal paternal love is the technical or theological equivalent to adoption as sons or daughters through faith is a question beyond the scope of this book; my personal belief is that the two differ. But Jesus, who had a well-known affinity for outcasts like Hop-along, would surely have recognized him as a prospective younger brother, and that is what I believe to be the meaning of my prayer on the prison yard.

A final note: at the time of this writing, I have not yet returned to the yard for another contemplation session *al fresco*. To me that one day was a glimpse of the future I can reach if I persist in my daily silent contemplative prayer in my cell: with practice, I can begin to see what Father Thomas Merton saw when he wrote that "We are living in a world that is absolutely transparent / and God is shining through it all the time." Recognizing God in Hop-along is the first, distant glimmer of "transforming union," too. Only by doing the work of *kenosis*, disassembling the self bit by bit, can my mode of perceiving reality be transformed permanently to allow a continuous direct experience of God and his creation. "Offer [God] your very self in simple wholeness, all that you are and just as you are," the author of *The Cloud of Unknowing* tells us in *The Book of Privy Counseling*. "[Make that] your joyful gift . . . to God."

6—Centering Practice—The Analysis, Part 1

In a strange and sad way, "[o]ffer[ing my] very self in simple wholeness, all that . . . [I am] and just as [I am]," is also what I did on the night of my crime: I threw away my life for someone I loved, and as a direct result I damaged or even destroyed many other lives. If you are uninterested in this particular piece of my history, please feel free to skip the remaining chapters of this Book and proceed to the second Intermezzo. None of what follows is an integral part of this volume. If you choose to read on, I will share with you what I believe to be both the proximate and distant causes of my crime to illustrate the process of "making peace with our past" after the "unloading of the unconscious." Presumably your Centering Practice analysis of your own life will not have to deal with a history quite as tragic as mine, so I hope that my admittedly extreme example will inspire you to dig deeply and uncover even the deepest roots of self.

Self is indeed what flawed the gift I tried to make on the night of my crime—in my case, the secret selfishness of abject self-hatred. And I believe this hidden motive, this unrecognized part of *me*, caused all the illegal and immoral acts I committed, all the harm I inflicted under the guise of love.

Yet I do not and will not reject retroactively the overt part of my motivation that was pure and loving, the unreflected impulse to "lay down . . . [my] life for . . . [my] friend" (John 15:13). Of course I regret more profoundly than you, my reader, can ever imagine both the manner of my self-sacrifice and the suffering I thereby caused others and myself; but I do not regret my instinct to help someone I loved at a moment of greatest danger to her, no matter what the cost to myself. In fact, I *cannot* reject this conscious factor of my actions that night, any more than I can deny the unconscious factor of self-hatred, since both were part of my personality and my history at that time.

And through God's grace, the self-sacrificial impulse of that eighteen-year-old boy has meanwhile matured into the self-empty-ing prayer life of the thirty-seven-year-old man (at the time of this writing). Thus the same character trait that led to my downfall has, in a very real sense, also carried me to my inner resurrection, iron-ically giving me something to be grateful for amid the misery I brought on others and myself. If you too sensitize yourself to the mysterious, even mystifying work of the Spirit in your past and present as part of your Centering Practice, then you will gain the experiential certitude that it is truly "[i]n *all* things [that] God works for the good of those who love him" (Romans 8:28).

Nothing can change, mitigate or justify the tremendous dam-age I did to others' lives, of course. My point here is that "making peace with your past" must be *completely* honest: neither you nor I can merely indulge our selves in a brief orgy of self-recrimination and then just move on. This idea that we can "deal with" our his-tory and then "put the past behind us" is a terrible lie, a willing blindness to God's continuing work in our lives from past through present and on to future. Not only that, but such self-imposed ignorance also prevents us from positively and creatively trans-forming the cycles of our history. Insight into the past, both good and evil, is the goal of this aspect of Centering Practice, and con-scious, God-guided choices are its fruit.

Since we are about to examine my role in the Haysom murders, I must first address the common—and in my opinion misplaced—fear that uncovering the social and psychological causes of crime inevitably leads to an evasion of responsibility. My personal expe-rience has been completely opposite: the deeper I delved into my past, the greater became my sense of guilt and debt, and I have observed the same dynamic in other inmates who participated in the Alcoholics Anonymous group or the innovative sexual offend-er treatment program at my current prison. Turning poverty, addiction or neurosis into an excuse is almost always the hallmark of those who have *not* done the hard work of self-examination and discovered that "each one is tempted . . . by his own evil desire" (James 1:14).

To me the key words in the preceding sentence are "each one": *all* of us re-enact Adam's fall in our early childhood and henceforth carry an ever-growing burden of sin and pain. As we come to understand the destructive role of our own self in this decline, we are inevitably sensitized to the suffering and often far heavier burdens of others. Not only does this insight greatly reduce the self's natural tendency to shift blame away, but it also increases our compassion for those who have attempted to help us but failed, those who never tried at all, and even those who accidentally or intentionally harmed us. Our friends and our seeming enemies all struggle with the same devils we do, and I have come to see that I hurt both groups at least as much as they may have hurt me.

In the following chapter I will have much to say about how my mother's alcoholism shaped my relationship with Elizabeth Haysom, and how the tragic interplay of these factors made my crime possible. Possible or even probable does not mean unavoidable, however: I and I alone am responsible for breaking both human law and God's law that night. Understanding the preconditions that led to my crime—some character traits formed in my youth, the diagnosed mental illness of the young woman I loved— gives me the opportunity to avoid similar dangers in future, not evade responsibility for the past.

Nor should you ever forget, as I certainly never do, that both my mother and even the nineteen-year-old Elizabeth Haysom were, in *very* different ways, wonderful human beings as well as God's beloved children. My mother was an unusually warm-hearted, giving, generous person of high intelligence and great wit: she excelled at the many official representative duties of a diplomat's wife and managed to raise two sons who graduated at the tops of their respective classes in spite of having attended schools on three different continents. And at age nineteen Elizabeth was both the "queen bee" of the honors student dormitory, according to one of her professors, and a writer of considerably more talent and imagination than I can ever hope to be. Neither my mother's alcoholism nor Elizabeth's heroin addiction and mental illness can or should detract from their many positive qualities.

To blame my crime on my mother would be absurd; she was a victim, primarily *my* victim. But I do not even agree with those who hold Elizabeth Haysom responsible for my illegal and immoral acts. While the lead investigator on my case once told a newspaper, "[n]o doubt [Elizabeth] manipulated him," the truth is that I literally begged her to use and abuse me, as we shall see.[25]

Below I will use the conceptual framework of the co-dependency / adult children of alcoholics literature, since I have found that to be the most useful in understanding specifically my crime. Of course my mother's disease did not "make" me break the law, nor did I "suffer" as a boy; all families have *some* problem(s), and my fellow prisoners' tales of their youths have taught me much about the bestial depths of childhood suffering. But growing up with an alcoholic parent inevitably creates certain emotional and behavioral patterns whose very predictability and ubiquity have made the co-dependency / adult children of alcoholics movement so helpful for millions of people. These same emotional and behavioral patterns—these parts of *me*—played a pivotal role in my crime, not by "causing" my actions, but by creating some predispositions. I could and should have acted differently, and I will always regret that I failed to do so.

7—Centering Practice—The Analysis, Part 2

I distinctly recall knowing before age seven that *something* was wrong with my mother, and that this something was somehow connected with the way her breath smelled after drinking from the bottles my father tried to keep locked in the living room cabinet. Since I was too young to understand any more than that, I quickly developed the behavior patterns typical of children of alcoholic parents:

- I instinctively assumed that my mother's strange mood swings were caused by some fault or mistake of mine;
- I became incredibly well behaved in hopes of regaining her favor;
- I tried to prevent future episodes of depression and withdrawal with childish attempts to make my mother proud of me;
- I learned at the center of my being that nothing I did was good enough, because my mother kept on drinking.

None of these themes of my early development were in any way unusual, of course; my younger brother trained himself to be a "goody two-shoes" just like me.

Since alcoholics will drink in spite of the rest of the family's sometimes quite elaborate efforts to avoid triggering a binge, both my brother and I became unrestrained overachievers. The long list of my prizes, awards, etc. in the university scholarship program's 1984 brochure shows just how compulsive my attempts to earn approval became. But none of it was good enough. I vividly recall becoming interested in psychology in my mid-teens when I ran across the terms "guilt complex" and "inferiority complex" somewhere—magic words that encapsulated what I was feeling all the time. Unfortunately, I never learned why I experienced those emotions, nor did I stop feeling that it was my responsibility to "fix" all the world's problems. My teachers came to rely on this trait of mine whenever they needed someone to organize some club or activity, so they presumably did not notice the low self-esteem and depression that motivated me. But the infamous diary letters I wrote Elizabeth four months before the crime reveal just how florid my self-hatred could become.

Much of the teen angst I unloaded in those diary letters was precipitated by my parents' particularly intense verbal arguments during that Christmas vacation. Like so many elder sons, I had begun to side more and more with my mother during the countless shouting matches of previous years. (I now realize that both my parents suffered equally.) Then, during my senior year in high school, my mother and I remained at my father's previous post of Atlanta, Georgia, while he and my brother moved to Detroit, Michigan, his new post. This was a lonely time for my mother, so I had repeated opportunities for taking care of her and lying about this to my father afterward. Straightening out the messes made by a substance abuser and keeping her secrets—I was in training, so to speak!

Literally one day after leaving my mother and going to college, I met Elizabeth Haysom, a heroin addict, and only a couple of months later, I had become her co-dependent caretaker. (An aside for Freudians: *all* of my [few] girlfriends were more than a year older than me, a significant age difference for teens.) What initially attracted me to Elizabeth was that she had suffered as an addict and a runaway, and yet had survived and even prospered: from a boarding school dropout to the most sought-after girl in the honors student dorm. Of course, like all junkies, she claimed to have stopped using drugs because my love was now enough, but she continued to do so surreptitiously. And she allowed me to perform the usual caretaker duties, like proofreading her college papers, paying for her (our) meals and rescuing her from her many crises, great and small. I knew in the very marrow of my bones that love has to be earned, so I was never tempted to use the impossible word "no" with her.

Elizabeth knew how to exploit this trait, of course: when I failed to be on time for a meeting with her at the library, she "punished" me by displaying a needle mark on her arm later that night. And I believed she was right to blame me. I should have put "my" addict's needs first.

After endless re-writing I have not found a more accurate way of saying this: on the night of the crime, Elizabeth engineered a crisis that required an immediate solution, and she left it to me to straighten out her mess. Being a caretaker, I did. And, being an overachiever, I had to "fix" the problem in a better, more spectacular way in order to make "my" addict proud of me. I had to be her knight in shining armor.

It is important to understand, I think, that I not only felt responsible for solving the problem Elizabeth had created that night, but actually felt responsible for having allowed the problem to arise in the first place. Since I had already failed in my caretaker duty to prevent the problem, it was obviously my fault "we" were in this mess and my duty to get "us" out.

This is not an attempt to shift blame, but the simple truth of how our individual psychodynamics fit together. Like so many addicts, Elizabeth actually enjoyed creating highly dramatic emotional situations to observe which way others would jump. And, like all co-dependents, I liked jumping on command.

In fairness to Elizabeth, I am convinced she did not "plan" the crime in the usual sense of the word, simply because her thinking was so disorganized and often failed to distinguish clearly between fantasy and reality. For instance, when I proofed her college papers, I found them brilliant but a mess. This, I understand from my more technical reading, is typical of borderline schizophrenia / borderline personality disorder.

Unlike Elizabeth, I was not a schizophrenic, borderline or otherwise; and while my background as a co-dependent caretaker predisposed me to help "my" substance abuser that night, I could and should have done so in a way that was not illegal and immoral. I am not seeking to excuse my actions but attempting to explain why an academic scholarship winner and "perfect little gentleman" chose to break the law.

On that night I honestly believed that others had already committed horrific felonies and that, if I did not act immediately, still worse crimes would be perpetrated against Elizabeth. Losing her, the source of my sense of self-worth, would have made my life literally worthless. Throwing away this otherwise worthless life in order to protect my life's center was, to me, the obvious solution.

That is what my crime felt like to me at the time: like a glorious self-sacrifice. I understand how almost blasphemous this sounds in retrospect, in view of the enormous suffering I caused others by my acts. But at the time I was only aware of how freeing it felt to ignore my own interests and values so completely. I did not see myself as *above* the law but *below* it, too unimportant to consider. And whereas others had already broken the law for their own sake, I could feel noble for committing my crime to protect "my" substance abuser!

That concludes my discussion of the causes of my crime. However, I would like to point out that the character traits of the co-dependent caretaker are, in themselves, wonderful qualities that my parents consciously and successfully instilled in me, especially by example. Taking care of and helping others, achieving beyond what is expected, being responsible to the point of straightening out the messes left by others, and putting others' interests ahead of one's own—my mother and father not only preached but practiced these principles, and I am grateful to them for having done so.

Now, at last, I can *choose* to live my life by these values; but when I had to make a split-second decision about Elizabeth's (and therefore my own) survival on the night of my crime, I made no such conscious choice. Instead, out of my unconscious came roaring the caretaker's credo:

- "I must protect my addict."
- "I must do so better than anyone else."
- "It's all my fault anyway, so I have to fix this mess."
- "To save my addict, I'll throw away my own interests, my values, my life—so I'll break the law, too."

These urges were so strong precisely because I did not consciously understand them. For instance, I was so possessed with the downright need to burn at the stake for Elizabeth that I never even thought of the incredible pain I would thereby (i.e., by my crime) inflict on others. But even though I was unaware of these dynamics, I *did* know better than to break the law, no matter how "noble" the purpose, and I alone am to blame for the terrible consequences.

The discipline of psychology does not—or in my view should not—promise to change fundamental character traits like those discussed above. Instead, Freud argued that making the unconscious conscious will give us a measure of control over those inner forces we cannot change (much). Even the practice of contemplative prayer cannot completely eradicate the grooves worn into the soul by the self and the past, and I do not believe that this is entirely a bad thing: as I suggested earlier, it is by these sometimes murky, sometimes sparkling waters of the rivers of our lives that we encounter God.

And like the course of a river through the alluvial plains, so too can the course of a life change. New perspectives emerge as a hill by the banks becomes an island midstream or a wave-topped creek bed turns into a dry, shallow valley. In my case the slow erosion of the *kenotic* process has washed away the hurt and the sense of betrayal that the mere mention of Elizabeth's name used to evoke, and revealed instead some bedrock truths about my own responsibility. And as a result I now feel, not a need for me to forgive her, but a desire to ask her for forgiveness.

All else aside—and I more than most realize that this is saying a lot—the plain fact is that Elizabeth was suffering from a recognized mental illness in the months before the crime. Two nationally known English forensic psychiatrists and one respected Virginia forensic psychiatrist diagnosed a borderline schizophrenia / borderline personality disorder in her, a finding confirmed by my prior personal knowledge of Elizabeth as well as an admittedly amateur's study of psychiatric literature. Although I was completely ignorant of such things as an eighteen-year-old, I could and should have realized that she needed some sort of professional counseling when she showed me the nude photographs her mother had taken of her. But I did nothing, and I now see my supposed "sensitivity" and "respect for her privacy" as selfishness, fear and a lack of real compassion for the young woman I claimed to love. (Ironically, Elizabeth was the one who, by showing me those pictures, had broken through the barriers of self, overcome her fear and reached out to me in love and in trust.) Without this cowardice, without this massive moral failure on my part, Derek and Nancy Haysom would still be alive, and Elizabeth and I would have normal, productive lives today (whether together or, perhaps better, apart).

Nor can I mitigate my guilt by appeal to some mental illness of my own. *After* the Haysoms' murders, under the overwhelming psychological pressure of keeping this terrible secret from others and even myself, I developed what the two English psychiatrists mentioned above diagnosed as a *folie à deux*, an extreme symbiotic relationship with Elizabeth to the extent of sharing her paranoias and fantasies. But *before* the crime I was fully in touch with reality, as my joking references in letters to Elizabeth's "p.o.t.'s" or "perversions of truth" clearly show. I was, unfortunately, suffering from nothing worse than . . . self. And it was because of self that I failed so miserably in my plain duty as a human being, as Elizabeth's lover and as the sane(r) one of the two of us to get her the psychiatric help she needed.

Once the crisis was at hand on the night of the murders, I again failed to do what would have been in retrospect best for Elizabeth and everyone else. So she, like me, has had to spend over a decade and a half in prison (at the time of this writing), suffering and no doubt regretting her past every day as I do. That is to a large extent my fault, and I am sorry.

By saying this, I do not mean to diminish the Haysoms' suffering in any way. Of course Derek and Nancy Haysom are the true victims of this crime, as are their other children, family members and friends. Even my own father, mother, stepmother and brother are secondary but genuine victims of, in their case, my crime alone. The pain of all of these victims is inexcusable, and I deeply regret the harm I did and the anguish I caused them.

By describing my feelings of guilt regarding Elizabeth in some detail, I do not wish to detract from the real victims' suffering at all, but simply to demonstrate that I have not reserved a corner of my heart for hating the person who has hurt me more than anyone else. If the Way of the Prisoner is not to be a dead end, then I cannot limit my empathy to exclude anyone; the true test is whether you "[l]ove your enemies, [not just] those who love you" (Matthew 5:44, 46).

Converting those noble sentiments into deeds, in a life lived as *kenotic* prayer through Centering Practice, is the subject of Book III. There my regret and sense of debt toward Elizabeth will manifest themselves in a specific act that will, I promise, shock you deeply—and hopefully inspire you as well.

Notes

1. Strong, James, op. cit.
2. Anonymous, trans. Johnston, W., *The Book of Privy Counseling* (New York: Image/Doubleday, 1973).
3. Climacus, John, trans. Luibheid, C., *The Ladder of Divine Ascent*, XXVII (Mahwah, NJ: Paulist Press, Missionary Society of St. Paul, 1982).
4. Keating, Thomas, *Open Mind, Open Heart*, op. cit.
5. St. Teresa of Avila, trans. Kavanaugh, K., and Rodriguez, O., *The Interior Castle*, IV, III, 7 (Mahwah, NJ: Paulist Press, 1979).
6. Pseudo-Dionysius, *Divine Names*, VII, 3, op. cit.
7. Meister Eckhart, op. cit.
8. St. Teresa of Avila, *Interior Castle*, V, I, 3–4; V, I, 6–8; V, III, 12; V, II, 8–11; IV, IV, 1, op. cit.
9. Quoted without attribution in Esther de Waal, "Attentiveness," in *Weavings— A Journal of the Christian Spiritual Life*, Vol. XVII, Number 4, July/August 2002.
10. St. Teresa of Avila, *Interior Castle*, IV, II, 4; VII, III, 2; VII, 1, 9; VII, III, 7; op. cit.
11. St. Teresa of Avila, *Interior Castle*, VII, I, 6, op. cit.
12. Meister Eckhart, op. cit.
13. St. John of the Cross, *Dark Night*, I, VI, 6, op. cit.
14. St. Thomas à Kempis, *The Imitation*, IV, 15, op. cit.
15. St. John of the Cross, *Dark Night*, II, XIII, II, op. cit.

16. St. Teresa of Avila, *Interior Castle*, V, III, 5, 3, op. cit.
17. Lewis, C. S., *Mere Christianity* (New York: Macmillan, 1952).
18. Meister Eckhart, op. cit.
19. Anonymous, *The Cloud*, XXVI, op. cit.
20. Anonymous, *The Cloud*, XXIX, XXXIV, op. cit.
21. Climacus, John, *The Ladder*, XXVII, op. cit.
22. Anonymous, *The Cloud*, XXVIII, op. cit.
23. Meister Eckhart, op. cit.
24. Hop-along's nickname and some personal characteristics have been changed to protect his privacy.
25. Zack, Ian, "Trial and Error," *Daily Progress*, January 21, 1996.

INTERMEZZO

I N ONE SENSE, the subject of this volume's first Intermezzo is April 30, 1986, the day I was arrested. The investigation, the trial and the appeals all hinge on that (for me) world-changing date. In this second Intermezzo, I want to share with you another turning point in my life which I now see as being equal in importance to the day of my arrest: February 19, 2003.

I write these lines perhaps too soon after that date to accurately judge the effects of what happened to me then. However, I *do* know that those effects continue to deepen and to broaden every day, making February 19 more, not less significant as time passes. This was no singular *event* but the beginning of a new transformative *process*.

Yet February 19, 2003, is also the fruition and possibly the end of another process that began on April 30, 1986. The former is, in a very real and deep sense, the product of the latter. On the day of my arrest, *everything* was taken from me; and on the day described below, I received *all* of it back—and more! The seventeen years in between were all about preparing me, step by painful step, to receive this gift.

What I am left with now is a sense of the *rightness* of it all. Below, you will read how a sense of rightness was one of the primary distinguishing characteristics of February 19, and it is precisely this feeling that has expanded since that date to encompass my whole life—past, present and future. Things were, and are, and will be truly as they *should* be; and they are *good!* As crazy as it sounds, I feel I have been undeservedly blessed with this life. I feel grateful and at peace.

If there is anything humorous about all this, it is how much of a surprise February 19 was to me. When I completed the second draft of Book I of *The Way of the Prisoner* in September of 2001, I believed that the process of contemplation as I described it in the *contemplatio* section of Book II would continue for me basically unchanged for as long as I practiced this spiritual discipline. Contemplative prayer worked like strip-mining, gradually wearing down the mountain layer by layer—so I thought. Secretly, I was convinced that all reports of a mystic's spiritual life being transformed by a single, extraordinary episode during prayer were . . . well, to put it charitably, mistaken. "Visions" struck me as figments of overwrought imaginations, as (particularly beautiful) distractions created by the mind.

Ooops! I was *wrong!*

Contemplative prayer does indeed work incrementally, but along with the strip-mining, it appears that God also secretly drills deep shafts and carves huge subterranean caverns. In the fullness of time, when those hollows are large enough, the land above caves in with a spectacular crash, transforming the surface geography all at once. This, in essence, is what happened to me on February 19, 2003, between 10:31 and 11:07 a.m.

Writing about such an "experience" during contemplation is far from easy for me. The first and greatest problem is, of course, to find words for the unnameable; even the term "experience" is problematic, hence the quotation marks. Then there is the danger of developing pride in the particular spiritual episode one has chosen to hold up for one's readers. And finally, concretizing a special session on paper risks establishing a benchmark that one may then attempt to reach again, with the inevitable resulting failure.

Nevertheless, I will try to recount the "experience" I underwent on February 19. One of my motives in doing so is to encourage relative newcomers with glimpses of what they too may encounter if they remain on the path of silent prayer. In addition, I have found value in the *vipassana* teaching that, after each session, one should fix in one's mind which turn one took at which fork in the road, so one can find one's way back. And, truth be told, I simply am compelled to write.

First, some background: during the third week of November, 2002, I experienced what Teresa of Avila would have called a "suspension of the intellect" of somewhat unusual length: roughly ten minutes. I believe this prayer session to have been the direct cause of an enormous burst of creative writing that lasted until mid-January, 2003. On February 7, I held a one-day contemplation "retreat" for myself, during which I prayed for nearly eight hours in an eleven-hour span. And then I entered a period of almost comically "bad" sessions, consisting just about entirely of rather intense sexual fantasies, which lasted from February 15 until the early morning of February 19.

Rather dreading another such episode, I sat down forty-five minutes early for my usual midday prayer, to get the expected unpleasantness over with. As always, I had no difficulty putting my attention on that cool, calm place—"the rest." Over the preceding few days, however, my mind had quickly swirled from this spot and, when led back, had refused to stay. This occasion was different, and if there is any value in this essay, it may lie in the following attempt to explain why.

First, I believe I may have placed slightly more emphasis on staying with the breath at the beginning of the session than I did during the preceding days, in hopes of avoiding failure. This contradicts to some extent what I have tried to practice (and suggested to others), since I clearly made *some* effort during the first few minutes. My thoughts on this now are that in the recent past I may have been taking my own advice on the (very real) importance of non-striving to an unwise extreme, by attempting to contemplate with absolutely no preparatory concentration at all. If I could instantly put my mind on the cool, calm place—as indeed I could, every time—why bother to settle down there and actually come to rest on the "the rest?" This I, now believe, was a form of greed: instead of barging through the open door and snatching up the gift with still trembling hands, I should have taken five minutes to conform my manner and spirit to the grace I was about to receive.

One technique for making myself ready for the gift that I have found particularly helpful—and that I used on this occasion—has been the careful monitoring of the subtle muscular tensions around the eyes and mouth. When these have abated, my inhalations and exhalations inevitably are at the smooth "baby's breath" stage, the "sign of concentration" in *vipassana* terminology. This takes so little time—five little minutes!—but it eliminates enough of the self's pushing and pulling to let me *stay* in the rest.

Settling down just a little more thoroughly on February 19 allowed me to experience once again the real pleasure of "sitting quietly [and] doing nothing." This chapter title from Alan Watts' *The Way of Zen* was for me one of those eye-opening rediscoveries of familiar principles which all of us make occasionally; in my case, I reconnected with this teaching during my one day contemplation "retreat." Somehow those five words opened up to me again the joy of stillness: there really, truly is "nowhere to go and nothing to do" because *everything* is right here in this moment, in the sitting and in the breathing.

If I sit and breathe with some spiritual goal in mind—if I treat the sitting as an "exercise"—then I completely miss the profundity, the universal significance of this humble, simple activity. Even words like "profundity," "significance" and "humble" distort the experience hopelessly, because they ring with inappropriate solemnity. Yet it is true that there is *nothing* more important I could possibly be doing than . . . sitting quietly and doing nothing.

By "doing nothing" I mean being attentive to nothing—or, perhaps more accurately, being attentive to the no-thing out of which God sometimes emerges in prayer. Here there are a couple of subtle distinctions that only practitioners can fully appreciate. On the one hand, concentrating gently on the breath during the first five minutes must not be confused with the being-attentive-to-nothing which follows. The former is a *curling inward* that requires slight but definite mental exertion, whereas the latter is a relaxed, straightforward *remaining with* whose essence is the absence of any effort—motionlessness, a calm abiding. On the other hand, there is a palpable difference between sitting quietly and attentively with the nothing, and stopping the mind from wandering off the nothing. The latter again requires some effort and, in my experience, is neither necessary nor helpful. If a part of the mind wants to roam around like an unruly puppy, I say, "Let it!" Chasing after the puppy to try to bring it back is definitely not "doing nothing"; but if I sit still with the nothing, the puppy comes and lies down at my feet and is quiet. The common element here is *doing nothing*: neither bringing the puppy to heel through con-centration, nor keeping a leash on it once it has settled a little.

That sounds excessively passive, but in practice it is not. To be genuinely attentive is actually a marvelously oxymoronic phenom-enon, an inactive activity. At its purest, it means giving myself entirely to someone or something *outside* myself—without, howev-er, seeking to lose myself in or to possess that someone or some-thing. My own thoughts, feelings and sensations no longer matter; what matters is that other to which I devote my time, my self. Without moving, without acting, I thus *step outside my self*.

While others may pay attention to a beautiful girl or a Renaissance painting, those of us who sit quietly and do nothing spend all our time on . . . nothing. The absence of any perceptible object is, of course, the key to this discipline—and also its greatest difficulty, since the mind tends to produce graven images for us to worship, or to "scatter" and "space out," or to turn back in on itself

to resume concentration. What had troubled me lately was the latter, I think; when my mind drifted off the cool, calm place, I tried
to bring it back by attempting to sweep out the distractions with a
prayer word. My attention was on the distractions, not on the
nothing, as it were. In the midday session on February 19, however, I somehow avoided that error and instead *remained with the nothing*. Those distractions that did arise then quickly faded for lack of
interest.

The nothing I mean in this context is a blank spot on the inner
screen of my eye. Following *vipassana* teachings, I choose one such
spot and then "connect" my breath to it, so that each exhalation
goes to it, and each inhalation returns from it, like a weaver's shuttle. This has been the single most helpful prayer "technique" I have
ever been taught. It permits a smooth transition from curled-in
concentration to straight, effortless expansion (contemplation),
and it somehow establishes as an inner reality that God is not only
within me but also outside of or beyond me.

I cannot find the Spirit only through concentration, by going
deeper and deeper within myself; I must also turn my attention outward, expand my awareness to that spot of nothing which I can
never reach. My breath, my life shuttle between these two
extremes of complete immanence and total transcendence, and it
is in this tension that God will find me.

On the methodological level, all of this means keeping my
inner gaze raised during contemplation and looking the nothing
straight in the eye. "Press earnestly into that nothing," the author
of *The Cloud of Unknowing* told his readers, and while I believe the
verb "press" implies too much effort, this piece of advice has
become the star by which I steer the ship of my prayer. What works
for me is a relaxed seafarer's gaze: I scan the horizon through my
inner telescope, paying constant and calm attention without press-
ing the brass eyepiece into my eye with effort. Out to the horizon
goes the exhalation, and back comes the inhalation (though I do
not look down to watch it turn back to exhalation). I am looking,

always looking, but I know that my attention cannot force Moby Dick to the surface. So I wait patiently and ignore the dolphins and seagulls that occasionally cross my field of vision.

Human beings cannot do anything without grace, of course, but it seems to me that one *can* learn this skill and thereby reach the cool, calm place without specific help from God. All that is required is:

- putting slightly more emphasis on the breath (concentration) during the first five minutes;
- "sitting quietly and doing nothing," enjoying just this moment and nothing else;
- letting the puppy of the mind roam a little without tugging on the leash; and
- looking with a level, relaxed gaze at the spot of nothing, without fixedly staring at it or "spacing out."

With these means, I believe one could even enter "the rest" without understanding where one really is—somewhat like Columbus, who stepped onto a new continent in the firm belief he had landed in India.

But those who practice contemplation know well what I mean by "the rest," the cool, calm place. Its first sign is an awareness of that mysterious dark light, a light that can only be felt, not seen, as it fills the darkness with invisible energy. Earlier, I described "the rest" as the baseline state of silent prayer: although the mind may still murmur quietly in one corner, I am mostly conscious of an enormous, veiled Stillness that gently…not draws, but perhaps invites me closer. Its calmness extends to me and quietens me—it gives me its own peace.

In some ways, this mysterious Silence feels like an Absence—not just a lack of the usual mental chatter, but a hole in the interior universe created by my mind. None of us can truly know reality itself; all we have is the mental image of an external world that the mind constructs out of the five senses' input. Whether my eye really sees a house, or whether my optic nerve is being fed a hallucination, is something I cannot discover. However, because the facsimile of reality created by my mind has a uniform "feel" and seems to "work," I normally assume that this mental construct is reality. Until I enter the cool, calm place, that is—for there I encounter a Something whose "feel" is entirely unlike anything else in my inner cosmos. My mind cannot process this foreign Presence, so it perceives it as a veiled darkness. Yet there can be no doubt that a new Reality has pierced into my interior universe and presented my mind with an irrefutable fact: I am not alone.

Moreover, this Presence is not only there, and real, but is...loving, though not in any common sense. Certainly it gives me a marvelous gift: this cool, calm rest, this peace. And it definitely asks me to come closer, though not with any compulsion at all. In human terms, I would call its attitude toward me extremely respectful and considerate, gentle and solicitous—exactly, in fact, as a father would treat his infant child. What else can this be but Love?

During the ten-minute "suspension of the intellect" I underwent in November of 2002, this loving Presence seemed in some way to unveil itself. In fact, it gripped me so powerfully that I could not sit down (having been required to stand in the middle of my prayer for a prison count procedure). Yet the word "gripped" may suggest more compulsion than was truly there; perhaps it would be more accurate to say that it never occurred to me to sit down during those ten minutes. I was there, and that was enough.

On February 19, no such unveiling of the Presence took place. Instead, after five or ten minutes in the baseline, "veiled Presence" state, "the rest" suddenly became very intense and somehow more focused. I had never before experienced this "supercharged" version of the cool, calm place, but as new and powerful as it was, I nevertheless recognized it as heightened form of a familiar contemplative state. I believe at some point (or points) I may have briefly been absent—that is, lost conscious awareness of myself. How long this phase lasted, I cannot say; perhaps somewhat longer than the preceding "normal" stage, more ten minutes than five.

And then, without warning, something new and completely surprising happened; instead of feeling myself falling toward the surface of the pond, as described in Book II, and then pulling back in panic, this time there was an almost physical sensation of running face-on into a liquid wall—or, more accurately, being *sucked into* a liquid wall. The area of my "body" that entered the water included the front of my head (face, back to the ears), the front of my upper arms, and the front of my torso down to a point just above my solar plexus. As when a pebble is thrown into water, my head and chest made a circular impact-wave that flowed away from me quickly. I felt both the impact and the wave, and I could "see" the departing wave like a widening circle of light out of the corners of my "eyes."

At that point, I also knew *very* powerfully that I had suddenly gained *enormous* clarity of vision. I cannot say what I saw; I would tend to say I saw nothing; but I saw this nothing with an amazing sharpness. The nothing had become totally transparent to me all at once, so that I could see very deeply into the nothing.

In some strange, perhaps "spiritual" way, my eyes felt as if they were extremely open, with lids pulled way back. My mouth also appeared to be open, and my head seemed turned slightly to the left. However, I am certain that, physically, my eyes, mouth and head did not move.

I was also instantaneously aware that my penetration into the liquid was only partial: the back of my head, my back and the back half of my arms were all "dry." This did not distress me in any way but struck me as right, as appropriate. In fact, the whole event seemed very right and good to me, though not in any exciting way. I did not feel scared, or happy, or curious, or bored: I simply felt *at home* in the nothing. More precisely, I did not feel as if I had arrived home from some other place, but simply that I was (and perhaps had been all along?) in the place I belonged.

That feeling of being at home is the reason, I now think, why it never occurred to me to question why my penetration into the water was "only" partial. On reflection, this too was precisely the way it should be: I am both body and soul, half in the physical world and half in the spiritual nothing. If I had passed all the way through and become fully immersed in the pool, I suppose I would have been "dead."

"Death," however, turns out to be an irrelevant concept. Entering the pool has given me absolute, experiential certainty about that. In some sense "death" is real, I suppose, but that sense no longer seems important to me.

"Death" does not matter because heaven and hell seemed to me to be the same place—the nothing. If at the time of my "death" I have already let go most of my worldly attachments—my Mercedes, my spouse, my sins—then the nothing will feel as it did on February 19, like *absolute* peace and *true* rest. But if I "die" still attached to the world and my sins, then the nothing—where there are no *things*—will feel like a barren waste that burns with my unfulfillable desires. To be in heaven, and to want to be somewhere else…this surely is hell. But "death" itself, that is irrelevant.

Of course, the last three paragraphs are merely my later reflections on this "experience." At the time, I did not "think" of anything but only enjoyed (if that is the right word) being *in* the nothing, after looking *at* it in contemplation for so long. There was a whole lot more of the nothing to see than before—so clear, so clear! In fact, so much nothing did I see that all sense of "me" seemed to vanish. There was no Seer, only Seeing.

After five minutes or so—about halfway through this phase, which was the longest of the three—the thought came to me that I could stop looking now. But I did not, and I simply continued to bathe in and look at the nothing. That was the right thing to do at the time.

Another three minutes or so passed, and I lowered my head, opened my eyes and prepared to lean forward to begin the Lord's

Prayer with which I conclude all my sessions. Before I could lean forward, however, I was given to understand *very* clearly that I was not supposed to stop yet. There was no verbal command, of course, but I received an unmistakable message. I cannot say whether I could have "chosen" to stop then; the issue did not present itself in those terms; I do know that I lifted my chin again, closed my eyes, and went back to looking at the nothing. After another three to five minutes or so, I was able (or allowed) to end the session.

During the concluding Lord's Prayer, I was overcome by a feeling of gratitude so intense that I actually repeated, "Thank you, God, thank you," over and over in my mind—something I had never experienced before. Next, I found myself telling God, "I don't deserve this, I don't deserve this," perhaps as Isaiah did during his call to prophecy: "Woe is me, I am doomed! For I am a man of unclean lips . . . yet my eyes have seen the King, the Lord of hosts!" (Isaiah 6:5). And finally, I experienced a strong wave of homesickness for the pool, a sense of being bereft that nearly brought me to tears. "Where have you hidden, Beloved, and left me moaning? You fled like the stag after wounding me," wrote John of the Cross in his *Canticle*.

For the next four to six hours, I felt somewhat dazed, though I was able to perform my work at my prison job. I was unusually quiet, however, and during the following week to ten days, I withdrew a little from my fellow prisoners; I needed some private time to adjust to my new perspective on reality. Oddly enough, I also felt lonely because I had no one with whom I could discuss what had happened to me, no one who had himself seen what I saw, no one who could appreciate the enormity of this "experience" and give me some reassurance. Of course both classical contemplative authors and modern psychologists give warning of such emotional reactions to major, life-changing events. As wonderful as a spiritual rebirth may be, it is also a major shock to the system!

After February 19, I felt out of place, somewhat at one remove from everything, as if I did not quite belong on this planet.

Entering that pool of water in prayer brought home to me in a fresh, intense way that, like all Christians, I too am a "stranger and alien on earth, [seeking] a better homeland, a heavenly one" (Hebrews 11:13, 16). Sometimes, during my regular activities, I found myself caught up in what the Czech novelist Milan Kundera called "the unbearable lightness of being": a powerful, almost physical sensation that, for all its apparent solidity, my life and indeed this whole world are mere wisps, just "shadows of the things to come" (Colossians 2:17). "You are a mist that appears for a while and then vanishes," wrote James in his letter (4:14).

Since February 19, this powerful new sense of the lightness of being has not faded for me. It is not so much that I have become accustomed to this feeling, but that I have learned to see the rightness of living at one remove from this world: this planet is not my home, this life is not my real existence. Sometimes I catch myself thinking—or, rather, feeling—that the prayer session of February 19 never ended, that I am in that pool still, that I am looking at the world *through* the water of nothing. (In fact, for a few days after February 19, I occasionally felt as if the circular surface of the pool, which projected a little beyond the width of my shoulders, might collide with a door frame as I passed!)

Another way to put into words this powerful feeling of being in the pool at all times is to say that *there is no pool and never was.* When I say that I look at the world through the pool of nothing, I could equally say that everything seems like nothing. I can see the nothing in all things; there is no difference from that perspective. But while everything is in the nothing, the nothing is greater than the sum of all things—so from *that* perspective, there *is* a difference.

Earlier I wrote that heaven and hell are the same place; only one's perception differs. One can extend that statement to say that heaven and hell *and this world* are all the same place—at least from one perspective. But the other perspectives are equally true. What is "new" is that I can seem to be able to "see" all of this *simultaneously* since entering the pool. . . .

I understand well that what I write may make little sense to you now; and I also understand that if you think it "makes sense" to you, then you may know less of what I am seeing than if you said it makes *no* sense. This is a new way of seeing, not understanding—and it is still rather new to me, too.

The thought occurs to me that perhaps I was not able to stop on the first try during the session of February 19 because whatever changes were being made in me had not yet been completed. Maybe new lenses were being installed in my eyes, and the glue had to set properly before I could be let go. And just possibly, the strong sense that I never really left the pool accounts for my strange lack of urgency in returning to the pool in prayer; I do not need to sit and close my eyes to "feel" the pool.

While I am on the subject of prayer, I should mention that all of my contemplation sessions since this extraordinary one have been unusually "good" by the standards of prior sessions. My contemplative baseline state—the cool, calm place, "the rest"—has definitely become more easily accessible in prayer, and much clearer as well. Possibly as a result, all three of my daily sessions now last roughly ten minutes longer than before, without my intending this.

My first and strong impression upon closing my eyes in prayer nowadays is indeed that I am back in—or, more precisely, *still* in—the pool; sometimes I can even feel the waterline on my neck. Then the puppy barks, and I calm it down gently, following the breath for about five minutes. Of course the puppy goes roaming even after I settle down and sit quietly, doing nothing; but at that point, it hardly matters, and eventually the pup shuts up. I keep my eye trained on the nothing on the horizon—*that* is the key, "press on into that nothing"—and I let the occasional cloud pass by. Those skies have been unusually clear lately. . . .

At the time of this writing, just about every fourth day since February 19 has been marked by at least one (in two cases, two) unusually intense contemplation session. By "intense" I mean that these prayer periods:

- included one or more definite and definable "experiences," as opposed to the featureless and therefore "experience-less" clarity of the pool of nothing;
- were characterized by a powerful sense of being gripped or held *externally* by God;
- concluded with strong feelings of gratitude and homesick-ness; and
- left me a little tired and withdrawn for the next couple of hours.

All but one of these sessions consisted of approximately twenty minutes of very good but unremarkable contemplation, followed by ten minutes or so of spiritual fireworks. While I can report that the intensity of these "experiences" exceeded anything I had undergone prior to February 19, I believe it would be misleading to attempt to describe the apparent content of these prayer periods here. Subjectively, each of these sessions seemed like a unique miracle and blessing, beautiful beyond my poor literary abilities to describe. But, as spectacular as they were, they did not show me anything new, much less transform my whole outlook on life as February 19 did. So I think they may well have been little more than growing pains, symptoms of a hidden process of adjustment to the great shift that occurred five weeks ago.

This shift, this new perspective seems more significant to me than the occasional ten minutes of rapture in prayer. In this Intermezzo's opening paragraphs, I mentioned the profound sense of rightness or goodness suffusing my life now: moments of stillness and peace sneak up on me several times a day because, at least on one level, *my search is over*. There was a point and meaning to those seventeen years of suffering, after all! In his incomprehensible mercy, God chose me to lose everything, one after another after another, until I was left with nothing—nothing but Him, all at once, in all his enormous, glorious mystery. What can I do, then, but whisper, "Thank you"?

You have sunk to the center of your own poverty, and there you have felt the doors fly open into infinite freedom, into a wealth which is perfect because none of it is yours and yet it all belongs to you.

And now you are free to go in and out of infinity.[1]

Notes

1. Merton, Thomas, *New Seeds of Contemplation*, 31 (Norfolk, CT, and New York: New Directions, 1961).

BOOK III

Lectio

Give us today our daily bread.
Forgive us our debts
    as we have also forgiven our debtors.
And lead us not into temptation
    but deliver us from the evil one.

(Matthew 6:11–13)

In bringing many sons to glory, it was fitting that God, for whom and through whom everything exists, should make the author of their salvation perfect through suffering.

(Hebrews 2:10)

Now if we are children, then we are heirs—heirs of God and co-heirs with Christ, if indeed we share in his sufferings in order that we may also share in his glory.

(Romans 8:17)

Now I rejoice in what . . . [I] suffered for you, and
I fill up in my flesh what is still lacking in regard to
Christ's afflictions, for the sake of his body, which
is the church.

(Colossians 1:24)

———

Meditatio

1—Our Crosses Just Might Be Our Blessings

Can we who are prisoners of our own lives' tragedies, as Christ was
a prisoner of Pontius Pilate, be "ma[d]e perfect through suffering"
like our older brother Jesus (Hebrews 2:10)? Can we too "rejoice in
what . . . [we] suffered" if we experience our pain "for the sake of
[Christ's] body," the younger sons and daughters of our common
Father (Colossians 1:24)? Can our broken, needy humanity—our
want of "bread," our yearning for "forgive[ness]," our struggle with
"temptation [by] . . . the evil one"—be the prisoner's way of
"shar[ing Jesus'] sufferings in order that we may also share in his
glory" (Matthew 6:11–13, Romans 8:17)?

I believe so; in fact, I believe that emptying the self through suffering for others' sake is in many ways truer to the spirit of Christ's
divine sonship than union with the I AM during contemplation.
Certainly Jesus himself did not stay in the desert after his battle with
the devil to commune silently with his Father, but instead "returned
to Galilee" and embarked on his road to the cross (Luke 4:14). And
as we saw in Book II, advanced contemplatives like Teresa of Avila
always stressed that "[t]his is the reason for prayer . . .: the birth
always of good works, . . . [even] to lay down [one's] life."

Of course silent inner prayer is a crucial spiritual catalyst in the
kenotic process, opening our eyes to the meaning of our prisons, our
suffering, and deepening our relationship with the Spirit who is
Love. At least in my life, however, my cross came to me long before

contemplation did, and my chains had to teach me my need to seek God in the nothing. Once I was finally ready to receive the marvelous gift of Centering Prayer, this discipline then gave me the strength to bear the even greater burdens that have meanwhile been placed upon me. But my cross was and remains my primary teacher, contemplation "only" my indispensable homework tutor.

Unfortunately, the contemplative tradition's classic literature has almost nothing to tell us about "the fellowship of sharing in Christ's sufferings, becoming like him in death, and so, somehow, to attain to the resurrection of the dead" (Philippians 3:10, 11). Yet the voluntary acceptance of specifically *undeserved* suffering is a central element of both Christ's messianic role of Suffering Servant and of our mission as his followers:

> For it is commendable if a man bears up under the pain of *unjust* suffering because he is conscious of God. . . . To this you were called, because Christ suffered for you, leaving you an example, that you should follow in his footsteps.
>
> (1 Peter 2:19, 21, emphasis added)

Since "being transformed into [Jesus'] likeness" is the explicit goal of silent inner prayer, I would have expected the contemplative masters to have focused on passages like these two, which point to the role of unmerited, self-sacrificial pain as another means of "becoming like [Christ]" and "follow[ing] in his footsteps" (2 Corinthians 3:18).

Of course those of us who are prisoners of some sort know from bitter, daily experience that our chains are constantly tearing down our selves, whether we like it or not. Our bodies ache, our hearts break and our minds capitulate, because no one can answer in human terms: *why is this happening to me?* Yet it is here, in our agony, on our own cross, that we "become like [Jesus] in death," because our helpless cry of *why* echoes his call at Golgotha, "My God, my God, why have you forsaken me" (Mark 15:34)?

His question, like ours, can have no reply beyond the divine mystery: to gain eternal life, the self must first die. "I tell you the truth," Christ said to his disciples, "unless a kernel of wheat falls to the ground and dies, it remains only a single seed. But if it dies, it produces many seeds" (John 12:24). Our minds, our selves cannot accept such an explanation, and that is precisely why the unanswerability of our anguished *why* is the perfect chisel to break down the self.

So, paradoxically, we prisoners actually have a head start in the process of self-emptying over those whose primary means of *kenosis* is contemplation. God has done so much of the work already through our agony that we need only finish the job during silent inner prayer. What a refreshing change of perspective: our crosses just might be our blessings, *if* we can find a way to serve others through our suffering.

This is the central idea behind my concept of Centering Practice as the necessary counterpart to and complement of Centering Prayer. Martha and Mary must indeed become one, as Meister Eckhart and Teresa of Avila pointed out, because *both* can serve to transform us into the image of Christ by emptying the self. In fleshing out this theory, I have identified three interrelated ways in which our lives' prisons can further the process of *kenosis*:

- through the hard inner work of "making peace with our past," with the emotional traumas that inevitably come to light during the "unloading of the unconscious" phase of Centering Prayer. This is what I attempted to demonstrate for you in the Centering Practice section of Book II, dealing with my case and self-analysis.
- through the self-emptying effect our crosses have even without our conscious awareness of the process. In Book I's Centering Practice section, I tried to show how my father's willing acceptance of great suffering for my sake slowly freed and opened him, though he was neither a practicing

Christian nor a contemplative during those years. This *meditatio* section is devoted to a more detailed case study of another subject which, I hope, will help you develop practical ways of maximizing the kenotic potential of your own life's tragedies.

- through the conscious transformation of our crosses, our prisons, into a vehicle for emptying ourselves and imitating Christ, by making our suffering an act of service. Throughout the first three Books of this volume I have repeatedly suggested that writing *The Way of the Prisoner* and sharing the great gift of contemplative spiritual practices with you, my fellow "prisoners," fulfills this purpose in my life. Deliberately harnessing my own pain to help others—and thereby to further the process of *kenosis*—is the hardest thing I have ever done, but I believe it is precisely this that Jesus meant when he commanded us to "[l]ove each other as I have loved you" (John 15:12). If you find that prospect a little daunting, never fear: this Book's *contemplatio* section, like the previous ones, presents a specific spiritual exercise that anyone can—and, scripture tells us, should—perform to train the self and soul in this Christ-like love.

All three of the forms of Centering Practice above are, I believe, marked by four guiding principles or "themes": voluntary acceptance of, honesty about, non-attachment to and service through the cross or prison God sends us. Though I cannot provide you with classic contemplative texts to illustrate these concepts, I shall in the following paragraphs demonstrate their derivation from Christ's self-sacrificial death for us. My hope is that studying the application of these four laws of Centering Practice to the case study presented in the next three chapters will allow you to transform the chains that tie you down into rope ladders that pull you up.

The first and most important of our four key elements is, of course, that counterintuitive but necessary step toward our pain. As we saw in Book I's case study of my father's life, this means not merely facing or enduring suffering, but willingly embracing it as Jesus did his: "The reason my Father loves me is that I lay down my life . . . *of my own accord*" (John 10:17, 18, emphasis added). Experiencing our cross not as an enemy to be fought but as an avenue to God is, I believe, the greater goal of both Centering Prayer and Centering Practice—and the supreme lesson of Christ's passion.

Of course this voluntary acceptance of pain should never turn into self-deception or denial, a pretense that our cross does not hurt or that our prison is really a "good" thing. Our suffering is *real*—that is what gives it the power to break down our selves and transform us. Just as Jesus admitted to his closest friends that his "soul is overwhelmed with sorrow to the point of death," just as he asked his Father that "this cup be taken from me," just as he "cried out again in a loud voice" on the cross itself, so must we too experience our agony fully and honestly (Matthew 26:38, 39; 27:50).

The opposite extreme of denial is "attachment," and after our study of Centering Prayer you will not be surprised to learn that this methodological error must be avoided in Centering Practice as well. Recognizing the disguises this subtle spiritual foe may take is no easy trick: the annals of medieval monasticism are full of misplaced pride in the severity of penances, and all of us know sincere do-gooders who bitterly resent any rejection of their insistent acts of "kindness." By contrast, Christ never took personal credit for his ultimate sacrifice, emphasizing instead that "I do nothing on my own but speak just what my Father taught me" and "do exactly what my Father commanded me" (John 8:28, 14:31).

Finally, Centering Practice must always include a strong element of service—indeed, altruism is this discipline's distinguishing characteristic. If Jesus had "la[id] down his life" merely for the purpose of "leaving the world and going back to the Father," his crucifixion would still have been selfish, since only he would have benefited from this (re-)union with God (John 15:13, 16:28). Only because he "g[a]ve his life as a ransom *for many*" did Christ's agony and death "draw all men to [him]self" and embody divine, self-giving love (Matthew 20:28, emphasis added; John 12:32).

In the following chapters we will examine the application of these four key principles of Centering Practice—bearing one's cross *willingly*, *truthfully*, *dispassionately* and *altruistically*—to our case study: the first fifteen years of my incarceration. I believe the history of my gradual self-emptying through physical, emotional, intellectual/conceptual hardships can be of direct and specific help to you because the great variety of my troubles behind bars almost certainly includes an easily translatable parallel to your personal prison:

- 1986–1990, *kenosis* on the physical level. During the nearly four years of extradition proceedings from England to Virginia, my attorneys told me many times that their efforts to protect me from the death penalty were sure to fail, that my extensive "confessions" would inevitably convict me, and that I should expect to die in the electric chair in the foreseeable future. It seems to me that my experience with confronting the end of my physical existence may well be of use to you if the chains you wear take the form of a terminal illness or similar life-and-death issue.

- 1990–1997, self-emptying on the emotional level. On the other hand, you may feel imprisoned by the trauma of having been attacked or violated in some way, or by the sense of abandonment and loss following a loved one's death or degenerative illness. If so, then learning how I coped with my near-rape by another inmate and with a long series of abandonments and losses during these years may benefit you in your struggles.

- 1997–2001, *kenosis* on the intellectual/conceptual level. Having your sense of identity ripped away through a bitter divorce, an unplanned ending of your professional career, or an episode of mental illness can easily seem like a prison, I imagine. In these last few years my concept of who I am was attacked on the same fundamental level: by the denial of any reading material in my native language, by an eleven-month stay at the harsher of Virginia's two super-max penitentiaries and by the U. S. Supreme Court's decision to refuse me justice and condemn me to living death. If this volume can be taken as evidence that some portion of me has survived, then perhaps my account of these experiences can help you heal, too.

Before we begin to dissect my past along the lines of Centering Practice's four guiding principles, however, I want to assure you that I am *not* attempting to solicit your sympathy with tales of woe from the dungeon. Personally, I find "prison stories" intensely boring after more than fifteen years of living through them myself, so I have selected only those few which can be of practical use to you. The sole purpose of this case study is to provide you with raw material to develop your own ways of carrying your personal cross in the spirit of Christ. Nor should you read ingratitude or pride into my discussion of life behind bars. I am well aware of how incredibly fortunate I was not *actually* to be executed, raped or psychologically crushed during the past fifteen years, and I am equally conscious of how others overcame much greater hardships than mine with more nobility of spirit than I could ever hope to develop.

My hope is that this Book will reveal to you the patterns and themes underlying all of our lives and thus give you a sense of both the meaning and the spiritual necessity of your own suffering. The closer you look, the more clearly you too will see the *kenotic* process at work everywhere: in you, in others and even in the three petitions of the Lord's Prayer with which we began this Book. Praying those old, familiar words in the spirit of self-emptying, as calls through the grates of our jail cell or as pleas from the cross to which we are nailed, is surely what Jesus intended us to do all along.

- "Give us today our daily bread." Only we prisoners can make this seemingly simply appeal with its true, proper urgency, because only we have experienced our total dependence on God for even the basics of physical survival. Whether our death sentence came from a judge or a doctor, we now know in the very fiber of our soul that the self is helpless, that only our Father's will must be done.

- "Forgive us our debts as we have also forgiven our debtors." So we all pray, though in practice we find perverse satisfaction in hating ourselves or nursing our grievances. But those of us who are about to break under the weight of those inner chains can sometimes find the courage to obey Christ's command, to accept or to grant the balm of forgiveness, to let go and thus free ourselves of our heart's pain.

- "And lead us not into temptation, but deliver us from the evil one." As should be clear by now, the "evil one" often works through the self to separate us from God. Prisons and crosses can indeed be our Father's means of delivering us from this enemy within, but without his help and guidance, our suffering may destroy instead of purify us. As I walk through the fire that is my life, I find myself praying ever more fervently that the I AM may protect me from being consumed by my anguish, that the dying to self may not become a death of the soul.

And if my prayer is granted and my *kenosis* continues to deepen, I may reach the "Amen" at the end of the Lord's Prayer, that free assent to our Father's will which is the ultimate goal of every spiritual journey, every prison, every cross. Meister Eckhart described this surrender and acceptance nowhere more beautifully than in his Sermon 12:

> A person who is so established in the will of God wants nothing else but what is God and what is God's will. If he were sick, he would not want to be healthy. All pain is joy to him, all multiplicity is simplicity and unity, if he is really steadfast in the will of God. Even if the pain of hell were connected to it, it would be joy and happiness for him. He is free and has left himself.[1]

2—1986–1990, *Kenosis* on the Physical Level
"Give us today our daily bread."

"Show me, O Lord, my life's end, and the number of my days; let me know how fleeting is my life," one psalmist prays, another adding, "Teach us to number our days aright, that we may gain a heart of wisdom" (Psalm 39:4, 90:12). But what a heavy price we must pay for this "heart of wisdom": our very lives, torn from us far too soon by cancers, viruses or sometimes even judges. No matter how divine the knowledge we may gain from early, unjust death, it seems a bitter consolation prize, compared with all we are about to lose.

Eternal life could surely have waited a few decades more—at least until we kissed our first grandchild, or visited Jerusalem, or tasted divine union during contemplation. And we are right to rage against the loss of our world, because it is only here, among the splendors of our Father's holy creation, that abstract divine love becomes manifest and real in human love. "No one has ever seen God: but if we love one another, God lives in us and his love is made complete in us" (1 John 4:12). While death may indeed reunite us with the Spirit-Breath, our passing robs us of the opportunity to reveal in our own lives why and how the invisible I AM's love is actually warm and concrete like a father's.

I offer you no words of comfort because I know very well that there can be none. For two and a half of the three and two thirds years I spent in prison in England, I was in exactly the same place as someone diagnosed with, say, cancer: on death row, fighting to save my life with legal briefs instead of with chemotherapy. So I know what it means to hear someone tell me, "I'm sorry, but I have bad news. . . ." I understand what it feels like to depend on strangers with college degrees and cool demeanors to protect me from the enemy's grasp. I too had to learn how to stop *screaming* at family and friends each time they said, "Oh, you're so bràve," or "Everything will be okay." And I too have lain in my bed at night and wished for death, just to end the uncertainty, the waiting. I am acquainted with the night. I know.

Nor should you think that the European Court's extradition ruling in 1989 somehow saved me from the hangman. Twelve years later the U. S. Supreme Court effectively reinstated my death sentence with a method of execution far crueler than Virginia's electric chair: lonely, hopeless, joyless old age in a cage. Not one of the years of my remaining "life" in here will be worth fifteen minutes at my mother's graveside out there. So I am still with you on death row; my dying will just take a little longer than yours.

If I have any advantage over you at all, it is simply my prior experience with awaiting death by electric chair between 1987 and 1990. Grappling with the imminent end of my physical existence *voluntarily*, *honestly*, *non-attachedly* and with some element of *service* during those years began the still-ongoing process of *kenosis*, the gradual freeing of my soul from the chains of self, earth and time. That kind of freedom is of an entirely different nature than the worldly joys we are losing, but it is no less real—and is certainly longer-lasting. My hope is that studying my experiences and the four key principles of Centering Practice will help you break through to this freedom as well.

Of course, much of what I could tell you of prison life, if I had the time and if you had the interest, is not very relevant to our specific subject: how I spent two uninterrupted weeks in an underground holding cell—no window, no toilet, no sink, no shower, no change of clothes—with an LSD addict who stood on his head almost all the time; or how a "screw" (English prison slang for guard) named Bronco at Her Majesty's Youth Remand Center Ashford used to encourage us to hurry up in the shower by directing a cold hard spray of water from a garden hose at our genitals; or how adult inmates at Her Majesty's Prison Brixton broke my thumb and wrist "accidentally on purpose" in 1986 and 1989, the second time so badly that it required re-breaking and surgery. No doubt these and the countless other incidents of those years had *some* effect on my self and soul, but I doubt it was *kenotic* in nature.

What is perhaps more germane here are the general and continuous conditions of my incarceration, since this background music helped shape the melody of my struggle with death just as the details of your daily routine—pill schedules, injections, dietary changes—inform your battle with terminal illness. During the period in question, I was housed in A-Seg and F-Wing of HMP Brixton and the remand wing of HMP Wormwood Scrubbs, two enormous facilities built in the mid- to late 1800s and then left to decay. Normally, pre-trial (or "remand") inmates only spent six months here awaiting court and subsequent transfer to a civilized, rehabilitation-oriented "convicted" prison. But because my extradition proceedings took so long, I spent three years and eight months in buildings and circumstances unchanged since Charles Dickens' days: one hour outside per day, weekly showers, weekly changes of clothes, "piss buckets" instead of toilets in the cells, jars and bowls of water instead of sinks, twice daily "stew" or "curry" that looked like vomit and tasted almost as good, and everywhere the stench of over one hundred years worth of sweat, urine and feces.

Showers and clothing exchanges were somewhat more frequent in one of my three locations, Brixton's A-Seg, because this area housed high-level organized crime and terrorist suspects whose pre-trial detention lasted longer than average. Another "privilege" of my maximum security classification throughout my years in England was a single cell, though the absence of libraries or TVs in "remand" prisons made the twenty-one to (more often) twenty-three hours of daily solitude difficult to bear. With nothing to distract me and no one to talk to day after day, year after year, I fell to brooding about the past and, even worse, about the future.

One of my lawyers' primary arguments against extraditing me to America under a death penalty indictment was the method of execution then in use in Virginia, the electric chair, so they submitted grisly descriptions of judicial electrocutions as part of their legal briefs. Since copies of these documents were sent to me too, I spent much of my endless spare time reading and re-reading vivid accounts of the smell of fried human flesh ("like bacon"), eyeballs popping out, tongues bitten off, scorch marks and flames, three or four jolts over twenty minutes in "botched" executions and so forth. During my months in F-Wing, these previews of my own approaching death were visually enhanced by the cells' all-night, bright red observation light, which turned the white and green speckled walls the color of blood until dawn. But even in A-Seg and the Scrubbs, "screws" and inmates never let me forget that I would soon "get a *charge* out of life," "have a *shocking* experience," or "need to save up your pennies for the *electricity* meter"—ha, ha.

Not surprisingly, I developed several obviously unhealthy ways of relieving stress: I gained twenty-five pounds through overeating, yet had diarrhea every single day between 1986 and 1990. ("Scared sh*tless" was my fellow prisoners' diagnosis of the latter problem.) While fighting your own rearguard action against death, you may well experience similar ancillary symptoms of battle fatigue and, like me, find yourself unable to control them in spite of your best efforts. But control and effort are among the first crutches of self which we must relinquish in this final struggle, so I would suggest that you treat such relatively minor setbacks or failures with compassion. As your own Centering Prayer sessions will keep reminding you, distractions and obstacles are actually an integral part of the *kenotic* process, more teachers or allies than outright enemies.

I myself certainly made many mistakes during the thirty months I waited to be sent the electric chair. In fact, even my primary coping mechanism, the very first one discussed below, must be approached with a great deal of caution and should not be used as a model by anyone. But I can hardly keep silent about my earliest attempt at Centering Practice, which, though clearly inappropriate, also *worked*. In my opinion this seemingly equivocal circumstance actually reflects the familiar contemplative principle that the tool matters less than the spirit in which it is employed—that the choice of prayer word, for instance, is much less important than its gentle, consistent use. I also hope the following account will encourage you to "think outside the box" as you develop your own Centering Practice, though obviously not as far "outside the box" as in my case.

Willing. Throughout the two and a half years of death penalty extradition proceedings, I prepared a "suicide kit"—bedsheets torn into strips and woven into ropes, etc.—every time another court was about to release its ruling on whether I would be sent to Germany and live or go to the U. S. and die. My lawyers had convinced me that my execution was a foregone conclusion when— not if—I returned to Virginia, so it was obviously wisest to "cheat the hangman" *before* American death row guards took me under round-the-clock observation. Since my case came before Bow Street Magistrate's Court, the High Court of Appeals, the House of Lords, the European Commission on Human Rights and the European Court of Human Rights—and since there was a "window" of several weeks or sometimes even months during which each of these courts' decisions could have been announced any day—I actually spent a considerable portion of my total time in English prisons quite literally sleeping with death, in the form of homemade ropes, hidden in my mattress. And even in the intervals between these periods, I believed the inevitable was only being delayed, that I would soon have to acquire another set of bedsheets and make new ropes.

Being a good German and a former "genius" scholarship winner, I mapped out my hanging with great care and precision: timing the guards' rounds (easy, so easy), setting my bed frame on end
and tying the top to the window bars to make a sturdy gallows
(need extra ropes for that), attaching the rope with the noose
(learned how to tie a hangman's knot in summer camp as a boy),
moving the dresser next to the bed as a scaffold, kneeling on top of
it and attaching the ropes with slip-knots from my ankles to my
belt loops (tying up my feet would allow a longer drop), putting the
noose around my neck (not at the back but at the side, to break the
spine), slipping my wrists through another set of rope loops at my
waist (to prevent any involuntary attempts at untying the noose),
and then . . . Except for that last, never-completed leap into freedom, I can still remember every detail of my test runs as if they
happened yesterday instead of twelve and more years ago. Even
now, as I write, I can *see* the small puffs of dust rising from the hard-
as-cardboard beige sheets as I tear them into strips, I can *feel* the
burst of cold air on my face when I open the window to attach my
bed frame–gallows to the bars, I can *taste* sour copper on my tongue
as I try on the noose. And most of all, I recall my eagerness, my
almost passionate anticipation of the end of my suffering.

In a strange, sick way, I had fallen in love with death. Christ
had not yet found me at that time, so I sought solace and guidance
from Marcus Aurelius, Epictetus and especially Seneca, who made
suicide sound romantic as well as reasonable in his Letter XXVI:

> "Rehearse death." To say this is to tell a person to rehearse
> his freedom. A person who has learned how to die has
> unlearned how to be a slave. . . . What are prisons, warders,
> bars to him? He has an open door. There is but one chain
> holding us in fetters, and that is our love of life.[2]

Oh, how seductive are words like these to inmates of cancer
wards or penitentiaries, crawling toward painful death and longing

for release! But those of us who have been awakened to the Spirit-Breath flowing through us even in our prisons can easily recognize the terrible flaw in Seneca's argument and therefore in my own flirtation with suicide: "love of life" is *not* a "chain holding us in fetters" but the very essence of the I AM, the reason why our Father created the universe and sent his Son to reveal his loving nature.

Without this "love of life" to guide us, self-murder can indeed seem both a reasonable means of ending pain and a noble assertion of human dignity and ultimate self-control. Thus suicide becomes a kind of celebration of the self, the only problem being that the guest of honor does not survive his own party! *With* love of life and grace, on the other hand, we can recognize the final passing of the self as an opportunity to conquer death by becoming truly one with the I AM. Christ showed us how: by making our last days and hours, when we know our kindnesses can never be repaid, into a time of service to others.

This is what the Stoics of old and I, in my English prison cell, simply failed to realize. Although planning my own death allowed me to embrace my cross, the one-sided focus on escaping my anguish would have turned my suicide into the self's final trap. Real freedom, on the other hand, requires reaching out beyond the self *especially* at the end of life, so love of God and humanity can flow through us and carry our soul back to its Source.

But before we can even begin to demonstrate and join the I AM's nature in our dying, we must first make and continue to take that all-important step toward our pain. Otherwise, service to others can become just another way of avoiding the reality and enormity of death, really no better than anaesthetizing ourselves with trashy TV shows (or, in my case, with heavy Russian novels). As wrong-headed as my suicidal fantasies were, at least they kept me focused on and grounded in the fact that my self and soul would very soon be separated forever.

Staying centered on our dying and refusing to distract ourselves is precisely what lets God "[t]each us to number our days aright, that we may gain a heart of wisdom"—a heart no longer tied to self and world (Psalm 90:12). Instead of praying in the tombs like Anthony of Egypt, or meditating on decomposing corpses in a charnel house as some Buddhists do even today, we death row inmates can use the contemplation of that fatal virus or the electric chair to break down every attachment of body, heart and mind. This unusual form of terminal *kenosis* works very well, as I found out in English prisons, because we who are dying must struggle with the literal, physical end of our existence, while monks and nuns of whatever stripe are limited to considering death in the abstract. Though none of us would have sought this spiritual gift of our own will, it would be silly to refuse the very real sense of freedom and detachment God now offers us in our passing.

Truthful and Dispassionate. Admitting the full extent of our pain, yet maintaining some emotional distance from it, are two standard coping techniques advocated even by secular grief counselors, but in this context honesty and non-attachment are also useful auxiliary tools that help us maximize the *kenotic* effect of our cross, our passing. On the one hand we must accept the full horror of our imminent death, since only this suffering can break down the self's chains and prepare us for our reunion with our Father; on the other hand, we cannot let our anguish become our god by descending into self-pity or indulging our lusts in a final frenzy of hedonism. *Apothesis*, the gentle letting go we practice each day during silent inner prayer, should also be our model for relinquishing life—with a clear recognition of what we are losing, but without the clinging so characteristic of the self.

During my years of waiting for death by electric chair or improvised gallows and rope, I was blessed with abundant opportunities to maintain and deepen a truthful and dispassionate attitude toward my nearing end. Almost every week a very kind Vice Consul from Germany's embassy in London came to visit me and allowed me to express all my despair and fear in conversation with her, an amazing act of compassion that kept me in touch with the reality of my emotions. And in between these verbal venting sessions, I spent two or three hours each day writing about my past in Proustian detail, so I could step back from my anguish and examine it more objectively. As simple and obvious as these methods of maintaining inner balance are, I believe I could not have stayed sane or indeed survived without them.

Unfortunately, their very modesty makes it easy to underestimate just how effective they can be—and how much continuous effort and discipline are required to reap their benefits. As all of us who have experienced a major tragedy know, the grieving process quickly reaches a stage where we do not want to voice our pain yet again even to the patient ears of our pet goldfish, nor do we feel like sitting down to compose one more dreary entry for our daily journal. But it is precisely at these points of inner resistance, when we are in danger of conscious avoidance or unconscious denial, that an honest, non-attached confrontation with our cross can purge us of essentially *self*ish responses like withdrawing into black, silent self-pity or pridefully pretending that we are handling our agony nobly, manfully, even stoically. Just as contemplative prayer is not meant to produce an immediate feeling of happiness or joy, so are Centering Practice techniques like talking and journaling not intended to be "fun"; they are disciplines that require dedication and perseverance if we want to reap their *kenotic* fruit.

The Old Testament provides us with models for both of these coping techniques, incidentally: the book of Job and the psalms of lament. Instead of letting himself be consoled with the thought that God must have had some secret plan for inflicting hardship on him—something all of us prisoners have surely heard enough to make us vomit!—Job never let go of his cross but kept insisting that his pain really was *wrong*. His fundamental truthfulness about his feelings, his refusal to mitigate or minimize his outrage were, of course, the driving force behind his relentless demands to see God, who finally rewarded Job for his persistent pursuit by unveiling divine omnipotence in all its mysterious splendor in Chapters 38 to 41. Job's response to the infinite, incomprehensible I AM was appropriately self-emptying: "Surely I spoke of things I did not understand, things too wonderful for me to know. . . . My ears had heard of you, but now my eyes have seen you," he concluded, suggesting once more that *kenotic* suffering can lead to a direct, unmediated experience of God as well as can self-emptying prayer (Job 42:3, 5).

As far as writing about one's pain to gain inner distance is concerned, the many psalms of lament in our psalter bear eloquent witness to the effectiveness of this technique for letting anguish guide us to our Father. Almost all of them move from complaint and even despair to trust or confidence in God, revealing in a few short verses how these ancient poets used quill and papyrus as tools to step back from self and turn to the I AM. Only in this context of frighteningly honest self-disclosure and soul-searching can we even understand why the author of Psalm 137, "By the rivers of Babylon...," felt he could not simply leave out the shocking last verse of his song, "O Daughter of Babylon, . . . happy is he . . . who seizes your infants and dashes them against the rocks" (Psalm 137:8, 9).

While Paul for obvious reasons had greater insight into the power of pain to unite us mystically with Christ and God—see this Book's *lectio* section—he never made the mistake of pretending to others or himself that to "share in [Christ's] sufferings" did not actually *hurt*. Hardly one of his letters fails to mention that "I die every day—I mean that, brothers," and in his sad final note to Timothy we can trace the same movement from acknowledgment of pain to confidence in God that we see in the psalms of lament:

For I am already being poured out like a drink offering, and the time has come for my departure. I have fought the good fight, I have finished the race, I have kept the faith. Now there is in store for me the crown of righteousness. . . .

(1 Corinthians 15:31; 2 Timothy 4:6–8)

This, I think, is the distinguishing characteristic of real saints, before the hagiographers do their misleading, prettifying work: they enter their pain but do not get lost in it, they weep without drowning in their tears, for they know that it is in the truthful, dispassionate acceptance of their own cross that they find themselves coming closest to Jesus on his.

Altruistic. While we cannot emulate Christ in saving *all* humankind through our dying, Centering Practice does require that we use our final day to serve our brothers and sisters, who are death row prisoners just like us even if they do not realize it yet. The insight that altruistic, self-sacrificial love can transform our seeming end into a new beginning is what sets us followers of Jesus apart and gives us hope even in the depths of our own final anguish, as Paul explained to the Corinthians:

> For we who are alive are always being given over to death for Jesus' sake, so that his life may be revealed in our mortal body. . . . All this is *for your benefit*, so . . . *[t]herefore* we do not lose heart. Though outwardly we are wasting away, yet inwardly we are being renewed day by day.
>   (2 Corinthians 4:11, 15, 16, emphasis added)

Christ only broke through to me nearly five years after my return to Virginia, so I was unable to use his example to guide me while I lived in the shadow of the electric chair. Even without my awareness, however, providence led me to implement at least an agnostic form of Centering Practice's fourth basic element of altruism. Not only did this help me survive emotionally at the time, but I believe it also allowed me to prosper spiritually over the long run by preparing my soul for my eventual conversion.

Ironically, the same spite that persuaded me to plan to "cheat the hangman" through suicide also inspired me to try to "stay human" and compassionate, if only because circumstances seemed to have conspired to fill me with hatred and bitterness. Simply to resist an unjust fate and to annoy "the system," I decided I would make a special, continuous effort to keep my heart warm and alive by helping others when I could—beginning with that detoxing LSD addict who stood on his head almost continuously during the two weeks we spent together underground at the very, very start of my long prison career. He needed someone to listen to him talk about dropping acid at Stonehenge; I had enjoyed "psychoanalyzing" my friends ever since high school and entered college as a psych major; so I made it a habit to provide what I thought of as an "open ear," a shoulder to cry on for the surprisingly high number of prison inmates who are eager to unburden themselves and almost pitifully grateful to anyone who will listen without judging.

I quickly learned that the only skill required of me was to shut up; neither youngsters nor adults needed my advice or insight but merely my concern, the simplest of all gifts—though perhaps not the smallest. As anyone who has practiced this form of service knows, it has the interesting effect of making the giver feel better immediately and without fail, even more powerfully and reliably than chocolate (my own mood-altering drug of choice).

Of all the men to whom I provided an "open ear" in those early years, the one I remember best was an Irish terrorist awaiting trial for several bombings. Like all the "freedom fighters" I met—and I encountered a variety of Irish, Arab, Iranian, Sikh, Kashmiri and Tamil bombers—he truly believed himself to be a deeply moral man, a future hero of his oppressed people, a David fighting cruel Goliaths, a soldier who simply hand-delivered his explosives instead of dropping them from expensive warplanes. I do not think we ever became friends, since he showed no interest in my struggle with approaching death, but I know his need for my patience and non-judgmental listening was greater than anyone else's during my time in English prisons. And I really do believe that I was able to help that man unblock a case of emotional constipation that seemed to have existed for decades, simply by giving him space and attention.

As I watched him fight his way toward some hard truths about himself and his past, I was quite aware that his gift to me far exceeded mine to him. He allowed me to be of use, to do real and perhaps lasting good behind the walls of Her Majesty's Prison Brixton—even as my own life seemed all but over. So, more than anything else, I felt and still feel gratitude to him, for giving what seemed to be my final days a greater purpose than mere passive waiting for the grave. In a very real sense, he helped save my soul.

3—1990–1997, Self-emptying on the Emotional Level
"Forgive us our debts as we have also forgiven our debtors."

All forms of emotional suffering are rooted in guilt: either we sinned or we were sinned against, and the weight of our responsibility or sense of grievance drags us down more heavily than chains of iron ever could. Blaming ourselves for failing to check our daughter's seatbelt or faulting our spouse for not braking quickly enough is what gives power to guilt's younger cousins, fear of driving any car again or grief that murders every hope of healing. And of course we know quite well that only a writ of pardon, forgiveness accepted or granted, can free us from the prison of our bitter, lonely heart.

But somehow we cannot bring ourselves to take that step beyond the confines of self-hatred or resentment, because deep down we *know* that punishment is justified. "There is no one righteous, not even one," Paul reminds us, "there is no one who understands, . . . no one who does good, not even one" (Romans 3:10, 12; quoting Psalms 14:1–3; 53:1–3; Ecclesiastes 7:20). This profound awareness of our existential guilt, the knowledge tainting all of us since Adam's bite into that apple, now seems to justify our clinging to the lash with which we whip ourselves or—at least in our minds—our debtors.

So long as we remain attached to our rancor and feed the fire of our anger, we cannot face and deal with, much less be transformed by, the feeling of bereavement that follows every tragedy.

Sometimes our seemingly justified resentment can even be a means of avoiding or denying loss, as when the hatred of (and civil suit against!) the other car's driver distracts us from our daughter's ever-empty bed. But this fundamentally human experience of finding our hands empty—of being deprived of our daughter, or our innocence or trust—is in many ways the main purpose of our soul's short stay on this planet.

As excruciating as our losses may be, they can also be God-given opportunities for relinquishing another bit of self and making more room within for the divine *pneuma*; in fact, the greater our deprivation, the greater our *kenotic* potential. Your heart *screams* at this thought, I know, and your objection is quite true: I do not know the enormity of your pain, your prison of emotions, your grief. But I dare say that the magnitude of what "the Lord has taken away" from me may at least come close to yours:

- nearly half of my life already spent in prison for a crime I did not commit;
- no realistic hope of ever being released; and
- the loss of my brother and mother, and the certain prospect of losing my few remaining family members and friends.

"Each heart knows its own bitterness," Solomon taught us, so I will not compare my pain with yours; but I hope that our shared experience of extreme bereavement can serve as a place where you and I can meet as fellow sufferers, as prisoners on the same chain gang (Proverbs 14:10).

Being a real convict in a stone-and-steel penitentiary, I know better than to give advice to another inmate such as you; that would be tantamount to "dissing" or "disrespecting" you, in American ghetto and prison slang. "Old heads" or long-termers like me can sometimes spark ideas in others, however, even when their external circumstances differ drastically from ours. If I somehow managed to let go of my grief, accept the emptiness of my hands and find God sparkling in my tears, then maybe there is some hope that you can be transformed by your anguish as well. Your heart has already been pierced, your cross is already on your shoulders, so why not see if you can find some meaning and perhaps even freedom in your sorrow?

As in the previous chapter, the key to success in this *kenotic* quest is once again the imitation of Christ through the implementation of Centering Practice's four laws. Painful feelings, no less than the approach of physical death, can be accepted voluntarily, honestly, non-attachedly and in a spirit of service, as he demonstrated for us on his cross. What tied these four qualities together into an effective spiritual tool against specifically emotional suffering was, of course, forgiveness: Jesus pardoned both the sin committed against him ("Father, forgive them...") *and* the sin whose guilt he bore ("Christ was sacrificed once to take away the sins of many" [Luke 23:34; Hebrews 9:28]). But precisely how do these two forms of the gift of pardon reflect or incorporate an emptying of the self?

Granting Pardon. In the first instance, forgiving others, we can easily recognize the familiar theme of relinquishment, in this case of the anger, fear and pain we feel as the result of others' actions. This initial release is difficult enough, as we all know, but it cannot bring us lasting freedom and inner peace if we do not also let go of our deep-seated attachment to the seeming justice of our cause and the apparent malevolence of our adversary. So long as we cling to the conviction that we were "right" and the person who injured us intentionally did "wrong," our sense of grievance will persist and may even deepen. After all, if we are noble enough to relinquish our pain and "forgive" the driver of the car that killed our daughter, then that son-of-dubious-parentage should have the decency to admit that he ran the red light out of pure insolence!

Now, it may in fact be true that the traffic light had turned to red just before the other driver ran the crossing, and it may even be true that you are God's firstborn Son instead of a rabble-rousing rebel—but the sad and hard-to-accept truth is that those who harmed us almost always thought they were justified in their actions, or at least not intentionally unjustified. "[F]or they do not know what they are doing" is the crucial qualifying clause that Jesus added to his plea that his crucifiers be forgiven (Luke 23:34). But while we can probably agree that the Pharisees honestly believed they were protecting the integrity of their religion by ridding themselves of a blasphemous troublemaker, few of us have the *kenotic* dispassion to admit that the driver who killed our daughter really did not see that the traffic light had just turned—especially when that driver aggressively insists on his innocence because guilt is secretly gnawing at him.

Whether he accepts our forgiveness (and therefore his own responsibility) is a separate and frankly secondary issue, of course. Freeing ourselves of the barbed wire prison of our outraged righteousness only requires that *we* develop the largeness of heart, the emptiness of self, to continue acknowledging the possibly mistaken or even twisted, but nevertheless *real* "good faith" of those who hurt us. Though that may in some cases require extraordinary moral empathy and imagination, my personal experience has been that *all* my enemies thought they were doing nothing wrong when they injured me—including the inmate who tried to rape me in 1991.

By the time "Flickin' Joe" turned his amorous attention toward me, I had already survived:

- a cross-Atlantic extradition and the subsequent trial, as described in the first Intermezzo;
- ten months at the Bedford County Jail, only slightly larger and no more sophisticated than Andy Griffith's in Mayberry; and
- another ten months at a correctional department reception center, where I was often the only white inmate not paying protection money, because my appearances on tabloid TV shows made me "all right, man."

In the summer of 1991, however, I reached Mecklenburg Correctional Center and lost any immunity my notoriety had leant me until then. Here I was nothing more than another "fresh fish," a pudgy guppy among highly experienced and hungry sharks.

Mecklenburg was at that time Virginia's only supermax facility, and for reasons that will become clear in the next chapter, I need to tell you now why I consider it to have been a comparatively successful and well-run prison. Although it housed inmates with very long sentences and disruptive, violent institutional records, it offered even these "no-hopers" incentives and opportunities to improve themselves: two tailor shops, vocational training in printing and computers, evening college courses in addition to the regular high school equivalency classes, decent law and regular libraries, and separate recreation yards for each of the five relatively small housing units. Keeping these unstable prisoners in pods of only a dozen single cells reduced violence proactively to the minimum practicable while allowing staff a maximum of supervision and control. Because superior quality costs extra even in departments of correction, Virginia unfortunately converted Mecklenburg into a double-celled, incentiveless reception "warehouse" shortly after I left in 1994.

Of course, even in 1991, while it was still being put to the use for which it had been designed, neither Mecklenburg nor its inmate population was perfect, and "Flickin' Joe" was less perfect than most.[3] He was a "gunner," a usually harmless subspecies of penitentiary *fauna* that spends its time cutting peepholes in shower curtains or standing at cell door windows to "gun down"—that is, masturbate on—the ever-increasing number of female correctional officers. Since Joe was absolutely enormous and had the physique of a professional bodybuilder, no one objected to his unusual form of foreplay: flicking his foot-long erection with his middle finger through his skintight Spandex biking shorts in the middle of the pod day room, in full view of the women guards and, of course, his fellow convicts. To his credit, however, he was an equal opportunity pervert, so he sometimes also became infatuated with a new "*phat* young white boy" such as yours truly.

I thought I had already learned how to parry advances like "Flickin' Joe's" and plot each day's excursions from my cell around his field of fire—but time was on his side, and eventually I slipped up. One day after leaving the shower, I suddenly found myself pinned against the top tier railing in a "full nelson" wrestling hold, with Joe's erection pressed against my lower back and his voice growling in my ear, "What choo gonna do if I drag you in mah cell *right now*?" Whatever I screeched in response—and I simply cannot recall what magic words I used, though they must have been extraordinarily eloquent even for me—induced Joe to let me go, and I "hauled *ss on away from there," to use a singularly apposite prison idiom.

Since I had not yet figured out that the "convict code" in Virginia's penitentiary system means that *everyone* snitches, I actually kept my mouth shut about this episode; in fact, I could not talk about it at all for several years. But someone must have heard and then told something, because a few days later I was moved to another pod. Shortly thereafter, a sixteen-year-old "*phat* young white boy" who had been tried as an adult became the new love in "Flickin' Joe's" life, saving my "booty" by sacrificing his.

My initial reaction to this close encounter of the foot-long kind was as inappropriate as the overeating and gastrointestinal problems of my *de facto* death row experience in England had been: I began jogging and working out with weights fanatically, as if it were really possible to run away from anyone in prison or to fight someone twice my size. But this otherwise ineffective coping mechanism also became my means of *voluntarily* embracing my new cross, my fear of and anger at Joe—by becoming his frequent weightlifting partner for the next three years. As bizarre as that may sound, I believe our loose cordial relationship helped me overcome my pain, by practically forcing me to acknowledge that he was not a monster but just another human being with a few good sides. That awareness, in turn, made forgiveness and healing possible for me, though the process took several years.

Naturally I planned none of this. Through God's guiding hand the weights simply happened to be on the small outside recreation yards next to the buildings; the cold winter wind usually kept everyone inside the building but Joe and me; and since one cannot do benchpresses without a "spotter" to back up the lifter, we *had* to work together and trust each other. Could I have split his skull with a dumbbell while he was lying on the bench and struggling with his "max" weight? Of course. But what would have been the point? And besides, the man I came to know during our brief "conversations" between sets was not such a terrible fellow. He knew a lot about doing time and next to nothing about everything else— including the immorality of rape, which he seemed to consider a normal part of the natural order of life. When I heard years later that Joe was dying of AIDS, I actually felt a little sad.

My near-daily weightlifting sessions kept me *truthful* about my painful feelings in that each trip to the "rec" yard forced me to face my fear and anger again; that little twitch in my stomach prevented me from convincing myself that I had bravely fought off my attacker instead of yelping in terror. What helped me develop emotional distance or *non-attachment*, on the other hand, was my sense of humor, though retrospectively I believe this may have become almost compulsive. For five or six years I turned virtually every remark or conversation with other inmates into a homosexual joke, a trait I have also noticed among many other prisoners who were less fortunate than I. The above account of my near-rape shows that even today I am simply unable to describe this episode without the defense of humor.

Finally, whether any of the above can be construed as implementing Centering Practice's fourth element of *service* seems highly doubtful to me. I wish I could have saved the sixteen-year-old "fresh fish" from Joe, though even today I cannot imagine how that miracle might have been accomplished. Nor can I be sure that my association with Joe was of any benefit to him at all, apart from a marginal increase in his muscle mass due to my spotting. But my failure in this regard need not prevent you from reaching out to others as you struggle with fear, anger and the granting of forgiveness.

Receiving Pardon. How to accept forgiveness and stop hating myself is something I have only begun to learn recently, as the continual practice of *letting go* during contemplative prayer has begun to bear fruit in other areas of my life. *Taking* blame is my specialty, as you know by now, while accepting the release of God's pardon is something I find particularly difficult. Rather than leaving my tears and my sins at Jesus' feet and then "go[ing] in peace" like Mary Magdalene, I—that is, my self—prefer to cling to the illusion of power and autonomy, the strangely comforting fantasy that I could have shaped my fate differently *if only.* . . . Oddly enough, as we shall see below, it was my brother who finally taught me how to relinquish, not my guilt, but my attachment to it, how to abandon myself to God's mercy, accept his forgiveness and "get up, take . . . [my] mat and go home" (Mark 2:10).

Of course this does not mean that I have "forgiven myself," a modern notion so evil and blasphemous that it occasionally provokes me to lose my contemplative cool. "God alone . . . can forgive sins," though "the Son of Man has authority on earth" to exercise this divine prerogative, as do those to whom he has entrusted "the keys to the kingdom" (Mark 2:7, 10; Matthew 16:19). When we "forgive . . . our debtors" on a personal level, it is God's love flowing through us that reconciles the offender to ourselves; we are just the vessels of his spirit, powerless on our own (Matthew 6:12). Attempting to usurp the power of pardon by "forgiving ourselves" merely extends the characteristically selfish ethic of instant gratification to the realm of morality—"I want to feel good about my bad acts *now*"—but it can never truly release us from the prison of guilt.

One thing that has made the thirteen years of my American imprisonment (at the time of this writing) so difficult for me is precisely this moral autism of my fellow prisoners, the often violently expressed conviction that the only standard of good and evil is what each one lusts after at this very moment. By contrast, the high-level organized crime figures and terrorists with whom I spent most of my nearly four years in English penitentiaries actually recognized that there were a few human beings with rights of their own besides themselves: really professional (often *unarmed*) robbers considered it to be a point of Cockney honor never to injure the working-class guards protecting currency transports, and the bomb-layers preferred targeting political leaders to killing frontline soldiers who were only following orders. Of course their ethical systems were twisted and perhaps even delusional, but at least they possessed *some* form of that basic building block of any full human being: a conscience. This moral component of their personalities in turn made it possible for me to relate to them on something approaching a genuine level. I was not completely alone.

In the eyes of the Virginian inmates with whom I have now lived for more than a decade, on the other hand, neither I nor any other two-legged mammal can be anything other than:

- a *means* of stilling the desire of the moment, a "vic" or victim to be conned or robbed;
- an *obstacle* to instant gratification, such as the "*po*-lice"; or
- an *accomplice* or "stick man" whose help and admiration they need to indulge their cravings.

There are no human beings in this world, no concept that one person's "right" may have to be balanced against another's "wrong," no possibility of communication between equals. And saddest of all, I believe my fellow convicts do not even realize how profoundly isolated they are within the prisons of their stony hearts.

Over the years I keep cycling through the same emotional reactions to the self-obsessed strangers with whom I am crowded into a cage:

- pity for the inmates on psychotropic medication, who wander around in a pill-induced haze, are exploited sexually and financially by everyone, and literally fight over discarded cigarette butts so they can roll themselves "retreads";

- fear of the lone wolves and packs of hyenas, against whom I have no defense but my lack of an obvious weakness or exploitable vice—and, more importantly, the miraculous protection of providence;

- sadness when I hear three new peachy-cheeked child molesters argue heatedly, as if it were a point of honor, which one of them was abused worst by his father;

- disgust at the same three molesters ten or twelve years later in their prison careers, when they have progressed from being "punks" to "prison daddies" on the prowl for new "kids" to enslave;

- frustration when a forty-three-year-old convict learns how to spell his middle name by himself for the very first time—and then gives up on learning more, because he realizes (perhaps better than I ever could) how enormous the past failures and future challenges in his education really are;

- alienation from the countless addicts whose entire existence and every conversation revolves only around "my thing, man": marijuana, home-brewed "mash," gambling, tattoos, Dungeons & Dragons and even food; and

- loneliness each time I encounter another one of the "walking wounded," the many undiagnosed and untreated crazies who appear quite normal at first—until you notice that they wipe down their cells, from ceiling to floor, each and every day with a sponge they fastidiously dip in toilet water; or until they explain how they model their sanitary habits on the Neanderthals in Jean Auel's "Clan of the Cave Bear" novels (which means wearing no shoes, using no soap, and urinating on their feet to prevent athlete's foot fungus); or until they excuse themselves to use the pod day room telephone, where they then sit for an hour or two chatting happily . . . without ever having dialed a number.[4]

Any one of my feelings—pity, fear, sadness, disgust, frustration, alienation, and loneliness—could at least theoretically have served as a basis from which to embark on meaningful contact with my fellow prisoners, *if* they had shown the slightest inclination to leave the confines of their private little hells. But though I tried over and over and over again, I was not able to establish a genuine, perhaps even friendly relationship with even one other person between 1990 and 2000. Every single face I saw remained, if not an enemy, then at least a stranger in the most profound sense possible. In fact, I cannot think of anyone I knew during that entire decade whom I would not positively regret seeing again. Only since my transfer to my current medium security facility in 2000 have I encountered a truly tiny handful of exceptions to the above, though I have my doubts about some of them, too.

All of this background about my penitentiary existence has been necessary to give you some understanding of why I was so deeply hurt by a series of what I experienced as betrayals and aban-donments by friends as well as family members between 1990 and 1997. As someone who relates to others primarily through his emo-tions, I found the general loneliness of my life inside prison nearly unbearable, so each severing of another tie to the outside world seemed to me to be an unnecessary, undeserved cruelty that pushed me further and further toward complete isolation. Yet the blows kept coming, and every few months I would hang a towel over my head and cry.

- What I felt to be the greatest betrayal at the time was, of course, Elizabeth's testimony against me at my trial in 1990. Some extraordinarily naïve and stupid part of me had hoped she would save my life on the stand just as I had saved hers four or five years earlier, simply because it would have been the right thing to do. When she missed her opportunity to make a grand, noble gesture to help me, Elizabeth also seemed to diminish the value of my sacrifice for her, as if her failure in the witness box were the final proof that she really had not been worth my throwing my life away for. I see these matters somewhat differently now, but at the time my pain was . . . well, let me just say that on June 21, 1990, on the night I was convicted, I tied a plastic bag over my head in an admittedly halfhearted attempt to kill myself.

- Because of the enormous legal bills generated by my trial as well as by my parents' divorce, my father could not afford to visit me between 1990 and 1995, while my mother canceled one planned trip after another as her alcoholic descent deepened. The sudden end of regular face-to-face contact with my parents was a major and very painful change for me, since they had visited me often in prison in England. While I certainly did not blame them—in fact, I blamed myself—I could not help but miss them and long for them as I dealt with the "Flickin' Joes" and the tabloid TV reporters.

- In 1993 I was forced to bring proceedings against my trial attorney before the Michigan State Bar Association, which eventually suspended his license and reimbursed me $6,000 he had misappropriated. Not only had he betrayed me in 1992/93: according to the expert witness in criminal law who testified at my *habeas corpus* hearing and has meanwhile been elevated to a federal magistrateship, I would not even have been convicted in 1990 if my lawyer had done his job properly. This was the man to whom I had entrusted my life, my only hope for justice and freedom; his failure had in effect killed me.

- After my transfer from Mecklenburg Correctional Center to Keen Mountain Correctional Center in 1994, I was no longer allowed to receive telephone calls from my parents once a month. Letters scribbled at the end of hectic days could not provide anything like the same level of intimacy and immediacy in communication, so we ended up having several major misunderstandings by mail—and no way to resolve them quickly. For a prisoner totally dependent on family support, these disagreements were particularly frightening and stressful.

- My mother died of alcoholism in 1997, a death for which I initially blamed myself alone and even now hold myself largely responsible. But apart from my tremendous feelings of guilt, her passing also seemed to me like a precipitous abandonment at a time when there still seemed to be hope of vindication by the courts, as if she had given up on me. The last time I saw her was in 1989, and the last time I heard her voice was in 1994. My only mementos of my mother are five photographs: three of her from the 1970s, 1980s and 1990s, and two of her grave in Bremen, Germany.

- In the year my mother died, my brother also broke off contact with me because, so I assumed, he too blamed me for her much-too-early end. I wrote him numerous letters over the next four years, accepting full responsibility for causing her death and asking him to forgive me, but he never replied. As odd as it may seem, this rejection by my brother hurt the worst, because I truly believed he was right to hate me.

Of course not all was doom and despair between 1990 and 1997: my father and I grew much closer during our four annual visits of a week each between 1995 and 1998, while he was stationed in Papua New-Guinea, and an old friend from high school visited me once with his new Russian wife. But each of these visits reminded me forcefully of how much further and further the outside world was falling away from my penitentiary existence, how I was coming to resemble a flounder flopping on the sand after the tide had receded permanently. Once a year or so, I was allowed to taste water briefly and pretend I was still alive—and then it was back to the dry, dead desert, where the psychotics and predators and perverts crawled over the burning sand and each other.

To some extent my isolation and sense of loneliness must remain opaque to you, of course: when you lay down this book, the first person you see will almost certainly regard you as a fellow human being and may actually care for you, while your exposure to being treated as a *thing* will be virtually non-existent. For me the reverse is true; and, what is presumably unimaginable to you, it has been true *for over a decade and a half* (at the time of this writing). The weight of all those years of being told by the guards, the inmates and the very bricks and bars around me that "You are slime, nothing but slime" has a persuasive force than even I have not been able to resist entirely. As any old convict will tell you, "You start off doing time, but after a while, time is doing you."

In the preceding paragraphs you will have noticed that between 1990 and 1997 I continued to use some of the same coping mechanisms I developed during my years in English prisons. But I now think my primary response to the loneliness of my existence was my conversion from agnosticism to Christianity in late 1994. Because spiritual transformation behind bars is a well-documented phenomenon—though in my experience much rarer than one might think—I will give you only a brief account of how Jesus and the I AM found me, so we can concentrate on how my rebirth in Christ revealed Centering Practice's four basic principles as they apply to the acceptance of forgiveness.

Personally, I blame the Vicar of Christ and NASA for my conversion; the fault is theirs alone. If His Holiness, Pope John Paul II, had not officially condemned the movie *The Last Temptation of*

Christ in 1994, I would never have been tempted to buy the original novel by Nikos Kazantzakis; I would never have recognized my
own existential situation in this author's very human fictional
Jesus, a man who loved and doubted and laid down his life for his
friends; and I would never have picked up a New Testament seriously for the first time to search for the real Christ. Thank you,
John Paul! This in turn prepared me for the central spiritual insight
of my life, which took place upon seeing the first published photographs from NASA's Hubble Space Telescope: Both the physical
force of *gravity*, which sent all those beautiful galaxies dancing
around each other, and the emotional force of *love*, which
Kazantzakis had described in his novel, are forms of *attraction*: two
different manifestations of the same universal unifying principle—
the I AM THAT I AM—"for whom and through whom *everything*
exists" (Hebrews 2:10, emphasis added). "The heavens declare the
glory of God" because they too sing that "God is love"; without this
power "in [which] . . . all things *hold together*," electrons would fly
away from nuclei, man would never join woman, and planets
would leave their suns (Psalm 19:1, 1 John 4:15, Colossians 1:16,
emphasis added). Suddenly, intuitively and overwhelmingly, all
this made sense to me when I looked at those photographs from the
Hubble Space Telescope. So, thank you, too, Dan Goldin (Director
of NASA)!

What my conversion to Christianity allowed me to do was to
come to terms with the extreme loneliness of prison life in an
entirely new way. Instead of bewailing each new abandonment
and betrayal as another cruel blow by a blind, uncaring fate, I
now came to recognize both God's guiding hand in my anguish
and my own deeper, underlying responsibility—even in those
cases in which others had wronged me without any apparent justification. My guide in developing this *voluntary, honest, dispassionate* and *outer- or upward-directed* acceptance of my cross was
Jeremiah, whose Lamentations seemed to have been written
especially for me:

It is good for a man to bear the yoke
    while he is young.
Let him sit in silence,
    for the Lord has laid it on him. . . .
To crush underfoot
    all the prisoners in the land,
to deny a man his rights
    before the Most High,
to deprive a man of justice—
    would not the Lord see such things? . . .
Is it not from the mouth of the Most High
    that both calamities and good things come?
Why should any living man complain
    when punished for his sins?
Let us examine our ways and test them,
    and let us return to the Lord.
Let us lift up our hearts and our hands
    to God in heaven and say:
"We have sinned and rebelled
    and you have not forgiven."
          (Lamentations 3:27–28, 34–36, 38–42)

Embracing my suffering as Jeremiah did his brought me more comfort than nursing my grievances ever could have done, because each slide into deeper isolation led me closer to God: "[t]hough my father and mother forsake me, the Lord will receive me" (Psalm 27:10). Privately, within my soul, I dedicated my feelings of loneliness to those people I had failed, as a gift or offering to try to make good my errors. That did not lessen my pain, but at least now that pain made sense.

Sometimes I wondered, however, why I never experienced any sense of great joy or bliss to indicate that my repentance had been noted and rewarded with divine forgiveness. When the prodigal son returned home, his father slaughtered the fatted calf and organized a feast, so it seemed reasonable to expect that I too would be given some overt, noticeable sign that the burden of guilt had indeed been lifted. The only plausible explanation for this lack of an "official" proclamation of pardon seemed to be that I had not yet been punished enough, that I had to wait a while longer to receive mercy.

Of all people, it was my brother who showed me the error of my thinking in this regard: after four years of writing him unanswered letters of apology, I was finally informed that he had never blamed me for my mother's death in the first place. This unexpected absolution of my guilt toward my brother brought home to me very powerfully that the spiritual state of *being forgiven* does not require some obvious signal, either from the person one had (or thought one had) harmed or even from God himself. Not the subjective and temporary experience of joy, but the movement of faith that leads from the feeling of regret to the search for God is what saves. It was "while [the prodigal son] was still a long way off," but clearly on his way back, that his father "saw him and was filled with compassion for him," for God really "will not despise . . . a broken spirit, a broken and contrite heart" (Luke 15:20, Psalm 51:17).

If there is any seal of pardon, I think it is precisely this "broken and contrite heart" that stays focused on the need for God because "my sin . . . is always before me" (Psalm 51:3). When we, like David, cry out to our Father, "Create in me a pure heart," our prayers are in a sense already answered in the asking, since we could not turn to him if our former proud, self-reliant hearts still existed (Psalm 51:12). So I have stopped looking for fattened calves and instead pray that God continues to "teach me wisdom in the inmost place" by reminding me constantly that "I was sinful at birth, sinful from the time my mother conceived me" (Psalm 51:6, 5). And I thank my brother for the insight he gave me, though I wish I could tell him so in person.

4—1997–2001, *Kenosis* on the Intellectual/Conceptual Level
"And lead us not into temptation but deliver us
from the evil one."

Of the three types of pain that may become means of emptying ourselves, I personally have found the third, suffering on the intellectual/conceptual level, to have the greatest *kenotic* effect and transformative power. Unfortunately, this kind of pain is also the hardest to write about: the agony of death and the anguish of your own or others' guilt are easy to identify, but what exactly does "having your sense of identity ripped away" mean? In this Book's Chapter 1, I suggested that a bitter divorce, an unplanned ending of your professional career, or an episode of mental illness might seem like attacks on the core of your being, depending on how you define yourself. What really distinguishes intellectual/conceptual suffering from the previous two kinds, however, is not the external problem set or even the intensity of the resulting pain, but the feeling that the very foundations of our world are crumbling away.

By contrast, even the most severe physical and emotional anguish need not necessarily threaten to destroy our soul and wipe out our personality. While waiting on death in English prisons, for instance, I never doubted that it was *I*, Jens Soering, who was going to fry or hang, and I clearly knew that it was *my* heart that broke when Elizabeth testified against me and my mother died. The four trials I underwent between 1997 and 2001, on the other hand, actually came close to extinguishing that little flame of "Jens" that had struggled so hard to stay lit with the divine Fire. The child of God that exists at least potentially within us all very nearly died in me during these years.

For it is not only our Father who can give birth to the Son in us, in Meister Eckhart's beautiful phrase; I learned from personal experience that Satan can also give birth to Judas, the evil one, in the dead space of a heart crushed by sorrow. These things are living realities, not metaphors. All the devil needs is the right kind of suffering, that special sort of pain which makes us question everything we thought we knew about ourselves and our world—and suddenly it can seem perfectly sensible to sell out the Messiah himself for thirty pieces of silver.

Matthew suggests that Judas's deal with the chief priests was prompted by Christ's seemingly selfish decision to let himself be anointed by Mary instead of selling the perfume and donating the proceeds to the poor (Matthew 26:6–16). Along with the rest of the disciples, Judas had recently risked his own life by returning to Jerusalem with his leader, so Jesus' apparent misappropriation of a charitable donation may well have appeared like a betrayal of his own selfless loyalty by a pious con man whose secret weakness for aromatic nard had finally been revealed (John 11:16, compare 12:3). I imagine Judas suffered tremendously as he watched all his certainties crumble and the meaning of his own existence called into doubt, and having encountered the evil one myself, I cannot help but pity him in his failure.

But Judas Iscariot was not the only one who faced the ultimate test of an intellectual/conceptual crisis in the city of Jerusalem two thousand years ago. Like his betrayer, Christ too experienced the terror of seeming separation from our Father and cried out in desperation, "My God, my God, why have you forsaken me?" (Matthew 27:46). Personally, I believe it was not the centurion's whip or the nails through the hands that Jesus feared when he prayed earlier that "this cup be taken from me," but this moment of apparent abandonment by his Abba (Matthew 26:39).

Of course the cup could not be taken from him because, like all of God's children, he could only be made "perfect through suffering" by experiencing the perfect hell: the feeling, however brief, that our Father has turned away (Hebrews 2:10). Only at that point of complete uncertainty can any of us sons and daughters of Light make a decision that is based *purely* on faith, without any external or even internal sign that God will catch us when we jump. If we never reach this place of doubt and near-despair, we simply cannot know the true strength of our faith or the perfect joy of having it confirmed, of finding ourselves safe in our Abba's arms.

That is why the last petition of the Lord's Prayer, "And lead us not into temptation but deliver us from the evil one," has slowly changed its meaning for me in the last six years (at the time of this writing). Because I had never plumbed these depths before, I could not be *sure* at first whether I would be granted the grace to reach beyond myself to God as I hung on my cross, or whether I would resort to the seeming security of worldly treasures, silver coins or otherwise. But my initially faint hope turned to trust and then to reliance and lately even to serenity as our Father responded each time I cried, "[W]hy have you forsaken me?" So while I do not tempt God by *asking* to be led into temptation, I no longer fear the fiery oven or the lion's pit, because "I [now truly] *know* that my Redeemer lives" (Job 19:25, emphasis added). Sometimes I even find myself giving thanks for these opportunities to shed more attachments to self and to world and thus to grow closer to God, though I realize that must sound odd indeed.

Because only some of us have to pass through this kind of crucible, and because the Judas within comes in a different shape for everyone, the following descriptions of my three encounters with intellectual/conceptual suffering may not offer obvious and potentially useful parallels to your ultimate temptation, if and when it comes. I hope the remainder of this chapter will nevertheless be of some benefit to you by helping you identify at least some of the varieties of this test, since its many disguises are not always easy to recognize. Judas, for instance, only understood after Christ's crucifixion that he had betrayed and helped kill not only God's first and only begotten son but also the spark of divinity within himself (Matthew 27:3–5). And even if you never enter these deep and treacherous waters yourself, you may still pick up a few bits of sea lore from my sailor's tales that will help you navigate through your own storms.

1997: Denial of German Reading Material. In 1997, a policy change by the Department of Corrections effectively forbade me any further access to the German language newspapers, magazines and books that I had read regularly during the first eleven years of my incarceration. Of course I filed written complaints, and the German Embassy in Washington, D.C., even provided a written certification by a University of Virginia German professor to the effect that the publications I wished to continue reading posed no threat to security (they were the German equivalents of the *Washington Post, Time* and Shakespeare). The Department of Corrections thereupon made the Solomonic ruling that I would be permitted to *order* whatever German reading material I wished—but that I could not *receive* anything until I located a German-speaking correctional officer at my prison who was willing to censor each individual issue of a periodical and every single book on his own time and without pay. Because I was never able to find a guard who was fluent in German, my only contact with my native language since 1997 has been a brief monthly letter or postcard from my father and, of course, my German Bible (which technically is illegal, since it has never been censored).

This linguistic drought has had a significant negative impact on me on a purely practical level by creating nearly insurmountable obstacles to my at least theoretically possible reintegration into civilian life in Germany upon completion of my American prison sentence. After only six years (at the time of this writing), I have already lost much of my ability to communicate either by speech or in writing, and I assume nothing will be left at all if I serve another thirty years in Virginia. Should this state deport me home at that point—at age sixty-five, after forty-six years behind bars—I would not even know the words for "Salvation Army soup kitchen" or "social security office" in German.

More insidiously, the lack of German newspapers and magazines has left me completely uninformed about the political and social trends in my country, the sort of everyday cultural information all of us take for granted but could not do without in order to navigate around our world. What people wear, how they spend their free time, where they work, what towns look like nowadays—these things are mysteries to me. I barely even know who the chancellor of Germany is!

All of the above would be bad enough, but it does not even begin to describe the real horror—and that is not too strong a word—of losing my mother tongue. The first words I heard were German, my baby-babbling was *auf Deutsch*, I learned to think in German, even my dreams were *Träume* and . . . well, I have forgotten the German word for "nightmare," another casualty of the cancer that is eating away my mind's basic structure. Apart from the prayer of divine union, *all* human experiences can only be processed through the medium of language, so the breakdown of this most basic of mental tools really means losing one's grip on reality itself.

Imagine, if you can, struggling to think an idea without having the form or mold to contain it: you can sense the presence of a thought straining to emerge like a baby from the womb, but lacking a word to shape it and make it graspable, it remains an unborn conceptual fog, a constipation of the brain. Imagine the helplessness, the frustration and the panic of finding yourself in a prison whose bars you cannot see or touch or even *name*. Imagine the terror of sinking into the mental quicksand deeper and deeper each day, of feeling your mind's movements become slower and weaker, of watching the darkness grow.

On some level all this must remain a mystery to you, of course, but it is worth noting that some of the most eloquent passages in our own scriptures tell of the special pain of being held captive far from home:

> By the rivers of Babylon we sat and wept
> when we remembered Zion. . . .

How can we sing the songs of the Lord
> while in a foreign land.
>
> (Psalm 137:1, 4)

And when the prison gates were finally opened and the Israelites returned home, their leader, Nehemiah, encountered precisely the same kind of linguistic estrangement and consequent loss of identity that I described above:

> [H]alf the children [of the remaining Israelites] spoke the language of Ashdod or the language of one of the other peoples, and did not know how to speak the language of Judah. I rebuked them and called curses down on them. I beat some of the men and pulled out their hair.
>
> (Nehemiah 13:24, 25)

Whether "curses" and "beat[ings]" and "pull[ing] out the . . . hair" would be at all helpful in changing the minds of those who decided to deny me access to German reading material is something I must leave to wiser heads than mine. Certainly the authors of the Pentateuch had firm opinions on such matters:

> Cursed be he who violates the rights of the alien. . . . You shall not molest or oppress the alien, for you were once aliens yourselves in the land of Egypt. . . . So you too must befriend the alien, feeding and clothing him.
>
> (Deuteronomy 27:19, Exodus 22:20, Deuteronomy 10:19; cf. Exodus 23:9, Leviticus 19:33, Deuteronomy 24:17, Zechariah 7:10)

If you are hoping for some redeeming or hopeful end to this section, I must unfortunately disappoint you. To this day I am not allowed access to my native language, and I cannot pretend that I do not feel a stab of pain three times a day when I read my German

Bible. "In the beginning was the Word," John tells us, and the Word first came to me in German words; I will always pray to *dem Vater, dem Sohn und dem heiligen Geist.*

Perhaps the best that I can say is that in some sense even the loss of my mother tongue does not matter anymore, since I will never be released from prison and thus have no need to retain my language and culture. That central part of me that is *deutsch* may as well be killed now.

1999–2000: Eleven Months at a Supermax Prison. If any section of *The Way of the Prisoner* results in official retaliation against me, it will be this one—but I cannot leave it out, because my experiences at Wallens Ridge demonstrate especially clearly both the soul- and personality-destroying quality of intellectual/conceptual suffering *and* its immense transformative power. Looking back, I can honestly say that my stay at "Wally's World," as we called it, proved to be of immense spiritual benefit to me, though that does not in any way justify the treatment meted out to me and other inmates. Please bear with me, then, as I give you some background information that may protect me against the wrath of those Department of Corrections officials who will take my narrative as troublemaking of the worst sort.

After the 1993 election of Virginia's first Republican governor in many, many years, the DOC engaged in an immense and, as it turned out, wildly excessive prison building program in response to and preparation for the simultaneous abolition of parole. At the time of this writing, Virginia has three or four thousand unneeded prison "beds" that it rents out to the federal Bureau of Prisons and states with overcrowded systems like New Mexico, Wyoming, Indiana, Michigan and Connecticut. Both of Virginia's brand new supermax facilities, Red Onion and its twin sister Wallens Ridge, house significant numbers of "tourist" inmates, in the case of Wally's World *half* of the population (at least during my time there).

I stayed at Wallens Ridge during roughly its first year of operation, a difficult time for any institution. During this approximate period, the prison was under investigation by five[5] official bodies for alleged human rights abuses and the suspicious deaths of two inmates (the FBI, Amnesty International, New Mexico, Connecticut and Virginia). Only Amnesty International found any fire beneath all that smoke, but Connecticut eventually had its prisoners moved to another, less problematic facility in Virginia.

In fairness, I need to point out that the Virginia Department of Corrections has proved itself capable of operating a supermax prison in a safe and humane manner in the past: Mecklenburg Correctional Center, where I myself spent three years in the early 1990s. I met a good number of frontline guards, non-security staff members, medical personnel and one higher-level administrator at Wallens Ridge who were openly critical of the facility's plan and procedure and tried to help inmates in general as well as me personally, for which I am deeply grateful. Finally, even those correctional officers whom I observed abusing others and/or who abused me must be excused to some extent: almost all of them were simply young, uneducated coalminer's sons and daughters who had been told by their superiors that the *only* response to *any* problem was firing shotguns. Perhaps they should have known that dehumanizing others only dehumanizes oneself, but I myself had to learn from bitter experience how easy it is to lose one's moral bearings when one is convinced of one's own righteousness.

The real problem with Wallens Ridge is not its staff but its architectural and operational design, which consistently gets wrong everything that the old supermax, Mecklenburg, got right:

- Instead of deescalating tension and diminishing the potential for violence proactively by housing inmates in small pods of twelve single cells as at Mecklenburg, the "general population" (i.e., non-"segregation") pods at Wallens Ridge contain forty double cells, thus concentrating eighty of the supposedly most unstable prisoners in the state in an area perhaps three quarters the size of a typical high school basketball gym. If that were not bad enough, stress levels are raised yet higher by leaving the great majority of inmates locked in "behind the door" approximately twenty-two hours per day (not counting meals), because the pod day rooms are so small that only half of the cells can be opened at any one time. Even Saint John of the Cross and Saint Teresa of Avila would start beating each other over the head with their rosaries if they were locked into a bathroom-sized cubicle together for that length of time every day, day after day, year after year.

• In prison, sports are not a matter of fun and games but an absolutely essential means of safely burning off the frustration that penitentiaries are, after all, meant to produce as part of their punishing function. That is why experienced correctional officers like working around inmate-weightlifters—they almost never get into fights—and that is why Mecklenburg offered frequent access to a total of six separate rec yards for its five housing units. Wallens Ridge's two rec yards, on the other hand, must be shared by eight "general population" pods, which means that in practice prisoners are lucky to get an average of forty-five minutes outside per day. Without appropriate means to self-regulate tension, not only predators but also mild-mannered inmates like me experience a steady buildup of psychological and physical pressure that will eventually be released in some usually harmful way.

• The absolutely best, most effective way to control convicts' behavior is to give them a $30-per-month prison job picking up trash or washing pots in the kitchen; since the vast majority of inmates receive no family support, they will do anything to keep that minimal income stream coming. Instead of using this well-proven method of maintaining order, as Mecklenburg did with the usual success (and inevitable occasional failures), Wallens Ridge offers only a very few jobs—but plenty of shotguns with interlocking fields of fire. In fact, the new supermax is specifically designed so that prisoners can be shot anywhere, including in the shower, and the guards make frequent use of their weapons for any infraction of the rules.

No verbal warning is given: the first sign of trouble is an incredibly loud *BANG*, a blank warning round. Anyone who does not then immediately lie down flat on his stomach with arms spread out will be fired upon with a live round of rubber pellets. Throughout my eleven-month stay at Wallens Ridge, I found myself hugging the grass, the concrete, the snow and once even the slime of a shower stall floor for a wide variety of rules infractions by other inmates, such as:

- jogging across the concrete sidewalk on the outside rec yard (only walking across the sidewalk is permitted)—*BANG*;
- crossing a red line in the pod day room to get a bag lunch too soon (the guard had not been waving at the prisoner in question, but at the man next to him)—*BANG*;
- giving half a bag of coffee to a friend—*BANG*; and
- arguing without raised voices over a basketball game— *BANG*.

Not one of the many warning shot firings I witnessed was prompted by an act of violence, or even an attempt at or preparation for an act of violence.

Living under the gun at all times, with the constant expectation of hearing a *BANG* at any moment and having to dive for the dirt, does not reduce problem behavior at all, of course. In fact, raising the level of tension to such heights and with such consistency puts everyone on a hair trigger alert, with predictable results. When frightened, over-stressed and psychologically unstable prisoners crack under the pressure and act out, they do not thereby confirm how right Wallens Ridge's designers were to put guns everywhere, but merely prove that poking a stick at a pit bull—or for that matter a chihuahua—is liable to earn you a bite on the backside.

Finally, apart from the bribe of a $30-per-month prison job, the second-best way to control convicts is to offer them hope in the form of opportunities to improve themselves, as Mecklenburg did through various educational, vocational and incentive-pay skilled work programs. The abolition of parole has largely ended the efficacy of this method of behavior modification—some "counselors" now tell inmates that they need not participate in Alcoholics Anonymous, for instance, since nothing they do can shorten their sentences anyway—but because so many prisoners simply enjoy learning or working hard, they will restrain their disruptive impulses to maintain access to school and work.

In my experience, it is especially convicts with long sentences—the supermax type, supposedly—who often develop a real sense of responsibility after ten or twelve years behind bars. No prison kitchen or warehouse or school program, and certainly no prison furniture factory, could function without plenty of "old heads" who do all the real work while civilian supervisors sleep off their hang-overs or make nuisances of themselves. Whereas Mecklenburg used all this talent and energy, Wallens Ridge keeps it locked down or shoots at it, a profoundly depressing and eventually counterproductive policy that directly affected me, as you can imagine. A single vocational course in custodial maintenance (I am not making this up; we called it "Mopping 101") and the occasional basic literacy class shown on the day room television may satisfy the American Correctional Association's aptly-named "minimum standards," but the admittedly broken human beings at the receiving end of these allegedly educational programs understand the underlying message very clearly. The Virginia Department of Corrections' Director, Ron Angelone, said it best at the 1998 opening of Red Onion: "What are they going to be rehabilitated for? To die gracefully in prison? Let's face it: they're here to die in prison."[5]

While reading the last few paragraphs, you may have been asking yourself how a model inmate like me, with a perfect institutional record for over fifteen years, found himself on a bus to Wallens Ridge. Surely I must have done *something* wrong! But ironically it was my good behavior that earned me my transfer to hell: shortly after Wallens Ridge opened, many docile, cooperative prisoners were sent there to fill up the enormous excess of brand new but unneeded supermax cells, and to provide the virgin, barely trained staff an opportunity to practice their correctional skills on inmates who would not fight back if shot or beaten.

I was taken to Wally's World with a whole busload of essentially medium-security prisoners, some with very short sentences indeed. The first thing we saw on the loading dock as we pulled in was a German shepherd *with an erection*—and that was not a coincidence, as quietly disapproving guards later told us. Apparently the canine unit officers manually assisted the dog in producing this sign of welcome for all new inmates, to let us know how excited they were to see us (colloquially: "we have a h*rd-on for you").

Having laid on that bit of amateur theatrics, a lieutenant and an officer with a video camera entered the bus and screamed at maximum volume, "This is Wallens Ridge State Prison! This is unlike any prison you have ever been in! If you break any rule or disobey any order, we will respond with immediate use of firepower!" Thereupon two black-suited and helmeted riot squad members physically pulled us off the bus one by one to a glass cubicle inside the reception building, where we had to strip naked, squat and cough, and finally do an odd little dance in a circle, all in full view of a dozen male and female guards. Wrapped in handcuffs, leg irons and waist chains, we were then half-led, half-carried across the rec yard to our cells with the German shepherd barking hysterically at our side every step of the way.

The pod my group entered upon our arrival was brand new; there was still construction dust and debris everywhere, and over the next few months we cleaned this and several other new housing units. When I moved into one of these new cells—in D-1 pod on a Friday, as I recall—my cellmate and I discovered that no air was coming out of the air vent. This was our only source of oxygen, since the cell windows are glassed slits that do not open and the doors are solid metal with a relatively narrow gap at the bottom, so we asked to be moved to one of the empty cells with a functioning air vent until the maintenance man could fix this cell's vent when he returned on Monday.

Instead, we were left where we were for three days, sweating and gasping for air and swallowing aspirin by the handful to fight off the ever-worsening headaches. Every time the cell door opened—one minute every hour or two during the day, but not at all at night—we would stand in the doorway and fan our towels to try to circulate some fresh air into the cell and move the stale air out. Of course we filed "emergency grievances," but those were returned to us marked "unfounded" because, so we were informed, no immediate threat to life or danger of irreparable harm existed. After spending Friday, Saturday and Sunday inside that airless tomb, my cellmate and I finally experienced a kind of resurrection on Monday when the maintenance man unblocked the air vent.

This particular incident could perhaps be explained away as an exception if it were not part of a consistent pattern of petty cruelty, of which the following are only a few representative examples:

- Wallens Ridge is the only prison in the state that has frosted over those cell windows facing outside the facility; according to friendly correctional officers, the view overlooking the valley below was considered too beautiful for inmate eyes.

- Inmates at Wallens Ridge's twin sister, Red Onion, had to file federal suit to obtain shower stall curtains for both facilities; until then, all of us had to wash in full view (and direct shotgun firing line) of male and female guards, "counselors" and groups of visiting dignitaries from DOC headquarters.

- Supposed "security risks" are used to justify sometimes truly bizarre rules, such as the banning of soap (!) and the prohibition against putting one's hands in one's pockets even on snowy winter morning trips to the chow hall.

- The same correctional officers who thought it amusing to manually stimulate a German shepherd in order to send prisoners a message were also allowed to engage in unnecessary and unprofessional harassment of the "worst of the worst." To cite but one example among countless others, it was only during driving rain showers that inmates had to stand in single file for up to ten minutes outside the chow hall while the gun port officer serenaded us with jeers.

Incidents like the one just described were daily, sometimes even hourly occurrences throughout my stay at Wallens Ridge and eventually led to my being shot. While I was walking in circles in the pod day room—my primary form of exercise during those eleven months—I observed a newly arrived inmate empty his trash into the large bin next to the small guard's office. Of course the officer in the gun port shouted at him to *stop*—the prisoner had crossed the red line in front of the trash can without asking permission first, and crossing red lines was a shooting offense! The inmate thereupon referred to the guard by a common epithet for the anal opening, just barely loud enough for the officer to hear, and went on his way.

Only a few laps around the day room later, I heard the all-too-familiar *BANG* of a warning shot and immediately spread-eagled myself on the floor. As I began to swivel my head onto my chin, to allow me at least a partial view in front while still keeping some part of my head touching the ground as per prison rules, I saw all other inmates lying flat—except for the new man, who was half crouching and looking around to discover the source of the strange loud noise. He was definitely *not* making any hostile gestures or aggressive movements, nor was he standing close enough to anyone to pose a threat. (What he did wrong—apart from calling the guard with the gun a rectal cavity—was never explained to us.) At this point, while the prisoner looked around in confusion, the officer fired the live round of rubber bullets, knocking the man to the floor and scattering pellets all over that section of the pod day room.

Later I learned that several other bystanders were hit directly by the spreading cone of projectiles—their injuries were subsequently photographed by a guard—but the single black ball that hit me was only a ricochet. Although I realize this cannot be true, I seem to remember *seeing* the pellet flying toward me, smacking into my left bicep and then burrowing underneath my arm. The point of impact was only five or six inches from my face, since my arms were stretched out on the floor to either side.

Unlike those inmates in the direct line of fire, I cannot claim that getting hit by this rubber projectile hurt me physically in the least. Nor can the emotional damage inflicted on me be compared with that presumably suffered by those prisoners who experienced the full force of shotgun blasts on this and other occasions. But describing the comparatively minor effects of this incident on my psyche may give you some idea of how other inmates, who perhaps have fewer inner resources than I do, may have felt after they were shot.

Naturally I laughed the whole episode off at first as a particularly funny instance of correctional humor: a baptism-by-fire, "Wally's World" style! Over the next few days, however, I developed a strange combination of claustrophobia and agoraphobia—a strong urge to leave the cell but intense fear of entering the free fire zone again—as well as sleeplessness, depression, incipient panic attacks and a very greatly exaggerated sensitivity to any loud noise. These symptoms only began to fade after the paperwork for my transfer away from Wallens Ridge to my current medium-security facility was approved, but some other feelings lasted months and in one case even years.

Perhaps my strongest and scariest reaction to being shot was rage: not only had "they" locked me up for a crime I had not committed, but now "they" were even shooting at me for something I had not done! I felt myself approaching that dangerous "enough is enough" point where the urge to strike back becomes almost overwhelming, where the cornered animal wants to fight to the death. The more I brooded about "the slings and arrows of outrageous fortune," the more I wanted to hurt someone, anyone, as badly as I was hurting inside.

Thanks to my recently begun practice of Centering Prayer, I was able to let go of my fury eventually; twice each day, I relearned that my emotions were passing wisps of self—impermanent, unsatisfactory, and without substance—and that even my pain and rage would fade in time. What a miracle, that God had sent me this blessing just in time to help me at my lowest point! But without this gift of silent prayer or even the benefit of secular counseling, the overwhelming majority of inmates are, I fear, likely to emerge from similar experiences with a greatly increased propensity for future violence. That may help ensure that Virginia's excess prison capacity will eventually be reduced, but at what cost?

Self-disgust was another powerful feeling that grew in the bitter soil of this incident, and I have found it much harder to uproot than rage. While I do not consider myself an angry person by nature, I cannot persuade myself that fury was simply a foreign seed implanted in me. Clearly there had been rage latent within my heart all along, as in any human being—an ugly side of myself I had no wish to become acquainted with in such depth. To this day I resent that the Commonwealth of Virginia brought this dormant spore to life with the poisonous water of that shotgun blast.

I have no name for the last emotional consequence of being shot, nor can I properly describe it. All I can tell you is that before Wallens Ridge, I truly loved Bach and all baroque music, just about everyone's violin concerto, the usual romantic stuff by Liszt, Strauss, Rachmaninoff, etc., and the great ladies of jazz: Billie, Ella, Sarah, Lena and company. My tape collection was my most prized possession apart from my Bibles, because music breathed some beauty into the hideous world of the penitentiary every single day. After "Wally's World," on the other hand, I not only found myself unable to listen to any of my cassettes, classical or jazz, but experienced so strong an aversion to all music that I actually had to leave the cell whenever I tried to renew my former friendship with dear old Johann Sebastian, for instance.

How or why a single black rubber pellet could turn my love of music into hatred is a mystery to me, nor do I understand why this wound has not healed and faded as both rage and self-disgust eventually did. Perhaps something in me was broken permanently in Wallens Ridge State Prison. I do not know.

Love of music was not the only part of me that died at Wallens Ridge, however; I also lost my natural, hitherto unquestioned conviction that I was a full-fledged human being with inherent dignity and value. In spite of my arrest, my trial and my then thirteen years of incarceration, I had managed somehow to preserve a definite sense of my own worth, based on inner qualities such as compassion and intelligence, and on external factors, such as the love of family members and the respect of prisoners and even guards. I felt myself to be a man, and others treated me like one, too. Nothing could change that—or so I had thought.

What I learned during my time in supermax was that both the interior and exterior pillars of my supposed personhood were mere illusions. Although I was transferred to another prison before my compassion and intelligence were overcome by rage and self-disgust, I came close enough to being broken to know that I am not the man I thought I was. Nor am I the man I thought my fellow men believed me to be: in fact, they considered me so much of a monster that they built a seventy-million-dollar penitentiary just to teach me that I am no man at all.

> I am set apart with the dead,
>> like the slain who lie in the grave,
> whom you remember no more,
>> who are cut off from your care.
> You have put me in the lowest pit,
>> in the darkest depths.
>
> (Psalm 88:5, 6)

Perhaps my inability to listen to music stems from this hideous new-found knowledge that "in the lowest pit" nothing is certain, that "in the darkest pit" no one is inviolable. Somewhere in the back of my mind, I am still waiting for the next BANG!

Strangely enough, the very ferocity and violence of the super-max assault on my sense of identity proved to have an immediate and highly beneficial side effect for me personally. Approximately halfway through my stay in hell, I felt all my old, primarily intellectual ways of coping with reality to be so inadequate that I turned to something completely different, something non- (but not anti-) intellectual: Centering Prayer. And, miracle of miracles, it actually worked, even when I was shot a few months later.

Perhaps I should be grateful that the DOC's newest prison induced in me a level of anguish and desperation so deep that I finally tried out contemplative spirituality—but I am just a thankless wretch, I suppose. Or perhaps I am too honest to sugarcoat this bitter pill for myself or for you, my readers. The truth is that each one of my now three daily sessions of contemplation is also a quiet little reminder of Wallens Ridge, of the ugly discoveries I made there. And I cannot feel grateful for those.

Once upon a time, I *knew* I was a human being, as certainly as I knew my next breath would come. But now I have to *remind* myself that I am a real person, because in Wally's World I was not sure I was. They almost convinced me…

BANG!

2001: Denial of Final Appeal. Roughly six months after leaving Wallens Ridge, I underwent the fourth and so far last form of intellectual/conceptual pain on my own Way of the Prisoner: in January, 2001, the U. S. Supreme Court refused even to hear my attorney's final *habeas corpus* petition, thereby effectively ending any hope of justice and freedom for me. This decision not only robbed me of my future—I will never now work as an advocate for judicial and penal reform, nor will I ever have the opportunity to fall in love with someone sane and father a child of my own—but the court's ruling also stole my past—it officially and finally sanctioned the lie that I am guilty of Derek and Nancy Haysom's murders. Personally, I cannot imagine any crueler punishment than forcing a man to live for another three or four decades without purpose, without love, without truth and justice, without freedom and without hope. I would much rather be executed by whatever means the state finds convenient, for the Supreme Court's decision amounts to a living death sentence.

Letting go of my dreams of vindication by the judicial system was the most agonizing exercise in *apothesis* I have ever endured, and the fact that I practice contemplation does not mean that I am "at peace" with the monstrous and disgraceful injustice being inflicted on me. While Centering Prayer and Centering Practice help me preserve the integrity of my soul in circumstances that should by rights have driven me insane already, I refuse to resign myself to the violent crime being perpetrated against me this very minute: my wrongful imprisonment. Every single morning I wake up slightly surprised that I am not screeching uncontrollably, that I did not try to claw my way through the concrete walls with my fingernails as I slept. While I still had hope of vindication and justice, I could bear the loss of my native language and even Wallens Ridge because, so I believed, one day all my losses would be restored along with a cleared name and the public acknowledgment of my lack of guilt. But now that hope lies murdered in the vaunted halls of justice, *how can I go on?* I feel like tearing out my eyeballs so I will no longer have to look at the bars of my cage!

If that sentence shocks you, I have achieved my aim. I want you to feel, really feel just the tiniest pinch of the bowel-twisting agony that I experience every waking moment. Why? Because God helped me overcome even this suffering, as profound as it is—not escape it, because I continue to suffer every second of every day, but overcome it." And if he did this for me, he will help you as well.

All we need to do to allow God to transform and transcend our inner and outer prisons is to apply the fundamental method underlying both Centering Prayer and Centering Practice: we *accept* mental disturbances in prayer, we *embrace* our crosses in life, because we can only *let go* those apparent obstacles if we first refuse to attach to them negatively. This entirely counterintuitive principle is what lies at the heart of Christ's command to "love your *enemies* and pray for those who persecute you"; here, too, we are *stepping toward* our pain, our adversaries, in order to break the futile cycle of the self's grasping and rejecting (Matthew 5:44).

So that is what I decided to do when the U.S. Supreme Court in effect killed me: I began writing *The Way of the Prisoner* as a gift of love for those who are ultimately responsible for the hideous miscarriage of justice that ended my life—that is, for you.

You? Did you read that correctly? Do I really consider *you* my enemy? How can I blame *you* for the Supreme Court's ruling? Have I lost my mind?

Let me assure you that I am still in full control of my mental faculties, as I will shortly demonstrate. Imagine that you are suffering from a terminal illness that could have been prevented with some pills I have in my possession, and that I had earlier refused to give you this medicine—would you not rightly consider me your enemy? Well, from the perspective of my *de facto* execution—life in prison without parole—that is precisely what you did to me: you could have forestalled my death, but you did not.

Allow me to tell you the story of a man who was executed in Virginia in October of 2000, a well known case covered by state and even international media. In the week before his execution, this man's lawyers at last obtained permission to do a DNA test; the blood sample was found to have disappeared from the courthouse evidence file; the sample then reappeared in a different file, and in an opened evidence bag; the "sample" found in this bag was DNA-tested and determined to incriminate the suspect; and finally the man was executed, all in the space of one week. As incredible as it may seem, this actually happened in America in what was technically the first year of the twenty-first century. And of course this case is only one of many comparable travesties of justice in every state of the country. In these "law and order" times, there may well be another such outrage taking place in your local courthouse even as you read these pages.

Now, I have no earthly idea whether this man in Virginia was guilty or innocent, and I certainly make no plea for him. Nor do I tell you his story to argue that no society that calls itself civilized should ever permit an execution—or even a prison sentence—to be carried out under circumstances in which the integrity of the judicial process had been violated as grossly as it had been here. My point is, rather, that *you did not protest.*

Because this man was probably guilty—and I agree, he probably was—you turned your head and let him go to his death, when you *should* have been picketing the courthouse and the judge's home, organizing phone and e-mail campaigns, pounding down the doors of your local, state and national representatives with a dozen friends in tow, and buying ad space in your newspaper to publish an open letter from your committee of concerned citizens. Why should you have done all this? Certainly not for the sake of this one man, whose individual fate matters no more than does mine, but *to restore the integrity of your judicial system.* And the best way to do that is to shine the light of public attention onto dark, sordid affairs like this one: "[e]veryone who does evil hates the light, and will not come into the light for fear that his deeds will be exposed" (John 3:20).

Christ himself did precisely what I now accuse you of not having done, when he prevented the stoning of the woman caught in adultery—in those times a matter of criminal law, not a religious dispute. Although she was undoubtedly guilty of a capital crime, the adulterous woman's execution would nevertheless have been a miscarriage of justice because, as Jesus pointed out, the judicial process had become corrupted: "If any one of you is without sin, let him be the first to throw a stone at her" (John 8:7). The judges themselves had lost their integrity and thus had no standing to enforce the legally appropriate sentence.

But surely *you* cannot be expected to intervene in your society's court system as Christ intervened in his, can you? Well, let us see what scripture tells us:

> Speak for those who cannot speak for themselves,
>   for the rights of *all* who are destitute.
> Speak up and judge fairly;
>   defend the rights of the poor and needy. . . .
> Rescue those being led away to death;
>   hold back those staggering toward slaughter.
> If you say, "But we knew nothing about this,"
>   does not he who weighs the heart perceive it?
> Does not he who guards your life know it?
>   Will he not repay each person according to
>   what he has done?
>   (Proverbs 31:8, 9; 21:11, 12)

Oddly enough, there is no suggestion anywhere in this passage that only the innocent are to be rescued from execution—but that is merely an interesting aside. What matters to my quarrel with you is that feeble excuses like ignorance will not pass muster. Even if you have never heard of the case of the Virginia man I described above, you are certainly aware of similar mockeries of justices in your own state. And did *you* "[r]escue those being led away to death?"

Had you followed Jesus' example and done your Christian duty in at least some of these other cases, you would have sent a clear message to those who would like to manipulate the truth in order to achieve "justice": the ends do not justify the means, the rules apply to the "good" guys as well as to the "bad," the public prefers "honesty at all times" to "convictions at any price." Removing the pressure to bend, twist and break the law to achieve "success" may well have prevented the unnecessary, unjust ending of my own life by your country's legal system. If they had felt your eyes looking over their shoulders, the prosecution team members at my trial might not have dared change the size of the crucial "incriminating" sockprint so frequently, and the U. S. Supreme Court might not have been so quick to dismiss my lawyer's *habeas*. Who else but you, a citizen of the United States and a child of God, could have saved me from their possibly well-intentioned zeal to keep me in prison forever?

But it is too late now; I am dead, beyond your help and that of anyone else's. Of course Virginia's governor has the power to order me paroled at any time, whereupon I would be deported to Germany—but he would thereby be freeing a man whom the highest court in the land determined to be guilty of double murder, and no politician can afford to do that. And, yes, the governor also has the power to pardon me, to clear my name completely and perhaps appoint me as advisor to his new blue-ribbon commission on legal reform—but on what grounds would he take such an unprecedentedly courageous step? All the new evidence that has emerged since my trial does not exonerate me clearly, but only raises reasonable doubt; that would have sufficed to free me at a court-ordered retrial by a new judge and jury, but no governor will release me on what the voting public might perceive to be a technicality. And, in any case, who would persuade him to give me justice—*you*?

All I can do now is to try to use the ending of my life as a means to be "united with [Christ] in his death" by loving my enemies even as I hang on my cross (Romans 6:5). So I embrace this gravest form of intellectual/conceptual pain willingly, honestly, non-attachedly and in a spirit of service by giving you *The Way of the Prisoner*, in hope that this record of my own spiritual journey will convince you to try Centering Prayer for yourself. And part of this proof of my soul is to impress upon you that, if my thinking were still worldly or "natural," I would be drowning in such bitterness that even *you* would seem like another enemy to me— which of course you are not. If Centering Prayer and Centering Practice have shown *me* the rightness of helping my "enemies"— the taxpaying citizens of a country that imposed a living death sentence on me for a crime of which I am not guilty—then surely *The Way of the Prisoner* can also help *you* overcome the most severe challenges, the toughest "prisons," and become "transformed into [Christ's] . . . likeness with ever-increasing glory" (2 Corinthians 3:18).

———

Oratio

O Lord,
A barred slit in the wall leaks milky light
into a twilit cell, warming the stains
and scabs of double wounds that now lack sight,
recalling what was lost and what remains.

Delilah and the sun are gone; and yet
the God of light and love sneaks in to kiss

my face. If light is real, dare I forget
the Love divine whose earthly form I miss?

I can't forget what last I saw before
flames closed my eyes: her smile as she held high
my hair; two lips that once seemed like a door
to paradise. Was love always a lie?

The light I loved in her I thought was You,
O God. But if her love was false, was then
Your love untrue? Or did my lies undo
her love? Or is love not of God, but men?

In the great hall, the mothers of the sons
I slew scream hate, throw fruit, make me their toy;
their love wants death. O Judge Divine, which one
are you—their vengeful love, or mine of joy?

A thousand years from now, in Babylon,
Three scribes will claim I pushed the great hall
    down.
Well, prisoners need fairy tales, and gone
And buried will be doubts that plague me now.

A boy leads me from jeers and taunts to rest
against a pillar: childish hands so soft,
as once Delilah's were in mine. What's best,
to kill this boy, the crowds in stands aloft,

all for the sake of God? I touch my hair,
My link and pledge to You: what shall love dare?

What shall love dare? One answer to that question is Paul's letter to Philemon, a frequently overlooked part of our New

Testament whose significance I shall explain in the *contemplatio* section that follows.

> Paul, a prisoner of Christ Jesus, and Timothy our brother,
>
> To Philemon our dear friend and fellow worker, to Apphia our sister, to Archippus our fellow soldier and to the church that meets in your home:
>
> Grace to you and peace from God our Father and the Lord Jesus Christ.
>
> I always thank my God as I remember you in my prayers, because I hear about your faith in the Lord Jesus and your love for all the saints. I pray that you may be active in sharing your faith, so that you will have a full understanding of every good thing we have in Christ. Your love has given me great joy and encouragement, because you, my brother, have refreshed the hearts of the saints.
>
> Therefore, although in Christ I could be bold and order you to do what you ought to do, yet I appeal to you on the basis of love. I then, as Paul—an old man and now also a prisoner of Christ Jesus—I appeal to you for my son Onesimus, who became my son while I was in chains. Formerly he was useless to you, but now he has become useful both to you and to me.
>
> I am sending him—who is my very heart—back to you. I would have liked to keep him with me so that he could take your place in helping me while I am in chains for the gospel. But I did not want to do anything without your consent, so that any favor you do will be spontaneous and not forced. Perhaps the reason he was separated from you for a little while was that you might have him back for good—no longer as a slave, but better than a slave, as a dear brother. He is very dear to me, but even dearer to you, both as a man and as a brother in the Lord.

So if you consider me a partner, welcome him as you would welcome me. If he has done you any wrong or owes you anything, charge it to me. I, Paul, am writing this with my own hand. I will pay it back—not to mention that you owe me your very self. I do wish, brother, that I may have some benefit from you in the Lord; refresh my heart in Christ. Confident of your obedience, I write to you, knowing that you will do even more than I ask.

And one thing more: prepare a guest room for me, because I hope to be restored to you in answer to your prayers.

Epaphras, my fellow prisoner in Christ Jesus, sends you greetings. And so do Mark, Aristarchus, Demas and Luke, my fellow workers.

The grace of the Lord Jesus Christ be with your spirit.

Contemplatio

1—Ebed-Melech and the Gerasene Demoniac

We have nearly reached the end of our long journey, the Way of the Prisoner; I thank you for your patience and ask you for just a little more as we travel our road to its conclusion. In some ways, this *contemplatio* section is the most important part of the path—perhaps only indirectly for me, but hopefully directly for you.

As you will recall, the purpose of each Book's *contemplatio* section is to provide a specific spiritual exercise that allows us to absorb the relatively theoretical insights of the preceding *meditatio* sections into the very fiber of our souls, transforming our interactions with reality instead of merely adding another layer of facts and concepts. That approach worked very well with Centering Prayer and contemplation, but how are we now to find a common Centering Practice technique that trains us to bear our crosses voluntarily, honestly, non-attachedly and in a spirit of service? Surely my steel and concrete penitentiary is far too different from your prison, whatever it may be, for there to be a method we both can use with equal effectiveness.

Well, let us examine precisely how Centering Prayer and contemplation changed our inner worlds and see if we can transfer the underlying principle to Centering Practice:

- To help us break the self's physical, emotional and intellectual/conceptual attachments to the world, we confront those spiritual chains over and over and over again during Centering Prayer, until they fade away into near-nothingness.
- To teach us to let go of the concept of a self itself, we continually and repeatedly note the impermanence, unsatisfactoriness and lack of inherent substance of all the self's manifestations during contemplation, thus dissolving the bars of our inner cages in the acid bath of insight into their ephemeral nature.

So, have you spotted the solution? It really is so very simple: to learn how to carry your cross willingly, truthfully, dispassionately and altruistically—that is, to transform your metaphorical prison into your means of salvation—*you must go to a real penitentiary over and over and over again, as a tutor, visitor or even minister.*

- *Volunteering* to help convicts change their lives is a graphic and meaningful way of embracing your cross, your own prisonerhood.
- By giving three hours of your time every week to this spiritual exercise, you are training yourself to face your own captive suffering *truthfully*; each visit to jail is a vivid reminder that will last till the following week.

- Seeing your own life's figurative chains in the context of convicts' literal handcuffs and leg irons helps you develop *non-attachment* to your anguish.
- Most importantly, by giving of yourself to men and women behind bars, you transform your cross into a vehicle for *serving others* and thus imitate Christ in the purest form possible.

Becoming a prison volunteer in order to sharpen your contemplative skills, to practice *letting go*, is not as farfetched an idea as you may think. Father Thomas Keating, co-founder of the Centering Prayer movement, conducts workshops for convicts in Folsom Penitentiary; and Father Richard Rohr, another leading author and teacher in this field, also has an active prison ministry. For a more detailed explanation of the spiritual benefits of tutoring barely literate inmates in remedial English, say, we must however turn to that wise seeker of truth in silence with whom we began Book I of *The Way of the Prisoner*: the Dalai Lama. In 1999 His Holiness gave a speech expounding the famous *Eight Verses for Training the Mind* by the Tibetan sage Geshe Langri Tangpa (1054–1123), the fourth of which addresses our question of the advantages you may reap by "[r]emembering those in prison as if you were their fellow prisoners" (Hebrews 13:3):

Verse Four

When I see beings of a negative disposition
or those oppressed by negativity or pain,
may I, as if finding a treasure, consider them precious,
for they are rarely met.

You can then go on to apply this sentiment to society in general. Among ordinary people there is a temptation or tendency to reject certain groups of people, to marginalize them and not want to embrace them within the wider fold of the community. People who are branded as criminals are an example. In these cases, it is even more important for the practitioner to make an extra effort, to try to embrace them, so that they may be given a second chance in society and also an opportunity to restore their sense of self-esteem. . . . [I]f that person, instead of responding to you in a positive way and repaying your kindness, inflicts harm upon you, normally you feel, as an ordinary person, a sense of outrage. . . . For a true practitioner, it is suggested that one not give in to that kind of normal response but rather to utilize the opportunity as one for training, as a lesson or a teaching. The practitioner should regard that person as a true teacher of patience because that is when the training of patience is most needed. . . .

However, this is not to suggest that a true practitioner should simply yield to whatever harm or injustice is being inflicted upon him or her. In fact, according to the precepts of the *bodhisattva*, one should respond to injustice with a strong countermeasure, especially if there is any danger that the perpetrator of the crime is going to continue negative actions in the future, or if other sentient beings are adversely affected. What is required is sensitivity to context.[6]

Our context is a Christian, not a Buddhist one, of course, so we should examine carefully whether Jesus agrees with the Dalai Lama that we should "make an extra effort to embrace . . . [p]eople who are branded as criminals." As it turns out, Christ addressed precisely this issue in the Parable of the Sheep and the Goats:

Then the King will say to those on his right, "Come, you who are blessed by my Father; take your inheritance, the kingdom prepared for you since the creation of the world. For I was hungry and you gave me something to eat, I was thirsty and you gave me something to drink, I was a stranger and you invited me in, I needed clothes and you clothed me, I was sick and you looked after me, *I was in prison and you came to visit me.*"

(Matthew 25:34–36, emphasis added)

This injunction to visit prisoners is commonly misinterpreted as applying only to missionaries incarcerated for their beliefs, perhaps because common criminals are so obviously unworthy of Christian love. But while the New Testament contains many calls for support of persecuted proselytizers, the context *here* is entirely different. The prisoners Christ speaks of in this passage are in fact one of several different groups of people distinguished, not by their apostolic activity, but by their misfortune. The hungry are not starving themselves *for Jesus*, those without clothes did not become nudists *for the Messiah*, and the sick are not running a fever *for the son of God*; we are not supposed to help them because they are suffering *for Christ* but simply because they are in need. So there is no justification for limiting our charity for the last group, prisoners, only to those who are behind bars *for their faith*.

But, you may object, while Jesus claimed he did "not come to call the righteous, but sinners," we never see him visiting an actual *jail* in the gospels, so how can we be sure he really wanted us to help *criminals* (Mark 2:17)? My reply is that you do indeed see Jesus not only visiting but freeing prisoners on *two* occasions, the first of which occurred in the Gentile territory of the Gerasenes:

[A] man lived in the tombs, and no one could bind him any more, not even with a chain. For he had often been chained hand and foot, but he tore the chains apart and broke the irons on his feet. No one was strong enough to subdue him. Night and day among the tombs and in the hills he would cry out and cut himself with stones.

(Mark 5:3–5)

As soon as you encounter a few real inmates, as opposed to the caricatures seen on TV, you will immediately recognize the Gerasene Demoniac as a typical convict: possessed by an evil spirit, leading a life devoted to death ("liv[ing] in the tombs"), uncontrollable even with chains and bars, and—if you bother to look closely enough—"cry[ing] out and cut[ting] himself." I knew a man only a few years ago who spent his meager inmate wages on getting one tattoo after another of the name of his wife, for whose murder he was serving thirty years.[7] If this acquaintance of mine is not *precisely* the kind of man whom Christ released both from the physical prison-exile of the tombs and from the emotional prison of mental illness, then I have entirely misunderstood the whole point of the son of God's mission on earth, and you should throw away this volume immediately.

The healing of the Gerasene Demoniac, as wonderful as it is, cannot compare to the first occasion on which Jesus freed a jailbird, one of my favorite passages in all of scripture. To understand the significance of the following narrative from the book of Jeremiah, it helps to know that the Hebrew name "Ebed-Melech" means "Servant-King," one of the titles of our Messiah[8]; and that our Old Testament is full of such "Christophanies," appearances or pre-figurings of the Trinity's second person before his actual incarnation as Jesus:

So [King Zedekiah's princes] . . . took Jeremiah and put him into the cistern of Malkijah, the king's son, which was in the courtyard of the guard. They lowered Jeremiah by ropes into the cistern; it had no water in it, only mud, and Jeremiah sank down into the mud.

But Ebed-Melech, a Cushite, an official in the royal palace, heard that they had put Jeremiah into the cistern. While the king was sitting in the Benjamin Gate, Ebed-Melech went out of the palace and said to him, "My lord the king, these men have acted wickedly in all they have done to Jeremiah the prophet. They have thrown him into the cistern, where he will starve to death when there is no longer any bread in the city." Then the king commanded Ebed-Melech, "Take thirty men from here with you and lift Jeremiah the prophet out of the cistern before he dies."

So Ebed-Melech took the men with him and went to a room under the treasury in the palace. He took some old rags and worn-out clothes from there and let them down to Jeremiah in the cistern. Ebed-Melech the Cushite said to Jeremiah, "Put these old rags and worn-out clothes under your arms to pad the ropes." Jeremiah did so, and they pulled him up with the ropes and lifted him out of the cistern. And Jeremiah remained in the courtyard of the guard.

(Jeremiah 38:6–13)

What I love about this account is the telling details: the author even knew in which room of the palace the old rags and worn-out clothes were kept, leading me to conclude that he was actually involved in this incident. And note the gentleness, the concern Ebed-Melech showed by not only releasing Jeremiah but taking care to pad the ropes.

Since both the healing of the Gerasene Demoniac and the jailbreak of Jeremiah involved actually freeing the convicts concerned, the question naturally arises whether the *release* of prisoners should be the ultimate objective of prison volunteering. While the New Testament is relatively mute on this subject—perhaps because Christ's call to forgive sinners "seventy-seven times" was thought to suffice—the Old Testament contains several definitive statements on the correct Biblical parole and pardon policy for *reformed* ex-offenders (Matthew 18:22):

But if men are bound in chains
    held fast by cords of affliction,

he tells them what they have done—
    that they have sinned arrogantly.
He makes them listen to correction
    and commands them to repent of their evil.
If they obey and serve him,
    they will spend the rest of their days in pros-
    perity
    and their years in contentment.
                             (Job 36:8–11)

Of course recidivists "will perish by the sword and die without knowledge," but according to the Psalter, one "strike" definitely does not mean you are "out" forever:

Some sat in darkness and the deepest gloom,
    prisoners suffering iron chains,
for they had rebelled against the word of God
    and despised the counsel of the Most High.
So he subjected them to bitter labor;
    they stumbled, and there was no one to help.
Then they cried to the Lord in their trouble,
    and he saved them from their distress.
He brought them out of darkness and the deepest
    gloom
    and broke away their chains.
Let them give thanks to the Lord for his unfailing
    love
    and his wonderful deeds for men,
for he breaks down gates of bronze
    and cuts through bars of iron.
                       (Psalm 107:10–16)

According to Isaiah, God wants to "release from the dungeon those who sit in darkness," while Ezekiel claims that "if a wicked man turns away from all the sins he has committed, . . . [n]one of the offenses he has committed will be remembered against him" (Isaiah 42:5; Ezekiel 18:21–23). Who would have thought that the Old Testament was so "soft on crime"?

The strong, consistent scriptural emphasis on actually liberating *reformed* convicts has direct implications for today's prison volunteers, of course. For instance, since freedom is meaningless if released inmates are not given the tools to *remain* free, you may incarnate Ebed-Melech's spirit more truly by giving a parolee a job in your business than by holding weekly Bible study sessions behind bars. (Hiring ex-felons entitles you to significant federal tax breaks and free bonding services, by the way.)[9] If you become involved in criminal justice issues either by volunteering or by political action, I suggest you acquire your denomination's published statements on crime and social policy and visit the websites listed in this endnote.[10] Perhaps your involvement in this problematic area can be the first step to actually implementing a Christian penal policy in this country.

One of the first questions that will come to your mind when you study this subject is why the "land of the free" incarcerates a greater percentage of its own population than *any* other country on earth. As a European who has also spent several years in a European prison—albeit an outmoded pre-trial "remand" prison— I find it noteworthy that *all* European countries impose much shorter sentences on their criminals; require far more psychological treatment, education and training of inmates while serving time; and finally expend significantly greater effort on reintegrating offenders into society as taxpaying citizens with full voting and civil rights. The fact that European crime rates are also generally lower than America's may or may not be connected to these policy differences; you can form your own opinion by asking a few real convicts whether the thought of prison even so much as crossed their drug-hazed minds before they committed their crimes. As far as cost-effectiveness is concerned, the RAND Corporation and other policy think tanks have found without exception that as a means of reducing crime, treatment is not only cheaper but also more successful than jail by several factors of ten.[11]

That may all sound as if I advocate liberal correctional policies, but you might be surprised at the toughness of my own pet proposals for certain categories of inmates. After all, I have spent more than a decade and a half locked into cages with many men who truly should never see the free world again—*unless* they change, that is. For as Christians, we simply are not permitted to deny any potential child of God the opportunity to reform:

> If your brother sins, rebuke him, and if he repents, forgive him. If he sins against you seven times in a day and seven times comes back to you and says, "I repent," forgive him. . . . [I]f you forgive men their trespasses, your heavenly Father also will forgive you; but if you do not forgive men their trespasses, neither will your Father forgive your trespasses.
>   (Luke 17:4; Matthew 7:14, 15)

The persistent practice of forgiveness on our part, coupled with practical acts of charity, may in fact *induce* our seeming enemies to repent, according to Paul and Solomon:

> Do not take revenge, my friends, but . . . on the contrary:
> "If your enemy is hungry, feed him;
> if he is thirsty, give him something to drink.
> In doing this, you will heap burning coals on his head."
> Do not be overcome by evil, but overcome evil with good.
>   (Romans 12:19–21, quoting Proverbs 25:21, 22)

In the ancient Near East, placing hot coals on the head was a public sign of repentance much like wearing sackcloth and ashes, so what this passage suggests is that we can shame others into changing their ways by requiting their aggression with practical acts of love. Of course this technique works neither immediately nor every time, but you need not be a Mahatma Gandhi or a Martin Luther King, Jr., to practice it successfully. Even I have managed to use it to teach some truly reptilian sleazeballs how to show me respect, simply by *insisting* on treating them as the full human beings they might one day become.

Perhaps some such undeserved, almost unnerving gesture of kindness lay at the heart of Christ's healing of the Gerasene Demoniac. But regardless of what spiritual technique Jesus used on that Gentile tomb-dweller, I think it is important to realize just how central the Messiah himself believed the rehabilitation of outcasts and convicts to be to his ministry. In the keynote sermon he gave at the very beginning of his public career, just after he battled the devil in the desert, Christ featured the liberation of captives as one of the central planks of his program:

Jesus returned to Galilee in the power of the Spirit, and . . . went into the synagogue, . . . [and] stood up to read:

> "The Spirit of the Lord is on me,
> > because he has anointed me
> > to preach good news to the poor.
> He has sent me to proclaim freedom for the prisoners
> > and recovery of sight to the blind,
> to release the oppressed,
> to proclaim the year of the Lord's favor."
> (Luke 4:14, 16, 18, 19, quoting Isaiah 61:1, 2)

From that synagogue, Christ left to cure *real* blind people, heal *real* lepers and, in the case of the Gerasene Demoniac, free *real* prisoners; we do our older brother an injustice if we interpret his very first public sermon as being meant only metaphorically.

What I find especially interesting as a contemplative as well as a convict is that Jesus held this sermon *immediately* upon overcoming the devil's physical, emotional and intellectual/conceptual temptations during the prayer retreat we examined so long ago in Book I. This suggests to me that Centering Prayer not only leads to Centering Practice generally, but that there is a profound spiritual connection between freeing our souls of the chains of self during contemplation and liberating our "poor . . . [im]prisone[d] . . . blind . . . [and] oppressed" brothers and sisters from their quite literal bonds. It is no accident, I think, that Christ spent his last few hours on earth, not holding some eternal sermon from the cross, but conversing with "two other men, both criminals," on the crosses next to his (Luke 23:32). "Deep calls to deep" here, that much is clear; we cannot travel the Way of the Prisoner alone but must release our fellow captives, too (Psalm 42:7).

When I write "we" in this context, I mean not only you but myself as well. I practice contemplation with practically fanatical dedication, and I know myself to be a child of God; *I believe.* And since "the only thing that counts is faith expressing itself through love," I must *live* my convictions through *acts* of love (Galatians 5:6). "[F]aith without deeds is dead" (James 2:26).

So, how can I help free a repentant convict even from my own prison? By following the model that Paul gave us in his letter to Philemon, quoted in the preceding *oratio* section: a prayer-in-action that in our day and age would take the form of a letter of support to the parole board. The slave Onesimus was a criminal, after all, a thief who had stolen his master's property by running away. But since he was repentant and willing to take responsibility for his crime, Paul asked Philemon for clemency, for parole, for pardon. And, best of all, he did so from his own jail cell.

That is precisely what I have tried to do for Elizabeth Roxanne Haysom. On October 1, 2002, I sent a letter to the Governor of

Virginia, asking that she be paroled and deported to Canada if she admits her guilt and shows repentance as Onesimus did. This is what it means to travel the Way of the Prisoner to its end; this is the logic of the cross.

2—An Open Letter to the Governor of Virginia

Your Excellency, I respectfully request that you parole Elizabeth Roxanne Haysom to her Immigration and Naturalization Service detainer for deportation to her home country of Canada, conditional upon her institutional behavior and her full acceptance of responsibility for her crime.

Paroling Ms. Haysom at this time would be in accordance with the general Biblical injunction to let "[m]ercy triumph over judgment" (James 2:13), and with the circumstances which obtain in this case, to wit:

- Age: Ms. Haysom was only nineteen years old at the time of the crime, which in my home country of Germany would make her subject to the juvenile court system. While your country's laws and traditions obviously differ greatly, I hope you will take into consideration that she had not yet developed the judgment and wisdom of an adult when she broke the law.

- Drug abuse: Ms. Haysom claims she was under the influence of heroin and other mood-altering substances at the time of the crime, and I believe this to be true. While this is not a mitigating circumstance, it is worth noting that Ms. Haysom became addicted to drugs long before the present crime, when by law she was not fully responsible for her actions. Moreover, I understand that she has successfully completed a drug treatment program while incarcerated.

- Mental illness: According to a respected Virginia forensic psychiatrist—as well as two nationally known English forensic psychiatrists—Ms. Haysom suffered from a borderline personality disorder (borderline psychosis) when she broke the law, a recognized mental illness that may not qualify as legal insanity but certainly should—and in many of this country's states would—reduce her criminal responsibility to a considerable extent.

- Family problems / motive: In a letter she sent me shortly after the murders, Ms. Haysom wrote, "I thought we did this so I could be free"—but free from what? While her 1987 sentencing hearing revealed some testimony and even material evidence indicating abuse, we cannot know now with any certainty whether this played any role in Ms. Haysom's motivation. We do know, however, that problems within her family were sufficiently severe for her to run away from home as a teen with her girlfriend for over a year. Any crime occurs in a context, including this one; wisdom and mercy suggest that you factor this background information into your decision.

- Lack of premeditation: While Ms. Haysom undoubtedly fantasized extensively about her parents' deaths before the murders, this does not necessarily mean that she planned the crime rationally, and I personally do not believe she did. In fact, the choice of weapon (knife) and the frenzied nature of the attack (an excess of very shallow stab wounds along with exaggeratedly deep neck injuries) suggest that the killings were committed in the heat of passion, under the influence of drugs and mental illness—all fueled by her fantasies, presumably, but not premeditated. The primary symptom of a borderline personality disorder (borderline psychosis) like Ms. Haysom's is that its victims cannot clearly distinguish between fantasy and reality, and the further blurring of this line by the use of narcotics is almost certainly the immediate cause of this terrible tragedy.

- Possible presence of accomplices / primary perpetrators: Since the victims in this case were killed in non-adjacent rooms with a knife/knives, there logically had to be more than one perpetrator. Additionally, forensic evidence indicates the presence of more than one attacker at the crime scene: small sock- and shoeprints inside, and very large bootprints outside the house (all in blood). This other person / these other people may not only have been accomplices but possibly even the primary perpetrator(s), thus at least potentially reducing Ms. Haysom's culpability.

- Length of time served: Ms. Haysom has served over one and a half decades in prison at the time of this writing. Given her relative youth at the time of her arrest, she has therefore spent nearly half of her life behind bars. No amount of time can be "enough" to atone for this crime, so the question really becomes whether any useful purpose is served by continuing to incarcerate Ms. Haysom. Certainly no nineteen-year-old resident of Virginia will decide to kill her parents tomorrow because Elizabeth Haysom was paroled after "only" sixteen years in jail! At the time of her plea and sentencing, that number of years was considered the length of a typical life sentence.

- Public safety: Since Ms. Haysom will be deported to Canada if paroled and cannot reenter the United States, the citizens of Virginia will be completely and permanently safe from her. What is more, the recidivism rate of paroled domestic murderers—and that, after all, is what this case is—approaches zero. Ms. Haysom hated two very specific people who now, tragically, are dead, and I firmly believe she will not harm anyone else again.

- Institutional record: It is my understanding that Ms. Haysom has an exceptional institutional record. Sixteen years of good behavior cannot be faked, especially in the high stress environment of prison. If she were in any way violent or still abusing drugs, some sign of such problems would have emerged by now.

Your Excellency, I hope you will consider all of these factors and accede to my request to parole and deport Ms. Haysom, so long as you determine that she has demonstrated her rehabilitation and accepted full responsibility for her true role in the murders of her parents. You have an awesome responsibility here—"in the same way you judge others, you will be judged"—but also a wonderful opportunity—to "[b]e kind and compassionate to one another, forgiving each other, just as in Christ God forgave you" (Matthew 7:2, Ephesians 4:32).

Respectfully yours,
Jens Soering

PS: If you can find the time—or perhaps especially if you *cannot* find the time and feel "chained" to your desk—please read my book, *The Way of the Prisoner*. It teaches an ancient Christian form of prayer called contemplation, which may help you deal with the stress of your position, free your soul of its worldly attachments, and bring you closer to God. This letter to you is actually the grand finale of my book, a sort of living demonstration of the spiritual principles I advocate.

Why not give it a try?

3—A Concluding Note and Request to My Readers

I now pose the same question to you, my reader: why not give the Way of the Prisoner a try right now? You realize, of course, that Virginia's governor will pay no attention to my letter on Elizabeth's behalf because I am a mere convict. But if you and a couple of thousand other readers of this volume add your voices to mine, then the governor *may* relent and parole and deport her.

So take this opportunity to begin your own transformation into an Ebed-Melech, a younger brother or sister of Christ, and scribble out a few lines of support for your sister, Elizabeth. The governor's address is:

> Governor, Commonwealth of Virginia
> State Capitol Building
> Richmond VA 23219
> Tel.: 804-786-2211

You need not even insist on Elizabeth's "full acceptance of responsibility for her crime," as I did in my letter. Nothing she says can possibly help me anyway, because there is no legal vehicle for re-opening my case in any court. My friends and advisors insisted that I cannot plead for her release without requiring that she tell the truth, but *you* can be more generous than I. Perhaps she needs some *unmerited* grace or blessing before she can make that turn away from self and toward God. Can any of us claim that we have never benefited from undeserved grace ourselves?

Notes

1. Meister Eckhart, op. cit.
2. Seneca, trans. Campbell, R., *Letters from a Stoic* (New York: Penguin Books, 1969).
3. "Flickin' Joe's" nickname and some personal characteristics have been changed to protect his identity.
4. Some personal characteristics of all of these inmates have been changed to protect their identities.
5. Hammack, Laurence, "Connecticut settles lawsuits in supermax deaths," *The Roanoke Times*, March 15, 2002.
6. His Holiness the XIV Dalai Lama, Tenzin Gyatso, *Training the Mind* (Somerville, MA: Wisdom Publications, 1999).
7. Some personal characteristics of this inmate have been changed to protect his identity.
8. Strong, James, op. cit.
9. Work Opportunity Tax Credit: 877-USA-JOBS; Federal Bonding Program: 800-233-2258.
10. www.ncjrs.org—one of the best sources of information on criminal justice issues;
    www.albany.edu/sourcebook—statistical data on all aspects of criminal justice;
    www.ojp.usdoj.gov—information on crime trends and correctional policy;
    www.cjcj.org—reports by the Justice Policy Institute;

www.sentencingproject.org/news/usno1.pdf—international comparison of incarceration rates; also www.sentencingproject.org/brief/pub1035.pdf—*Facts About Prisons and Prisoners*;

www.deathpenaltyinfo.org—Death Penalty Information Center;
www.curenational.org/new—Citizens United for the Rehabilitation of Errants;
www.centurionministries.org—has won the release of twenty-five people wrongly convicted and sentenced to death or life in prison;
www.criminaljustice.org—National Association of Criminal Defense Lawyers;
www.crimelynx.com—criminal justice resource with news, links and forums; and www.prisonstudies.com—Centre for Prison Studies, King's College, London, UK

11. Caulkins, Jonathan P. et al., *Mandatory Minimum Drug Sentences: Throwing Away the Key or the Taxpayers' Money?* (Santa Monica, CA: RAND Corporation, 1997).

AFTERWORD

"Bᴜᴛ ɪs ɪᴛ ᴇɴᴏᴜɢʜ?" a friend of mine recently asked me. "If you really have to spend the rest of your life behind bars, is Centering Prayer enough to sustain you?"

"Of course not," I answered. "Teresa of Avila said, 'This is the reason for prayer . . . the birth always of good works, good works.' Without Centering Practice, self-giving service, Centering Prayer alone degenerates into spiritual self-indulgence."

"Then how will you live for another three or four decades behind bars? Can you help other prisoners, maybe teach them Centering Prayer?" my friend asked.

I had to pause for a moment before I replied, "I don't think so. We can't lift others out of the same hole we're in, any more than we can bootstrap ourselves out of it. To be someone else's Ebed-Melech, I would need to come from outside that person's hole, his prison, so I have some place to stand when I pull him up."

"Hm . . . Makes you wonder whether that little nun from Skopje would have become 'Mother Teresa' if she had *not* left home and traveled all the way to India, doesn't it?" my friend mused. I shrugged my shoulders, so he continued, "But I have to ask you again: how can you go on?"

"I don't know," I said. "I don't know if I *can* go on."

> I cry to you, O Lord;
>   I say, "You are my refuge,
>   my portion in the land of the living."
> Listen to my cry,
>   for I am in desperate need;
> rescue me from those who pursue me,
>   for they are too strong for me.
> Set me free from my prison,
>   that I may praise your name.
> Then the righteous will gather about me
>   because of your goodness to me.
>
> (Psalm 142:5–7)

A POSTCRIPT ON CENTERING TERMINOLOGY

AFTER COMPLETING THE MANUSCRIPT of *The Way of the Prisoner*, I had the astonishing effrontery to send it to Father Thomas Keating, from whose works I had learned Centering Prayer. And he had the even more astonishing kindness both to read my manuscript and to pass it on to his own publisher, who is now my publisher: Lantern Books. Not content to restrict his generosity to this act of literary assistance, Father Keating then entered into a lengthy correspondence with me about contemplation and writing. What a gift! No ordinary author would have bothered to read some unknown convict's scribblings, help him find a publisher and send him encouraging personal letters.

Father Keating's response to me is, I believe, the best possible proof of the truth of one of the central theses of *The Way of the Prisoner*: that the spiritual liberation brought about through Centering Prayer practically *compels* practitioners to help free "real" prisoners of their literal chains. Deep calls to deep! Of course Father Keating was conducting workshops in penitentiaries long before he ever heard of me, but this time it was Jeremiah Soering whom Ebed-Melech Keating pulled out of the cistern.

My correspondence with Father Keating has been both a priv-
ilege and a joy, but it has also revealed that we use the terms
"Centering" and "concentration" in slightly differing ways.
Because I encourage all of my readers to study Father Keating's
Open Mind, Open Heart very carefully, I believe it would be help-
ful to explain these variations in terminology:

1. I use "Centering Prayer" and "to center" in a comparative-
    ly restricted sense to refer to the process of letting go gen-
    tly of sensations, feelings and thoughts. This is also what I
    mean by "concentration": turning away from self and
    becoming attentive to God. "Contemplation," under my
    definition, is the state of *being* attentive to God; I call this
    the "expansion" phase of prayer, as opposed to the preced-
    ing "concentration" phase. While *becoming* and *being* are
    obviously very similar, I have found it useful to explain and
    teach them separately (in Books II and III of *The Way*,
    respectively[1]) because that is how I myself learned them. I
    believe most novices will similarly benefit from learning
    how to walk before they try to tango.
2. Father Keating uses the term "Centering Prayer" more
    widely both for the *becoming* and the *being* attentive to
    God, but especially for the *being*. He prefers using "atten-
    tion" rather than "concentration" for the *becoming*,
    because he understands concentration to involve acts of
    the will, imagery, concepts and reflections. As you will
    recall from the relevant sections of Books II and III of *The
    Way*, acts of the will (effort and "trying") are all manifesta-
    tions of the self that must be avoided, so I completely con-
    cur with Father Keating on this point—though perhaps
    not on his aversion to the word "concentration"!

Father Keating rightly emphasizes that both Centering Prayer
and contemplation are receptive practices that must not be con-

fused with a mantra-type discipline like Father John Main's. It is for this very reason, of course, that I advise my readers to use a graduated system of ever-subtler focal points—prayer word, breath, a blank spot of no-thing (Keating's "simple inward gaze")—to reach the state of "general loving attentiveness toward God" (St. John of the Cross). While I believe most people, like me, need to be eased into this spiritual discipline step by step, I agree that an effortless, simple presence to the Presence within is the essence of contemplation.

Whether you prefer to think of yourself as being "attentive to the Spirit (*pneuma*)" or "concentrating on the breath (*pneuma*)" is probably secondary. Here is the real test: is Centering Prayer transforming you into Ebed-Melech? Can you imagine lavishing as much care and concern on a mere convict as Father Keating has shown me? "For a tree is known by its fruit" (Matthew 12:33).

Notes
1. Book II, *contemplatio*, Ch. 7; Book II, *contemplatio*, Ch. 8; Book III, *meditatio*, Ch. 7; Book III, *contemplatio*, Ch. 4.

APPENDIX

The Method of Centering Prayer

© Thomas Keating

Theological Background

The grace of Pentecost affirms that the risen Jesus is among us as the glorified Christ. Christ lives in each of us as the Enlightened One, present everywhere and at all times. He is the living Master who continuously sends the Holy Spirit to dwell within us and to bear witness to his resurrection by empowering us to experience and manifest the fruits of the Spirit and the Beatitudes both in prayer and action.

Lectio Divina

Lectio divina is the most traditional way of cultivating friendship with Christ. It is a way of listening to the texts of scripture as if we were in conversation with Christ and he were suggesting the topics of conversation. The daily encounter with Christ and reflection on his word leads beyond mere acquaintanceship to an attitude of friendship, trust and love. Conversation simplifies and gives way to communing, or as Gregory the Great (sixth century), summarizing the Christian contemplative tradition, put it "resting in God." This was the classical meaning of contemplative prayer for the first sixteen centuries.

Contemplative Prayer

Contemplative prayer is the normal development of the grace of baptism and the regular practice of *lectio divina*. We may think of prayer as thoughts or feelings expressed in words. But this is only one expression. Contemplative prayer is the opening of mind and heart—our whole being—to God, the Ultimate Mystery, beyond thoughts, words, and emotions. We open our awareness to God whom we know by faith is within us, closer than breathing, closer than thinking, closer than choosing—closer than consciousness itself. Contemplative prayer is a process of inner purification leading, if we consent, to divine union.

The Method of Centering Prayer

Centering Prayer is a method designed to facilitate the development of contemplative prayer by preparing our faculties to cooperate with this gift. It is an attempt to present the teaching of earlier times (e.g. *The Cloud of Unknowing*) in an updated form and to put a certain order and regularity into it. It is not meant to replace other kinds of prayer; it simply puts other kinds of prayer into a new and fuller perspective. During the time of prayer we consent to God's presence and action within. At other times our attention moves outward to discover God's presence everywhere.

The Guidelines

1. Choose a sacred word as the symbol of your intention to consent to God's presence and action within.
2. Sitting comfortably and with eyes closed, settle briefly and silently introduce the sacred word as the symbol of your consent to God's presence and action within.

3. When you become aware of thoughts, return ever so gently to the sacred word.

4. At the end of the prayer period, remain in silence with eyes closed for a couple of minutes.

Explanation of the Guidelines

I. "Choose a sacred word as the symbol of your intention to consent to God's presence and action within." (cf. *Open Mind, Open Heart*, Chapter 5.)

1. The sacred word expresses our intention to be in God's presence and to yield to the divine action.

2. The sacred word should be chosen during a brief period of prayer asking the Holy Spirit to inspire us with one that is especially suitable for us. Examples: Lord, Jesus, Abba, Father, Mother. Other possibilities: Love, Peace, Shalom.

3. Having chosen a sacred word, we do not change it during the prayer period, for that would be to start thinking again.

4. A simple inward gaze upon God may be more suitable for some persons than the sacred word. In this case, one consents to God's presence and action by turning inwardly toward God as if gazing upon him. The same guidelines apply to the sacred gaze as to the sacred word.

II. "Sitting comfortably and with eyes closed, settle briefly and silently introduce the sacred word as the symbol of your consent to God's presence and action within."

1. By "sitting comfortably" is meant relatively comfortably; not so comfortably that we encourage sleep, but sitting comfortably enough to avoid thinking about the discomfort of our bodies during this time of prayer.

2. Whatever sitting position we choose, we keep the back straight.

3. If we fall asleep, we continue the prayer for a few minutes upon awakening if we can spare the time.

4. Praying in this way after a main meal encourages drowsiness. Better to wait an hour at least before Centering Prayer. Praying in this way just before retiring may disturb one's sleep.

5. We close our eyes to let go of what is going on around and within us.

6. We introduce the sacred word inwardly and as gently as laying a feather on a piece of absorbent cotton.

III. "When you become aware of thoughts, return ever-so-gently to the sacred word."

1. "Thought" is an umbrella term for every perception including sense perceptions, feelings, images, memories, reflections, and commentaries.

2. Thoughts are a normal part of Centering Prayer.

3. By "returning ever-so-gently to the sacred word," a minimum of effort is indicated. This is the only activity we initiate during the time of Centering Prayer.

4. During the course of our prayer, the sacred word may become vague or even disappear.

IV. "At the end of the prayer period, remain in silence with eyes closed for a couple of minutes."

1. If this prayer is done in a group, the leader may slowly recite the Our Father during the additional two or three minutes, while the others listen.

2. The additional two or three minutes gives the psyche time to readjust to the external senses and enable us to bring the atmosphere of silence into daily life.

Some Practical Points

1. The minimum time for this prayer is twenty minutes. Two periods are recommended each day, one first thing in the morning, and one in the afternoon or early evening.

2. The end of the prayer period can be indicated by a timer, provided it does not have an audible tick or loud sound when it goes off.

3. The principle effects of Centering Prayer are experienced in daily life, not in the period of Centering Prayer itself.

4. Physical symptoms:

    i. We may notice slight pains, itches, or twitches in various parts of the body or a generalized restlessness. These are usually due to the untying of emotional knots in the body.

    ii. We may also notice heaviness or lightness in the extremities. This is usually due to a deep level of spiritual attentiveness.

    iii. In either case, we pay no attention, or we allow the mind to rest briefly in the sensation, and then return to the sacred word.

5. *Lectio divina* provides the conceptual background for the development of Centering Prayer.

6. A support group praying and sharing together once a week helps maintain one's commitment to the prayer.

Extending the Effects of Centering Prayer into Daily Life

1. Practice two periods of Centering Prayer daily.

2. Read Scriptures regularly and study *Open Mind, Open Heart*.

3. Practice one or two of the specific methods for every day, suggested in *Open Mind, Open Heart*, Chapter 12.

4. Join a Centering Prayer Support Group or Follow-up Program (if available in your area).

a. It encourages the members of the group to persevere in private.

b. It provides an opportunity for further input on a regular basis through tapes, readings, and discussions.

Points for Further Development

1. During the prayer period various kinds of thoughts may be distinguished (cf. *Open Mind, Open Heart*, Chapters 6–10):

   a. Ordinary wanderings of the imagination or memory.

   b. Thoughts that give rise to attractions or aversions.

   c. Insights or psychological breakthroughs.

   d. Self-reflections such as, "How am I doing?" or, "This peace is just great."

   e. Thoughts that arise from the unloading of the unconscious.

2. During this prayer we avoid analyzing our experience, harboring expectations or aiming at some specific goal such as:

   a. Repeating the sacred word continuously.

   b. Having no thoughts.

   c. Making the mind a blank.

   d. Feeling peaceful or consoled.

   e. Achieving a spiritual experience.

3. What Centering Prayer is not:

   a. It is not a technique.

   b. It is not a relaxation exercise.

   c. It is not a form of self-hypnosis.

   d. It is not a para-psychological phenomenon.

   e. It is not limited to the "felt" presence of God.

   f. It is not discursive meditation or affective meditation.

For information and resources contact the national office:

Contemplative Outreach, Ltd.
9 William Street
P.O. Box 737
Butler, NJ 07405
Tel.: 201-838-3384.